Howard L Huebener
Lake Elmo

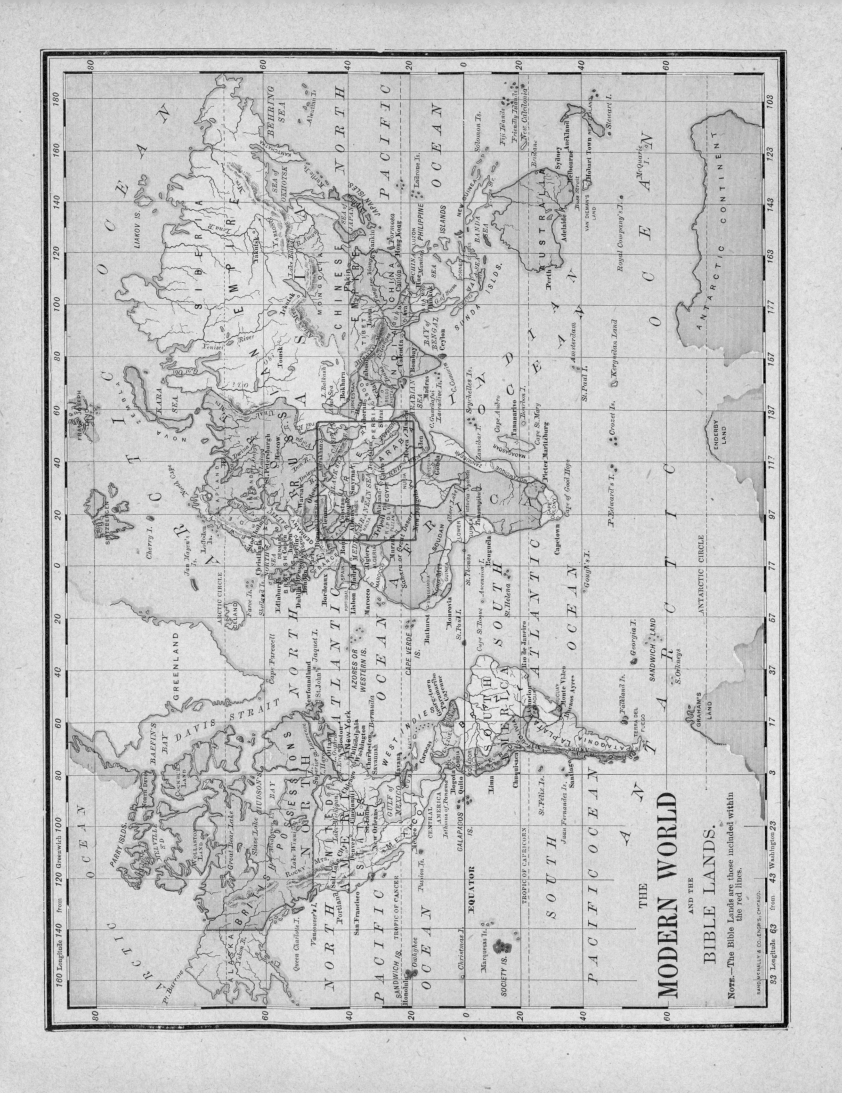

THE
MODERN WORLD
AND THE
BIBLE LANDS.

NOTE.—The Bible Lands are those included within the red lines.

RAND, McNALLY & CO. ENGR'S, CHICAGO.

BIBLE ATLAS

A MANUAL OF

BIBLICAL GEOGRAPHY AND HISTORY

ESPECIALLY PREPARED

FOR THE USE OF TEACHERS AND STUDENTS OF THE BIBLE, AND FOR SUNDAY SCHOOL INSTRUCTION, CONTAINING

Maps, Plans, Review Charts, Colored Diagrams,

AND

ILLUSTRATED

WITH ACCURATE VIEWS OF THE PRINCIPAL CITIES AND LOCALITIES KNOWN
TO BIBLE HISTORY.

REVISED EDITION.

BY REV. JESSE L. HURLBUT, D. D.,

AUTHOR OF "REVISED NORMAL LESSONS," "STUDIES IN THE FOUR GOSPELS," "STUDIES IN OLD TESTAMENT
HISTORY," ETC.

WITH AN INTRODUCTION BY

REV. BISHOP JOHN H. VINCENT, D. D., LL. D.,

CHANCELLOR OF THE CHAUTAUQUA UNIVERSITY.

CHICAGO:
RAND, McNALLY & COMPANY,
PUBLISHERS.

INTRODUCTION.

On this side of the sea we sit down with a big book in our hands. It is an old book. Nearly two thousand years have passed since the last word of it was written, and no one can tell how many thousands of years ago the records were made or the words uttered, out of which its first writer prepared his wonderful statements.

This old book is a singular book as to the variety of its contents,—ranging from dry chronological statement to highest flight of royal poetry. Many pages of it are simply historical, with lists of kings, and names of family lines through many generations. Geographical allusions descending to minutest detail are strewn thickly through its pages. There is no department of natural science which does not find some of its *data* recognized in the chapters of this venerable volume. Stones and stars, plants and reptiles, colossal monsters of sea and land, fleet horse, bird of swift flight, lofty cedar and lowly lily,—these all find their existence recognized and recorded in that book of "various theme."

As it is a long time since these records were made, so are the lands far away in which the events recorded are said to have occurred. We measure the years by millenaries, and by the thousand miles we measure the distance. The greatest contrast exists between the age and land in which we live and the age and lands in which this book found its beginning, its material and its ending.

To one familiar only with the habits, dress and customs of American life, the every-day events recorded in the book seem fabulous. We do not dress as the book says that people dressed in those far-away years and far-away lands; we do not eat as they did; our houses are not like theirs; we do not measure time as they did; we do not speak their language; our seasons do not answer to the seasons that marked their year. It is difficult, knowing only our modern American life, to *think* ourselves into the conditions under which this book says that people lived and thought in those long-ago ages. Their wedding feasts and funeral services differed utterly from ours. They lived and died in another atmosphere, under a government that no longer exists; made war upon nations that are powerless to-day as the sleeping dead in a national cemetery; and the things which we read concerning them seem strange enough to us.

In the changes which have taken place through all these centuries, it would be an easy thing, under some circumstances, for men to deny that the people of the book ever lived, that the cities of the book were ever built, that the events of the book ever transpired. And, if its historic foundation were destroyed, the superstructure of truth, the doctrinal and ethical teachings resting upon it, might in like manner be swept away.

This old Book — the Bible, a divine product, wrought into the texture of human history and literature with the gradually unfolding ages — is the old Book we study to-day on this side the sea.

It is a "Book of books,"—the Book out-shining all other books in the literary firmament, as the sun out-splendors the planets that move in their orbits around him.

It is a book that deals with man as an immortal soul; making known the beginnings of the race; going back of the beginning to God, who is from "everlasting to everlasting," and who "in the beginning created the heaven and the earth"; revealing the creative purpose and loving grace of God; tracing the fall and deterioration of man, the divine interposition in human history, the preparation of a family, a race, a nation, and a world at large, for the coming of the Redeemer; revealing the glory of God in the face of Jesus Christ; showing how the Christ came, what he did, what he said, what he resisted, what he endured, what he suffered, what he achieved; telling in simple way the story of the early church, from the little meeting of the bereaved disciples in the upper room to the magnificent consummation of Christ's coming, as seen in the prophetic visions of St. John on the Isle of Patmos.

It is a book full of history, of geography, of archæology, of prophecy, of poetry, of doctrine, of "exceeding great and precious promises."

In an important sense the foundations of this book are laid in human history and geography. However high toward the heavens it may reach in doctrine and promise, its foundations lay hold of the earth. If the children of Israel did not live in Egypt and Canaan and the far East, if the statements of their history as recorded in the book be not *facts*, if the story of Jesus Christ be false,—everything fails us. With the sweeping away of fact, we must also bid farewell to the words of doctrine and of promise here recorded; to the divine words of assurance which now give comfort to the penitent, hope to the despairing, strength to the feeble, and immortal life to the dying.

As we sit down on this side of the sea, it is well that we are able to look beyond the sea to the lands which gave to the world the book in our hands. And it is well, that, as we look, we are able to connect the book of to-day with those same lands as they now lie among the rivers and by the seaside, from the sources of the Tigris and Euphrates to the mouths of the Nile, from the palaces of Babylon to the dock at Puteoli and the prison at Rome. And it is well that the lands as they are found to-day correspond to the records of the Book as they were made centuries and centuries ago. The Book, on its human historic, geographical and archæological side, is true to the facts as in the nineteenth century they are presented to us in the lands of the East.

There are those who believe with firm faith, that, for these days of skepticism and of merciless and conscienceless historic criticism, the lands have been kept almost in their original condition, that the testimony of the modern skeptical traveler might (though unintentionally on his part, but necessarily) corroborate the teachings of the Bible. Have the mummy wrappings of Mohammedan domination held the far East unchanged through the centuries, that in these days of doubt the hills of Canaan, the plains of Egypt and the ruins of Mesopotamia might lift their voice in solemn attestation to the divine truthfulness of the sacred historians?

These lands are memorial lands. They are now what the Book says they once were. Although the sweeping away of ancient governments and the reign of anarchy have modified the face of the country, the evidences still remain that the most glowing descriptions of their prosperity were not exaggerated. Infidels have doubted, for example, whether Palestine could contain the immense populations which, in its prosperous days, according to the statements of the Book, were resident there. But scientists show that the soil of Canaan, under cultivation, is one of the richest and most fertile in the world. The broken terraces that may still be traced on the hill-sides, the walls of cities and other ruins that fill the land, sustain the account of the prosperous days and the immense populations of Bible times.

So little have the conditions of social life been modified, that one may live the old life over again in Canaan. Soil and scenery, the seasons of the year, Jacob's well and the Jordan, Ebal and Gerizim, the plain, the wilderness and the city, all give witness to the words of the Book.

The names of olden time still linger. One lands at *Yafa*, the "Joppa" of old; Jerusalem is now *el Khuds*,—"the Holy"; *Bahr-lut*—"the Sea of Lot" —is the Dead Sea in the Valley of Sodom and Gomorrah; *Bir es Seba* is the Beersheba of the olden time; *el Azariyeh* is Bethany, the home of Lazarus; *Beit-lahm* is still Bethlehem; and *el Khalil*—"the Friend" —is the name of Hebron, the home of Abram, "the Friend of God."

In the customs and costumes, in the habits of speech and the manners of the people, you read the same lesson. In the spring of 1863 I was permitted to spend forty days and forty nights in Palestine. I saw Abraham at his tent-door; Rebekah vailing herself at the approach of the stranger; the long caravan of camels and Midianites on their way toward the South. I saw the wailing mourners at the house of death; the roof that might easily have been broken up; the wedding procession; the grass on the house-tops; the sparrow making a nest for her young in the synagogues of Jerusalem. I saw the elders in the gates; David the shepherd, with his sheep, on the hill-side; the Jewish mother teaching Timothy the words of the old Book in the old city on the hill. Verily, it is the old land; it is the old life; it is the memorial presentation in concrete form of what the Book says was true there thousands of years ago.

As I stood on Safed, overlooking the Sea of Galilee and the lovely land about it, I turned and looked toward the north, and saw snow-sheathed Hermon, probably the Mount of Transfiguration, as it stood out that day against the blue sky of Syria. I thought of Ruskin's words: "These pure white hills, near to the heavens and sources of all good to the earth, are the memorials of the light of his mercy that fell snow-like on the Mount of Transfiguration."

I once saw the Alps glorified by the setting sun. I was standing on *La Flégére*, looking down upon the Valley of Chamounix, and upward upon the magnificent heights, above which towered the great Mont Blanc. A pall of mist had hidden the rough and unilluminated rocks; but, when that mist grew thin as a vail of delicate lace, I saw the Alps beyond, and they appeared as if on fire. I cried out in ecstacy, "Behold Mount Zion." Through the mists of earth I saw the splendors of heaven. The story of the transfiguration on Mount Hermon, in the days of Jesus, if taken literally, is not so marvelous as the history we call the life and character of Jesus. Both belong to the realm of the supernatural. The "life" granted, the transfiguration has no surprise in it. So I discover the strange blending of the natural and supernatural in the Land and the Book, — in the Land as to-day hallowed by the Book, — in the Book as to-day supported and made real by the Land.

It thus easily appears that every Bible reader should be acquainted with the outlines of Biblical and geographical antiquities. Without such knowledge it is impossible properly to understand the divine word. How often, through ignorance of sacred archæology, we overlook the force and beauty of the allusions which abound in the narrative, poetic and prophetic parts of Scripture. And there is, moreover, an air of reality imparted to all history by familiarity with the geography involved in it.

In view of the supernatural character of Bible history, acquaintance with Bible geography is particularly important. Once give its wonderful transactions an actual locality among the hills, valleys and cities which may still be found and visited, connecting and comparing them with the records of our present history, and our youth will readily distinguish the miraculous from the mythical, and discover not only clear illustrations of many portions of the Bible, but strong and irresistible evidence in favor of its divinity.

I therefore hail with joy the admirable presentation of the facts of Bible history and geography in this volume — a presentation so clear, and so abundantly illustrative, that the humblest teacher and most indifferent student may be interested and instructed.

The study of Bible history and geography must not be limited to the theological school, the pastor's study, or the advanced Bible class. It is a department pecul-

iarly adapted to our youngest children, and by them most needed, that they may secure the vivid realization of actuality in the Bible narratives. Boys and girls to-day may not take much delight in the advanced doctrinal teachings of the Bible; but it is possible so to connect its history with stories of modern travel, through the regions referred to in that history, that they will become interested in the one because of the pleasure they find in the other.

Our Sunday School libraries should contain the many books of travel through the far East which are published in these days. And our ministers should enlist young people, through special classes, in the study of Bible history and geography. In this way a "week-day hold" upon our young people may be secured.

During ten years of my pastoral life, wherever the itinerant system of my church placed me, I held on every Saturday afternoon, in the lecture-room of my church, a class to which old and young, and the representatives of all denominations, were admitted. It was called "The Palestine Class," and was devoted to the study of Bible history and geography. An outline of facts, prepared in catechetical form, was printed, and committed to memory by every pupil. Difficult old Hebrew names of lands, cities and mountains, were arranged in a rhythmic way, and chanted after the manner of the old-time "singing geography" classes. Answers were given in concert to help the memory, and personal examinations were afterward conducted to test it. The class constituted an "ideal company of tourists to the far East." The course of lessons was divided into five sections, covering the whole of Bible history. As each member, passing a personal examination, gave proof that he had thoroughly mastered "Section One," he was constituted a PILGRIM to the Holy Land, and given a certificate to that effect. Having studied "Section Two," and passed a satisfactory examination, he was made a RESIDENT in Palestine, and his name was associated with one town or mountain. In that way every principal place on the map was associated with the name of some member, who was held responsible to the class for information concerning its history and present condition. An examination in "Section Three" made our "pilgrim" and "resident" a DWELLER IN JERUSALEM. Having been examined in "Section Four," he was made an EXPLORER of other Bible lands, and was located on some mountain, or city of Egypt, Arabia, Chaldea, Asia Minor, etc. A final examination made him a TEMPLAR.

The songs, concert exercises, responses and ideal pilgrimage gave enthusiasm to the class, while the personal examinations guaranteed thoroughness. As I recall those Saturday afternoons of my early ministry, surrounded by earnest women and wide-awake boys and girls of all ages, I am amply rewarded for all the labor and time expended. The enthusiasm and delight, the perceptible growth in knowledge, the spirit of catholicity, the steadiness promoted in the frivolous, the gratification afforded on the occasion of public examinations and reviews, the increased appreciation of the Sunday preaching, visible on the faces of young and old, the grateful words that have come through the intervening years from those who were by these studies incited to a more intelligent and earnest Bible study — these are some of the results of those years of pastoral service. The plan is practicable for every pastor. The book which I now have the honor of introducing to the public furnishes to every minister a complete preparation for directing such classes — a preparation which, twenty-five years ago, would have been a great benediction to me.

One of these Palestine classes reported its imaginary tour through the village paper. These articles gave local interest to the movement, delighting the imaginary tourists, and (through no fault of ours) deceiving more than one simple-hearted reader in the community. From these letters I make a few extracts.

"PALESTINE CORRESPONDENCE OF THE 'INDEPENDENT WATCHMAN.'

"DEAR INDEPENDENT: In fulfillment of the promise made the night before our departure, I sit down to write the first of a series of letters detailing the most noteworthy incidents of our journey to the Holy Land, with such historical and geographical facts as are suggested by the localities we may be permitted to visit.

"As you are well aware, an association, which has for its specific object the study of Bible history and geography, was organized in your town some months ago. After a course of thorough preliminary training, arrangements were consummated for a tour of observation through Egypt, Arabia, Palestine, — the lands of Hebrew life and literature, the scenes of the early Christian history, and, later, the arena of Saracenic invasion and domination. We are now on the way thither. While the tide of mighty immigration is pouring westward toward the American desert, the Rocky Mountains, Pike's Peak and Cherry creek, a tiny rill of exploration is trickling eastward toward the desert of Sinai, the mountains of Egypt, the peaks of Lebanon, and the river of Jordan." * * * * *

After calling attention to two books which had just then appeared — "The Land and The Book," by Dr. Thomson, and "Palestine Past and Present," by Dr. Osborn — the Palestine correspondent continued:

"No class of literature is more refining and exalting than the records of cultivated minds made amid the sacred scenes of Palestine, and the not less interesting ruins of Egypt, Asia Minor and Greece. A taste for such mental pabulum is a better safeguard against the popular and polluting fictions of the day than all the mandates of the parent or the uncompromising denunciations of the pulpit. Preoccupy by the good, and there will be no evil to expel. Create a taste for healthful literature in our young people, and they will not crave the blood and fire potions now so mercilessly provided by the corrupt press. This is one object of our present pilgrimage to Palestine. We would open a new world — the newest and yet the oldest of worlds — to their view. We would unfurl bright maps and open new books, and delight them in a field of thought and research, in which healthful influences prevail, a field of fragrant and thornless flowers, of luscious and life-giving fruit. * * * * * The association to which I have referred is composed of about eighty pilgrims. On Saturday morning, the 25th, we left your quiet village, reaching Chicago the same evening. Tuesday morning found us on our way to New York, where we arrived early this morning. We shall sail on Saturday, April 2, for the Orient. In order to diminish our expenses, we forego the speed of the regular steam route, and have chartered the sailing vessel, the schooner 'Star of Bethlehem.' She is a new vessel, and a 'bright light' in her way. Well rigged, and ably manned, she is prepared for the buffeting of old ocean. Her captain is the distinguished and experienced *Hardstudy*, with whom, I am sure, you have some acquaintance. He is a true gentleman, and, I am told, has been an intimate companion of several Oriental travelers. He accompanied Dr. Robinson on both his tours. The 'Star,' built expressly for excursions to the Mediterranean waters, is a stout boat, and is provided with the modern conveniences and luxuries of travel. She is about 150 tons burden. I spent an hour on board of her this afternoon, and am much gratified with the neatness and elegance displayed in all her departments. The library and reading-room is a little palace. It contains about 1,500 volumes, chiefly of Eastern travel, which, together with a number of good maps and paintings, will afford us every opportunity to prepare for the interesting tour we are about making. All thus far are well. Remember us in our wanderings, and send us copies of your paper, directing to the 'care of the United States Consul at Alexandria.' Prepay to New York, and send 'Via Liverpool and Beyrout.'"

The next letter gives an account of the various pilgrimages which have been made to Palestine from the days of Abraham down to the present.

"Off Sandy Hook, 3.30 P. M.," our correspondent wrote. "The wide ocean is before us. We have passed the Battery, Brooklyn, Staten Island, the ruins of old quarantine and the forts, — feeble protection in cases of invasion, — and yonder to the east is Sandy Hook. The bell of the tug rings. In five minutes our friends who accompany us down will return to the city, and we shall be alone upon the wide, wide sea. The waters appear quiet; a faint west wind is rising; all the children are in good spirits. If they are as bright to-morrow it will be strange. Farewell, native land! Farewell!"

ROSIN PRODUCED FROM DEAD STUMPS BEI

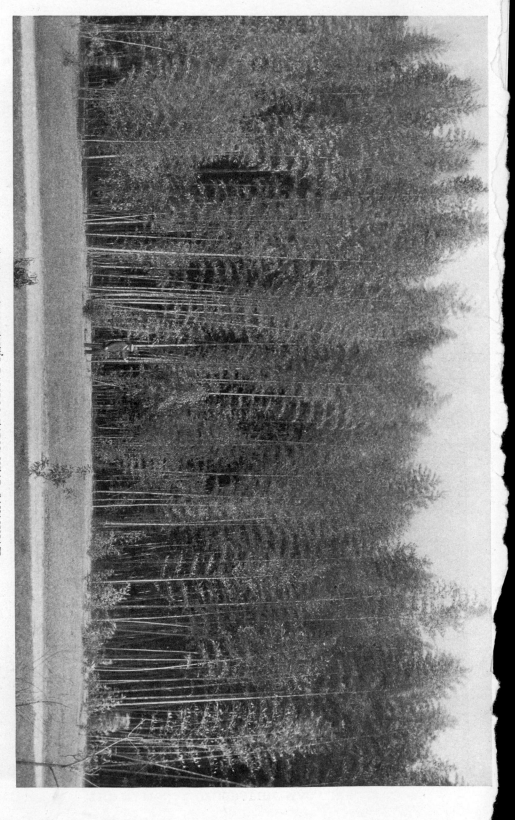

THE GOVERNMENT'S BAMBOO FARM NEAR SAVANNAH

This magnificent grove of canes has sprung from a single shoot of bamboo planted 35 years ago. From it the United States Department of Agriculture has shipped thousands of plants throughout the South and Southwest. Bamboo flourishes in the United States from Virginia to California (see text, page 295). Each plant in this grove attained its full height in a single season's growth. Some of the canes grew at the rate of from 12 to 17 inches in 24 hours.

The third letter opened with a quotation from Browning:

> "'In the dimmest northeast distance
> Dawned Gibraltar, grand and gray.'

"Schooner Star of Bethlehem,
"Harbor of Gibraltar, May 4, '59.

"Dear Independent: Thirty-two days ago we left the port of New York, and day before yesterday glided through the Straits of Gibraltar, casting anchor in this harbor. Our voyage was short and agreeable, all that could be desired, with the exception of the sea-sickness that prevailed among us for the first four or five days, and the alarm occasioned by the heavy gale of last week. For two days the storm raged so violently that our fears were much excited. On the evening of the 26th ult. the winds were lulled, the clouds broke away, and the rays of the setting sun hurried swiftly across the yet raging waves, to brighten their foaming crests with golden light, and bring hope to our hearts. Religious services were conducted each Sabbath by the chaplain, and our programme of study and reading was faithfully observed every day. All that we did, and all that we saw, cannot be reported in a single letter. Our young friends must themselves write about the wonders of the sea,—whales, dolphins, icebergs; sunset, sunrise, midnight; calms, storms, water-spouts; and all other sources of joy or terror in ocean life. Yesterday was spent in an excursion to the town of Gibraltar." * * * * *

After a description of Gibraltar, the writer says:

"The whole juvenile forces of our vessel have been invited to dine this afternoon with the officers of *H. M. S. Manchester*, in company with the British and American consuls of Gibraltar, and left an hour ago, under the charge of Captain *Hardstudy*, to comply with the gracious invitation, and I remain to prepare this letter for the morrow's steamer from Valetta to Liverpool. The sun is already sinking in the blue and gold waters of the Mediterranean. A fresh breeze has startled the sleeping waves into lively gambols, and our flag points eagerly westward and homeward. See our party of little travelers just off for the 'Manchester'! How their boats dance up and down over the water! 'Boom!' 'boom!' go the signal guns from the kind old ship! Now hear the thunderous volleys from the batteries on the huge mountain, proclaiming the hour of sunset!"

The letters which follow are from "Alexandria, Egypt, May 28"; from the "Steamer Rameses, River Nile, June 11"; from "Off Joppa, June 16"; from "Jerusalem, July 5"; from "Nablous, 'the City of Samaria,' July 12"; from "Beyrout, Syria, July 23"; and on Monday morning, July 25, our correspondent writes his farewell, as follows:

"Well, friend Independent, our travels are ended. We came on board the 'Star of Bethlehem' this morning. The steamer for Liverpool leaves this afternoon, and we shall send our letters ashore to be mailed. By the 30th of September we hope to be with you again. We have seen the earthly Canaan, with its degradation and defilement. Our minds turn toward the better Canaan. With Watts we sing:

> "'Look up, our souls, pant toward the eternal hills;
> Those heavens are fairer than they seem.
> There pleasures all sincere glide on in crystal rills;
> There not a dreg of guilt defiles,
>   No grief disturbs the stream
>   That Canaan knows,—no noxious thing,
> No cursed soil, no tainted spring;
> No roses grow on thorns, nor honey wears a sting.'"

Such devices as these help to inspire the young with an interest in sacred things. They may not yet be prepared to appreciate the night of prayer on the mountain, the agony of the Lord in Gethsemane, or the rapturous experiences of St. John on Patmos; but they may take delight in the land, its customs, its wonderful histories, read with gratification an account of journeys from Dan to Beersheba, with perils from robbers, and the pranks of native children, the lonely horseback ride from Jerusalem down to Jericho, the encampment by the "Fountain of robbers" north of Jerusalem, the loveliness of Nazareth, the beauty of the Sea of Galilee, and the glories of Lebanon and Hermon. Finding delight in these more human things, they may, incidentally, under the leadership of the divine Providence and Spirit, catch glimpses of his face who, by simile and word and spirit, sanctified the land from north to south and from Bashan to the sea.

J. H. VINCENT.

PREFACE TO THE REVISED EDITION.

During the fourteen years since this work was prepared great advancement has been gained in knowledge of the ancient Oriental world. In the light of recent researches it has become necessary to revise the entire book. The work has been done with care, every location has been reinvestigated, and the historical allusions have been compared with the latest and best authorities. In this revision the author has been materially aided by Prof. Robert W. Rogers of Madison, N. J., and Prof. Karl P. Harrington of Chapel Hill, N. C., to both of whom thanks are rendered. It is possible that some errors may yet remain, and if any appear to students who make use of this work, corrections or suggestions with regard to them will be gratefully received.

Jesse L. Hurlbut.

GENERAL INDEX.

TABLE OF CONTENTS.

LIST OF ILLUSTRATIONS.

ENTRY OF PILGRIMS INTO BETHLEHEM.

THE OLD TESTAMENT WORLD.

I. Extent. The Old Testament World embraces the seas and lands between 30° and 54° east longitude, or from the mouth of the Nile to that of the Persian Gulf; and between 27° and 40° north latitude, from the parallel south of Mount Sinai to that north of Mount Ararat. The total extent of territory is about 1,400 miles from east to west and 900 miles from north to south, aggregating 1,260,000 square miles. Deducting from this the space occupied by the Mediterranean Sea and other large bodies of water, the land will include about 1,110,000 square miles, or one-third the extent of the United States, excluding Alaska. Unlike the United States, however, nearly two-thirds of this extent is a vast desert, and uninhabitable, so that the portion actually occupied by man is less than an eighth of that included in the American Union.

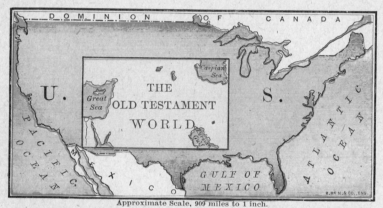

Approximate Scale, 909 miles to 1 inch.

COMPARATIVE VIEW OF UNITED STATES AND OLD TESTAMENT WORLD.

II. Seas. This world of the Old Testament embraces several large bodies of water. 1. The *Caspian Sea*, the largest body of water surrounded by land on the globe, occupies its northeastern corner. 2. The *Persian Gulf*, the outlet of the great rivers of the Old Testament history, is in its southeastern border. 3. The two arms of the northern end of the *Red Sea*, the Gulf of Suez and the Gulf of Akaba, are on its southwestern side. 4. The *Mediterranean Sea*, "the great sea toward the going down of the sun" (Josh. 1:4), forms a part of its western boundary. These are its largest seas; but besides these may be named three others, all salt lakes, imbedded in its mountain system. 5. The *Dead Sea*, called in the Bible "Sea of the Plain," and "Salt Sea," lying 1,290 feet below the Mediterranean, and situated in the land of Palestine; 6. *Lake Van*, anciently Arsissa, in Armenia; and 7. *Lake Urumiyeh*, in Media. Neither of the last two are referred to in the Bible.

III. Mountain Ranges. The nucleus of the mountain system is found in the land of Armenia, on the north of the map. Here five great ranges of mountains have their origin. 1 The *Ararat Mountains* are lofty masses, lying between the Caspian Sea and Asia Minor. They are arranged in three sections, nearly parallel: Mount Masius, on the south; Mount Niphates, north of Lake Van; and Mount Abus, still farther north. One of the peaks of this latter section is the traditional resting place of the ark (Gen. 8:4), and is the summit of the group, 17,750 feet high. 2. The *Caspian Mountains*, branching from Ararat, bend around the southern end of the Caspian Sea and extend eastward, forming the northern boundary of Media. 3. The *Zagros Mountains* also start from Ararat, and follow a direction generally southeast, to the northern shore of the Persian Gulf. They form the eastern watershed of the Tigris and Euphrates rivers. 4. The *Lebanon Range* starts from the western side of the Ararat group, and follows the Mediterranean coast through Syria and Palestine, then down the Sinaitic peninsula. Its general direction is west of south. In Syria and Palestine it is divided into two parallel branches, Lebanon and Anti-Lebanon, the latter on the east. Its highest peak is Mount Hermon, about 9,000 feet above the sea. South of Palestine it forms the remarkable Sinaitic group of mountains, upon one of which the Law was given. 5. The last range is *Mount Taurus*, which also branches from Ararat, in a westerly direction, and forms the southern coast line of Asia Minor.

COMPARATIVE HEIGHT OF BIBLE MOUNTAINS.

IV. Rivers. Passing by many unimportant streams, we notice the following, the largest of which have their

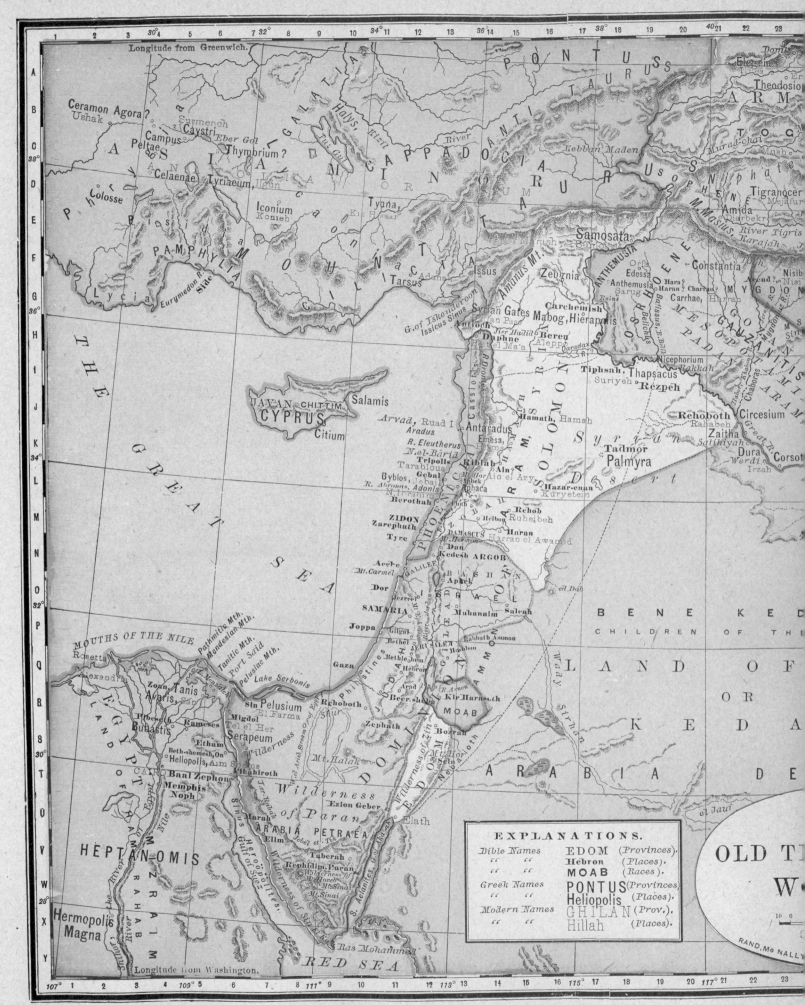

A
B
C
38°
D
E
F
36°
G
H
I
J
K
34°
L
M
N
O
32°
P
Q
R
S
30°
T
U
V
W
28°
X
Y

1 2 3 30°4 5 6 7 32° 8 9 10 34°11 12 13 36°14 15 16 17 38° 18 19 20 40°21 22 23

Ceramon Agora?
Ushak
Campus
Peltae
Colosse
Celaenae
Tyriaeum, Ilghin
Iconium
Konieh

Caystri
Surmeneh
Eber Gol
Thymbrium?
Tuz Gul
Halys
Kizil

ASIA
PHRYGIA
PAMPHYLIA
Lycia
Side
Eurymedon R.
Tarsus
Adana
Issus

GALATIA
CAPPADOCIA
LYCAONIA
MOUNTAINS
Tyana
Kir Hissar
Nazianz

PONTUS
TAURUS
Kebban Maden

ARM
Theodosio
Er
TO
Mush
Murad-chai
SOPH

SHEN
Tigranocer
Mejafur
Amida
Diarbekr
River Tigris
Karajah

Samosata
Orfa
Edessa
Anthemusia
Sarug
Ruins

Zeugnia
Carchemish
Syrian Gates Mabog, Hierapolis
Cilician Pass
Antioch
Daphne
Beit el Ma'a
Bereu
Aleppo

MYGDON
Hara
Haran?
Charran
Carrhae, Harran
Batissus, R. Belichus
Nicephorium
Rakkah

GAUZANITIS
GOZAN
PADAN
ARAM
Nisib
MESOPOTAMIA
M

THE
GREAT
SEA

JAVAN CHITTIM
CYPRUS
Salamis
Citium

Arvad, Ruad I.
Aradus
R. Eleutherus
N.el-Bárid
Tripolis
Tarablous
Gebal
Byblos, Jebail
R. Abrunas, Adonis
N. Ibrahim
Berothah

Antaradus
Emesa,
Hums
Riblah
M. Hor Ain el Azy
Anek
Aphaca

Hamath, Hamah
ARAM, OR SYRIA
Hazar-enan
Kuryetein

Tiphsah, Thapsacus
Suriyeh
Rezpeh

Rehoboth
Rahabeh
Zaitha
Dura
Werdi
Irzah
Circesium
Corsot

Tadmor
Palmyra

Syrian
Desert

ZIDON
Zarephath
Tyre

DAMASCUS
M. Hermon
Dan
Kedesh
Acche
Mt. Carmel
Dor
Jezreel
SAMARIA
Joppa

Helbon
Harau
Harran el Awamd

Rehob
Ruheibeh

ARGOB
BASHAN
Aphek
Mahanaim
Saleah
el Dah

BENE KED
CHILDREN OF THE

MOUTHS OF THE NILE
Rosetta
Alexandria
Pathmitic Mth.
Mendesian Mth.
Tanitic Mth.
Port Said
Pelusiac Mth.
Lake Serbonis

Zoan, Tanis
Avaris
San
Z. Menzaleh

Bubastis
Rameses
Migdol
Tel el Her
Serapeum
Ethan
Beth-shemesh, On
Heliopolis
Aim Shems
Pihahiroth

Gilgal
Bethel
Bethlehem
Hebron
Arad
Beer-sheba
Zephath
Bozrah

JERUSALEM
Rabbath Ammon
Heshbon
AMMON
MOAB
Kir-Haraseth
R. Arnon
Mt. Hor
Sela
Nebo

LAND OF
OR
KEDA
ARABIA
DE

EGYPT
Baal Zephon
Memphis
Noph

Wilderness
of Paran

Ezion Geber
Elath

ARABIA PETRAEA
Marah
Elim
Jebel et Tih
Taberah
Rephidim, Paran
Mt. Sinai

Wilderness of Zin
EDOM

HEPTANOMIS

Hermopolis
Magna

Sinai

RED SEA

107° 1 2 3 4 109° 5 6 7 8 111° 9 10 11 12 113° 13 14 15 16 115° 17 18 19 20 117° 21 22 23

EXPLANATIONS.		
Bible Names	EDOM	(Provinces).
" "	Hebron	(Places).
" "	MOAB	(Races).
Greek Names	PONTUS	(Provinces)
" "	Heliopolis	(Places).
Modern Names	GHILAN	(Prov.).
" "	Hillah	(Places).

OLD T
W

RAND, McNALLY

rise in the mountain system of Armenia. 1. The *Araxes*, not named in the Bible, but important as a boundary, rises in the northern section of the Ararat Range, and flows, in a general direction, eastward into the Caspian Sea. 2. The *Tigris*, called in the Bible Hiddekel, rises in Mount Niphates, of the Ararat Range, and flows in a southeasterly direction, following the line of Mount Zagros, unites with the Euphrates, and thence flows into the Persian Gulf. Its length to the union with the Euphrates is 1,146 miles; beyond the union to the gulf, at present, 100 miles, though anciently much less; and at a time within the limits of history the two rivers discharged by separate mouths. Their united stream is now called the *Shaat el Arab*. 3. The *Euphrates*, or the *Frat* (a word meaning "abounding"), is the great river of the Bible world. It has two important sources, both

the sea. 5. The *Jordan*, least yet most important of all, flows southward from the foot of Mount Hermon into the Dead Sea. It will be described in connection with the Physical Map of Palestine. 6. The *Nile*, the great river of Africa, rises in the centre of the continent and flows northward into the Mediterranean Sea, turning the desert through which it passes into a garden.

V. **The Lands.** These are not easy to determine, since their boundaries and names varied at different periods of the history. Yet their locations may be given, and their natural limits are generally known. They may be classified as follows: 1. Lands of the Mountain System, all north and east of the Zagros chain of mountains: Armenia, Media, and Persia. 2. Lands of the Plain: Assyria, Elam, Mesopotamia, Chaldea, Arabia. 3. Lands of the Mediterranean: Asia Minor, Syria, Phœnicia, Palestine, The Wilderness, Egypt.

I. LANDS OF THE MOUNTAIN SYSTEM.

MOUNT ARARAT.

1. **Armenia** is a name nowhere used in the original Scriptures, but in our version is a translation of the word "Ararat," which word properly appears in place of "Armenia" in the Revised Version. The province embraces the lofty plateau and mountain group between the Caspian and Black Seas, and north of Mesopotamia and Assyria, the source of four great rivers, the Araxes, Tigris, Euphrates, and Acampsis, the latter pouring into the Black Sea. Its boundaries are: upon the north, the Caucasus Mountains; on the east, Media and the Caspian Sea; on the south, Media, from which it is separated by the Araxes, and Assyria, from which it is divided by Mount Masius; and on the west, the Euphrates, separating it from Asia Minor. Tradition states that it was settled by Haïk, a grandson of Japhet; and the earliest history names it as tributary to Assyria. Excepting the resting of Noah's ark upon one of its mountains, few events of Scripture are associated with it.

in Armenia: one at a place called *Domli;* the other, the more distant and true source, at *Diyadin*, at the foot of a mountain called *Ala Tagh*, 20 miles west of Mount Ararat. It flows westward 400 miles, then southward about as far, then in a southeasterly direction 1,000 miles, uniting at last with the Tigris to form the *Shaat el Arab*. It is navigable for 1,100 miles, and has in all ages formed the principal means of travel between Eastern and Western Asia. At Babylon, it is nearly a mile in width, though for 800 miles it does not receive a single tributary, as it flows through a desert. It overflows its banks every year, rising as high as twelve feet. 4. The *Orontes* rises in Mount Lebanon, and flows northward parallel with the Mediterranean until, just before reaching Asia Minor, it breaks through the mountains and empties into

2. **Media** is in the original the same word as Madai, the son of Japhet. (Gen. 10:2.) Its boundaries are the river Araxes and the Caspian Sea on the north, the great salt desert of Iram on the east, Persia on the south, and the Zagros Mountains, separating it from Assyria and Armenia. A branch of the Zagros Mountains, running eastward, divides it into two portions, anciently known as Media Atropatene (the one northward) and Media Magna. In each of these provinces the principal city was called Ecbatana. The Medes were of the Aryan or Japhetic stock, and were always a warlike and independent people. Though conquered by Assyria, their land was never formally annexed to the Assyrian empire. In

B. C. 633 the Median kingdom was established, and soon became supreme over Assyria, Armenia, and Persia, and formed the Medo-Persian empire, which succeeded to the power of Babylon in the East, B. C. 536. After that date the history of Media is lost in that of Persia.

3. **Persia** was originally a small province on the Persian Gulf, still known as *Fars*. But Persia Proper included, besides the sandy plain on the gulf, a mountainous plateau north of it, and was bounded by Media on the north, by Carmania on the east, by the Persian Gulf on the south, and by Elam on the west. Its people were of the Aryan race, and at first subject to the Medes. They revolted under Cyrus the Great, and became the controlling power in the conquest of Nebuchadnezzar's dominion. The Persian empire arose to greatness at the fall of Babylon, B. C. 536, conquered and ruled over all the lands from India to Ethiopia, and was by far the greatest of the great Oriental monarchies. It was subjected by Alexander the Great, B. C. 330. The capital of the Persian empire was Susa, called in the Bible "Shushan the Palace" (Esther 1:2); which was, however, situated not in Persia Proper, but in Elam. The most important places in the province were Persepolis (its capital at one period), Pasargada, and Mesambria, none of which are named in the Bible.

II. LANDS OF THE PLAIN.

Of these, two are situated mainly between the Zagros chain of mountains and the Tigris river, Assyria and Elam; two are between the Tigris and Euphrates, Mesopotamia and Chaldea; and one is the vast Arabian desert.

1. **Assyria,** in the Hebrew everywhere Asshur, was properly the province now called *Kurdistan*, lying on the western slope of the Zagros Mountains, and extending across the Tigris to the Sinjar hills and the border of the Mesopotamian desert. The mountains separate it from Armenia; and the line of division from Elam, on the southeast, was near the place where the Tigris and Euphrates approach nearest before their separation. The land was occupied by people of various races, of which the Semitic were predominant. The earliest city was at Asshur, supposed to be *Kileh Sherghat*, where a dynasty of kings began to rule about 1800 B. C., while the Israelite tribes were in Egypt. The seat of government was afterward transferred to Calah, or Halah (*Nimrud*), north of Asshur; and finally a permanent location of the capital was made at Nineveh, which became the centre of the great Assyrian empire. This will be described more fully with the map of that empire, on page 91. The Assyrian kingdom was long in its duration, but passed through many vicissitudes, several times ruling all the lands of the Euphrates, and again, in a feeble condition. Its principal cities, besides Nineveh, were Calah, Resen (which may have been at *Selamiyeh*, three miles south of Nineveh), and Rehoboth. There is reason to believe that all the four cities named in Gen. 10:11, 12, were combined in the walls of Nineveh.

2. **Elam,** called Susiana by the Greeks, lay southeast of Assyria and west of Persia Proper, between the Zagros chain of mountains and the Tigris river. It included both a mountainous and a lowland tract, the latter very fertile. Shushan (Susa), the capital of the Persian empire, lay within this province, and was its principal city. The earliest conqueror named in the Bible, Amraphel, was the king of Elam, and held dominion over most of the lands as far west as Canaan. (See the map of his empire, on page 34.) This kingdom was not of long continuance as an independent state, but soon fell under the power of Assyria, though maintaining its own organization as a vassal state until the Persian period, when it became a province of the empire.

3. **Mesopotamia,** called in Scripture Aram-naharaim, or "Syria of the two rivers," was a land of indefinite boundaries. The name means "between the rivers," and hence it was often applied to all the plain between the Tigris and Euphrates, including even Chaldea and a part of Assyria. A more frequent use of the name restricts it to the northwestern portion of the region between the rivers, above the place where they approach and separate again. The Sinjar hills, crossing, divide it into two sections, a higher and a lower, the former mountainous, and the latter mostly a great desert. The upper section contained the cities of Orfa (Edessa), formerly supposed to be the birthplace of Abraham; Haran, the patriarch's resting place on the way to Canaan; Nisibis and Amida, now *Nisibin* and *Diarbekr*. The only time when Mesopotamia appears in Bible history as a kingdom was a brief interval during the period of the Judges. (Judg. 3:8.) Earlier it had been occupied by separate and warring tribes; later it was a part of Assyria.

4. **Chaldea** is also called Shinar and Babylonia. The name Chaldea, in its most accurate sense, belongs to the southern portion of the province, but is generally used with reference to all the Mesopotamian plain south of *Baghdad*. It is perfectly level, and by nature one of the most fertile places on the whole earth. Its earliest inhabitants, at least the ruling portion of them, were Cushites, of the stock of Ham. An early Oriental kingdom began at Ur (*Mugheir*) about B. C. 3900. It lasted, with varying fortunes, until B. C. 538. Babylon afterward became the capital, and in a later period was the greatest city of the East. (See diagram on page 93.) Other cities of Chaldea were Erech (*Orchoë*), Calneh, and Sepharvaim. Further details of its political history are given in the account of the Babylonian empire of Nebuchadnezzar, on page 92.

5. The desert of **Arabia** occupies more than half of the map of the Old Testament World. That portion of it included upon the map is a vast triangle, having for its base the 28th parallel of latitude, from the Persian Gulf to the Red Sea, the Euphrates on its northeastern side, and the border of the Lebanon chain of mountains for its western. It is called in the Bible "the land of Kedar." It is a high, undulating, dry plain, with few oases, and almost impenetrable to travelers. From the

2

days of Abraham until the present, the caravans have gone around it upon the north, following up the Euphrates to Tiphsah (Thapsacus), and then turning southward rather than face its terrors. Only once in history is it related that an army crossed it. This was when Nebuchadnezzar, while ravaging Palestine, learned of his father's death, and crossed this great desert by the most direct route, in order to take possession of the throne.

III. LANDS OF THE MEDITERRANEAN.

These lands will receive more extended treatment in connection with other maps, so that we give them only a brief mention here.

1. **Asia Minor** scarcely enters the field of the Old Testament, except as the "land of the Hittites." It will be noticed under the topic of the Journeys of the Apostle Paul, page 117.

2. **Syria,** in the Hebrew Aram, is a name of indefinite signification, sometimes embracing all the territory north of The Wilderness of the Wandering, and therefore including Palestine and the provinces around it. But Syria Proper seems only to indicate the territory bounded by the Amanus and Taurus ranges of mountains on the north, by the Euphrates and the desert on the east, by Palestine, beginning with Mount Hermon, on the south, by the Mediterranean and Phœnicia on the west. It reaches the Mediterranean only near the mouth of the Orontes. It consists of three portions: On the north an elevated tract, never thickly populated, having Carchemish and Samosata as its principal cities;

between the Lebanon and Anti-Lebanon ranges of mountains a great valley, called Cœle-Syria, "hollow Syria," forming the bed of the Orontes, flowing north, and the Leontes (*Litany*), flowing south; and on the east a level country reaching to the desert, containing the cities of Damascus on the south, Tiphsah (Thapsacus) on the north, and Tadmor (Palmyra) in the desert. During the times from Jeroboam to Jehoash, Syria was an independent kingdom, the rival of Israel, with which its political relations may be seen on the map on page 86. In the Old Testament period, Damascus was its principal city, and exercised sovereignty; but later, Antioch, in the north, became more prominent, and was the Greek and Roman capital of the province.

3. **Phœnicia** is a narrow strip of territory between the Mediterranean Sea and Mount Lebanon, north of Palestine and south of the Orontes. Its two great cities were, Zidon, the mother of Mediterranean commerce; and Tyre, her daughter. Its boundaries were never extensive; but its vessels traded with every land, and its colonies were planted all along the shores of the Mediterranean.

4. **Palestine** lies south of Phœnicia, between the Mediterranean and the desert. It will be described in connection with the Physical Map of Palestine, page 29, and Moab and Edom, near it, on pages 39 and 45.

5. South of Palestine is **The Wilderness,** a part of Arabia, in which the Israelites wandered during forty years. Its description may be found on page 42.

6. **Egypt** lies in the northeastern corner of Africa. See its description on page 41.

OUTLINE FOR TEACHING AND REVIEW.

1. Let the teacher state the EXTENT of the Old Testament World, and its comparison in size with the United States, as given in the description; the class taking down the figures in their note-books.

2. Let the teacher draw upon the blackboard the SEAS of the map, in presence of the class, describing each as it is drawn. If drawn in advance with an ordinary slate pencil, the mark cannot be seen by the class, but can be traced by the teacher with white chalk. Do not try to make the lines exact. A general sketch will answer far better than finished work. Write upon each its initial letter, but let the class give its full name; and at the same time follow the teacher by drawing the map on slates or in note-books. Review the names of the seas: *Caspian, Persian Gulf, Red Sea, Mediterranean* or *Great Sea, Dead Sea, Lake Arsissa* or *Van, Lake Urumiyeh.*

3. Draw next the most important of the MOUNTAIN RANGES, showing

their general lines, in blue or green color, naming each as drawn, requiring the class to repeat its name, and to review at the close all the names: *Ararat* (including *Masius, Niphates, Abus*), *Caspian, Zagros, Lebanon, Taurus.*

4. Draw the RIVERS in white chalk, and drill the class upon their names as the course of each is shown: *Araxes, Tigris, Euphrates, Orontes, Jordan, Nile.* Review the names of seas, mountains, and rivers, before beginning the next subject.

5. Show the LANDS in their three classes, and drill the class upon their names. (1.) MOUNTAIN LANDS: *Armenia, Media, Persia.* (2.) LANDS OF THE PLAIN: *Assyria, Elam, Mesopotamia, Chaldea, Arabia.* (3.) LANDS OF THE MEDITERRANEAN: *Asia Minor, Syria, Phœnicia, Palestine, Wilderness, Egypt.*

Review the entire map, from the beginning; then erase it, and call for the class to give the names as they are indicated by the pointer without marking.

ANCIENT WORLD, AND DESCENDANTS OF NOAH.

One of the most ancient and valuable accounts of the races of mankind is found in the tenth chapter of Genesis. It states the location and, in large degree, the relationship of the various families upon the earth, as they were known to the descendants of Abraham.

In the interpretation of this "Table of Nations" certain facts and principles are to be borne in mind. 1. It is *incomplete;* not undertaking to name all the races of mankind, but only those in the Hebrew, Egyptian, and Assyrian sphere of interest. Neither the yellow, the brown, or the black races are represented upon it, and only a portion of the ruddy or white race. 2. It is *popular* and not scientific. The Orientals never wrote with the precision of modern students. Hence find in this document terms employed in a general and indefinite manner. 3. It is, in reality, *geographical* rather than racial. For example, when it says "the sons of Canaan," we are not always to infer a literal descent, but a location in the land of Canaan. The names upon this table are generally not those of individuals, but of tribes. In some instances relationship may be indicated; but generally propinquity of settlement is all that can positively be affirmed. 4. It arranges the nations *according to zones,* in a general direction from northwest to southeast; not by continents, as was formerly supposed. The nations of the Japhetic family are found in Asia and Europe; the Shemites, or Semites, in Asia; the so-called Hamitic races, in Asia and Africa. After the deluge an instinct of migration took possession of the human family. From the original home (long supposed to be near the Caspian Sea, but now uncertain as to locality) clans moved in all directions, and nations arose, occupying different lands.

I. THE JAPHETIC NATIONS.

These belonged to seven families, who are called "sons of Japheth" in Gen. 10:2; and seven others, who are

BIRS NIMROUD (SUPPOSED TOWER OF BABEL).

spoken of as his grandsons in Gen. 10:3, 4. These statements are not necessarily to be understood literally. There may have been other sons and grandsons of Japheth; but these were the ones whose names are remembered as the founders of nations. The peoples descended from Japheth belong to what is called the Aryan or Indo-European race.

1. **Gomer** is named, in Ezek. 38:2–6, as a race opposed to Israel after the captivity. They were probably the people whom the Assyrians called *Gimirrai,* and the Greeks *Kimmerioi.* Their name is perpetuated in the *Crimea,* their early home. A branch of this race moving westward became the *Cimbri,* who were formidable enemies of Rome; and probably another, the *Cymry,* settled in the British Isles, and were the ancestors of the Welsh and the Irish. The Celtic races, to which the French partly belong, are descended from this family.

Three of the families descended from Gomer formed separate tribes, named, in the table of nations in Gen. 10:3, after Ashkenaz, Riphath and Togarmah. All of these had homes around or near the Black Sea.

(1.) *Ashkenaz* is the name of a people spread out of *Mysia* and *Phrygia* in Asia Minor. "Ascanios," a Greek form of the word, occurs in Homer as the name of a Mysian and Phrygian prince. It is, however, true that, in Jer. 51:27, Ashkenaz is located in Western Armenia, whither this people had later migrated. Here, also, the Assyrians located them.

(2.) *Riphath* was formerly supposed to point to the *Riphæan Mountains,* north of the Danube and west of the Black Sea, but this is very doubtful.

(3.) *Togarmah* (Ezek. 27:14; 38:6) is identified with the land of *Armenia,* whose people have a tradition that they are descended from Targom.

2. **Magog** (called, in Ezek. 38 and 39, *Gog,* the prefix *Ma* being thought to signify "land") is generally understood to designate the *Scythians.*

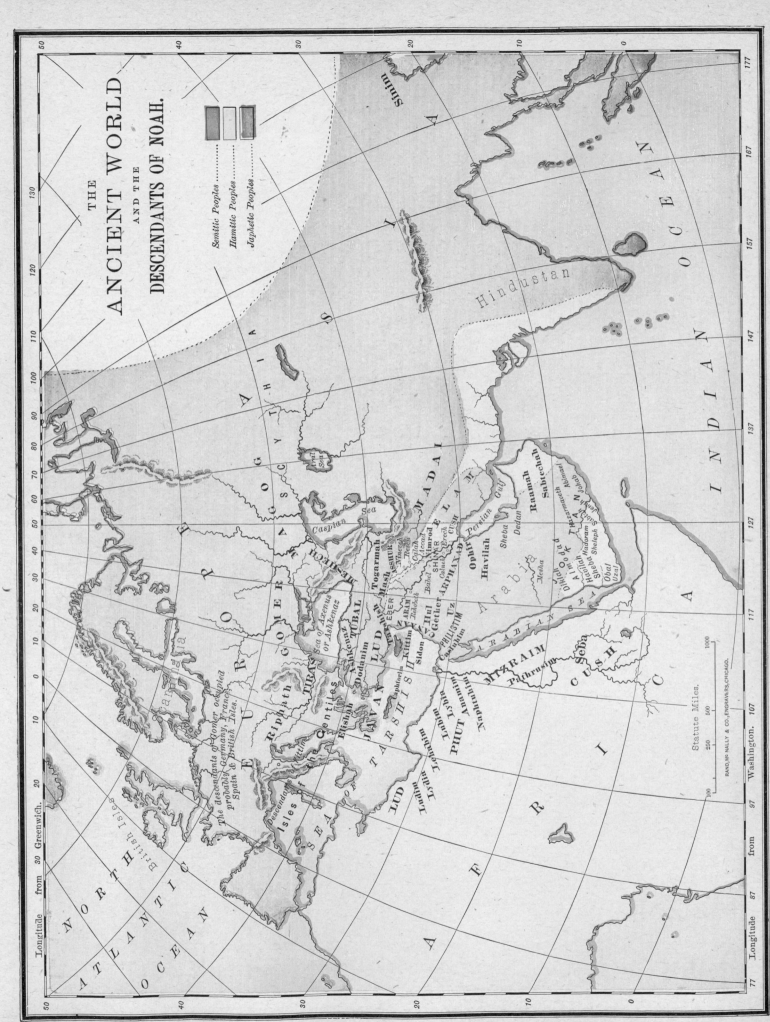

THE ANCIENT WORLD

AND THE

DESCENDANTS OF NOAH.

Semitic Peoples ....
Hamitic Peoples ....
Japhetic Peoples ....

Hindustan

INDIAN OCEAN

Sinim

SCYTHIA

EGOG

Aral Sea

Caspian Sea

MESHECH

TOGARMAH

MADAI

ELAM

ASSHUR

Raamah

Sabtechah

Persian Gulf

Sheba

Dedan

Havilah

Arabia

DIKLAH

Hazarmaveth

Abimael

Joktan

Obal

Uzal

JOKTAN

Ophir

SHINAR

Nimrod

Accad

Babel

Erech

Calah

Resen

Cush

Gether

Uz

Hul

ARPHAXAD

SALAH

EBER

PELEG

JOKTAN

ARAM

CANAAN

Sidon

Zidon

Kittim

Caphtorim

ARABIAN SEA

MIZRAIM

Pathrusim

SEBA

CUSH

PHUT

Anamim

Naphtuhim

Lubim

Lydia

Lehabim

LUD

Lydia

JAVAN

TARSHISH

Kittim

Tarshish

Dodanim

Elishah

TUBAL

Ashkenaz

Sea of Axenus
or Ashkenaz

GOMER

Riphath

TIRAS

Descendants of Kittim

Isles of the Gentiles

SEA OF TARSHISH

EUROPE

Carthage

British Isles

NORTH

ATLANTIC

OCEAN

The descendants of Gomer occupied
probably Germany, France,
Spain & British Isles.

AFRICA

Statute Miles.

1000
500
100

RAND, McNALLY & CO., ENGRAVERS, CHICAGO.

Longitude   from   30   Greenwich.

Longitude   from   Washington.   107   97   87   77

3. **Madai** is everywhere in Scripture the word translated *Medes*, whose early home was south of the Caspian Sea, whence they marched westward, and conquered the lands as far as the Mediterranean.

4. **Javan** is the Hebrew term for the *Greeks*, as is indicated by various references in the Old Testament. It is especially applied to the Ionians (originally called Iafon-es, the descendants of Iafon, or Javan), who were the Grecian people, with whom the Israelites were brought into commercial relations.

Five lands and races are named as subdivisions of the family of Javan in Gen. 10:4, all of which were situated near each other.

(1.) *Elishah* (or, as in Ezek. 27:7, "the isles of Elishah,") is supposed to refer to the *Æolians*, inhabiting the isles of the Ægean Sea, from which came the purple dye mentioned in Ezekiel's reference.

(2.) *Tarshish* was formerly supposed to refer to *Tarsus* in Cilicia of Asia Minor, on the authority of Josephus, but is now identified with *Tartessus* in Spain, embracing the coast land from Gibraltar to the Guadalquiver.

(3.) *Kittim*, or *Chittim*, was the name applied to the island of *Cyprus*, of which one of the cities was called Kitium. The name Chittim was also loosely given by the Hebrews to the shores and isles of the Mediterranean.

(4.) *Dodanim* (or, as in some copies of 1 Chron. 1:7, Rodanim). If the reading *Dodanim* be preferred, this may point to the *Dardanians*, a name often applied in the classics to the people of Troy, the famous city of Homer. The other reading, *Rodanim*, which is preferred by some critics, is supposed to point to the isle of Rhodes, in the Ægean Sea, a home of the ancient Greeks. Thus both Javan and all his sons who founded families were connected with the Greek race.

(5.) *The Isles of the Gentiles* (Gen. 10:5) in Hebrew refers not only to islands, but all lands bordering upon the sea. Here it refers to the Japhetic colonies on the coasts of the Mediterranean, the Black and the Caspian Seas.

5. **Tubal,** and 6. **Meshech,** are generally associated in Scripture. (Ezek. 27:13; 32:26; 38:2, 3; 39:1.) From their associations, they are to be sought near the Caspian and Black Seas, where Herodotus mentions the *Tibareni* and the *Moschi*.

7. **Tiras** (1. Chron. 1:5) was believed by the Jews to refer to the *Thracians*, southwest of the Black Sea. There is nothing to oppose this view, but no evidence except the similarity of name in its favor.

II. THE HAMITIC RACES.

These are named with greater particularity, because they were those which rose to prominence early in the history, and those with which the Hebrews were brought into closer relations, either as enemies or as friends. Four principal races are given, some of which were greatly subdivided. The homes of these races were in Africa, Eastern Arabia, with a fringe of seacoast along the eastern Mediterranean, and the great Mesopotamian valley, in which arose the earliest world empires. They have been sometimes called *Turanians*. It is by no means probable that all these nations should be regarded as the descendants of Ham, the son of Noah. In this list are evidently grouped together some races whose territory was contiguous, but whose physical appearance and language show no relationship.

1. **Cush** is, throughout the Bible, the word translated *Ethiopia*. Generally this refers to the region south of Egypt, now known as Abyssinia; but in Gen. 2:13, Isa. 11:11, and Ezek. 38:5, the reference must be to an Asiatic Cush, in Mesopotamia. The subdivisions of the Cushite tribes in Gen. 10:7-12, show that the earliest great Oriental monarchies were of this race. These subdivisions are as follows:

(1.) *Seba.* These were, probably, the Ethiopians of Meroë, on the Nile, anciently called *Saba;* in Isa. 43:3 and 45:14, connected with the Egyptians.

(2.) *Havilah.* This is supposed to refer to *Arabia*, or at least a part of it.

(3.) *Sabtah.* This may refer to the *Sabbatha*, or *Sabota*, of Pliny and Ptolemy, on the southern shore of Arabia.

(4.) *Raamah*, with whom are associated his sons or descendants, *Sheba* and *Dedan*, occupied the eastern shore of Arabia, near the Persian Gulf.

(5.) *Sabtechah.* This is unknown, but, from the relation of the previous names, may have been in the southeastern portion of Arabia.

(6.) *Nimrod* is named as a descendant of Cush (perhaps the only name of an individual in the list), and the founder of the early Babylonian empire.

2. **Mizraim** is the name everywhere used for *Egypt* in the Hebrew. The word is in the dual form, representing the two divisions of the country, and corresponding to the two crowns on all the royal effigies. Several branches of this race are especially mentioned.

(1.) *Ludim.* Not the same with the *Lud* of verse 22, but from its associations plainly in Africa. The location has been given as *Nubia*, but is very doubtful.

(2.) *Anamim.* An unknown people, whose identity was early lost in some other race.

(3.) *Lehabim.* These are elsewhere in Scripture called *Lubim*, and were the Libyans, or people of Libya, west of Egypt, on the southern shore of the Mediterranean.

(4.) *Naphtuhim.* Probably the *Na-Ptah* of the Egyptian monuments, having their home at *Memphis*, south of the Delta.

(5.) *Pathrusim.* Often referred to in the prophets as *Pathros*, or Upper Egypt.

(6.) *Casluhim.* An unknown people, perhaps in the vicinity of *Goshen*.

(7.) *Caphtorim.* Generally supposed to refer to the people on the island of *Crete*. With these, and not with the *Casluhim*, should the *Philistim* be connected. (See Deut. 2:23, Jer. 47:4, Amos 9:7.)

3. Phut. The word is several times translated *Libya*, and, from its association with other tribes, should probably be referred to that section in Northern Africa. (See Jer. 46:9; Ezek. 27:10; 30:5; 38:5; Nah. 3:9.) Some of these passages would indicate that there was also an Asiatic branch of this same family.

4. Canaan. The ancient inhabitants of Palestine and Lower Syria, from Gaza to Hamath. In their most flourishing period, just before the conquest by Joshua, they embraced six subdivisions or clans. (See map on page 36, and explanations.)

III. THE SEMITIC RACES. (Gen. 10:21–31.)

The descendants of Shem are placed last in the list of the table of nations, not because their founder was the youngest, but because out of their lines one family is chosen as the especial theme of the history, which thus receives a fitting introduction. Shem was the founder of five great races, and of many subordinate tribes.

1. Elam everywhere is recognized as the name of a province east of the Tigris and north of the Persian Gulf, called by the Greeks *Elymais*. The name was often applied, in later times, to the whole of Persia, whose capital stood within its territory.

2. Asshur is frequently mentioned in the Old Testament. It was located on the Tigris, having Nineveh as its capital, and its people at one time were rulers of all the lands westward to the Mediterranean.

3. Arphaxad, or *Arpachshad* (as in the margin of Gen. 11:10), has been supposed to be the ancestor of the Chaldeans, whose home was at the head of the Persian Gulf. The patriarch Abraham belonged to his race, and was born in "Ur of the Chaldees." Another of Arphaxad's descendants was *Joktan*, from whom arose thirteen tribes, named after *Almodad, Sheleph, Hazarmaveth, Jerah, Hadoram, Uzal, Diklah, Obal, Abimael, Sheba* (the most important of all in after history, absorbing most of the rest), *Ophir, Havilah*, and *Jobab*. All these occupied the southeastern and southern sections of the great Arabian peninsula. The fact that some of these names have already been mentioned in the Hamite genealogies may indicate that the two races became mingled.

4. Lud. This is believed by most scholars to refer to the *Lydians*, who dwelt on the southwestern border of Asia Minor, and under their king, Crœsus, became a powerful nation. Their history was short, as their empire was conquered by Cyrus the Great.

5. Aram. This is the word uniformly rendered *Syria* throughout the Bible. The Arameans, or Syrians, occupied the region between Canaan and Phœnicia, on the east, the Euphrates on the north, and the great desert on the west and south. Four branches of this race formed separate tribes. *Uz*, the race of the ancient Job, was settled in the middle of North Arabia, near Nejd. *Hul* and *Gether* are supposed (but with slight evidences) to have occupied the country near Lake Merom, where the *Geshurites* were afterward found. *Mash*, or, as called in 1 Chron. 1:17, *Meshech*, may have merged with the Meshech of the Japhetic line.

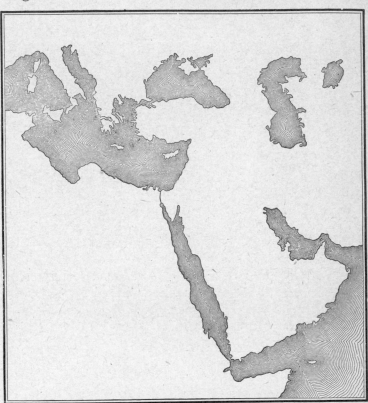

OUTLINE MAP FOR REVIEW.

OUTLINE FOR TEACHING.

1. The principal authorities for the map on page 24, and its explanations, are: "Ethnic Affinities," by Canon George Rawlinson; E. H. Browne, in "The Speaker's Commentary"; J. G. Murphy's "Notes on Genesis"; Dillmann, "Commentary on Genesis"; and "The Races of the Old Testament," by A. H. Sayce. To these the student is referred for more thorough discussion of the subject.

2. In teaching, draw on the blackboard a sketch map (no matter how roughly) of the outlines of the coast, as given above, and then write on each place the name of the people occupying it. Take, first, the great divisions of Noah's family; then, the subdivisions; then, the minor tribes. Review the locations as each family is finished. Write on the board only the first syllable of each name, as an aid to memory, as *Ar* for *Arphaxad*, *Cu* for *Cush*, etc. If the names of each of the three great races are written in chalk of a different color, it will make the distinctions more readily understood.

3. If practicable, by means of a duplicating process, print a sufficient number of copies of the sketch map to supply the class or audience, and let each person, with pencil, place on the map the names of the tribes as they are located. This will greatly add to the interest of the lesson.

REVIEW CHART—THE TABLE OF NATIONS.

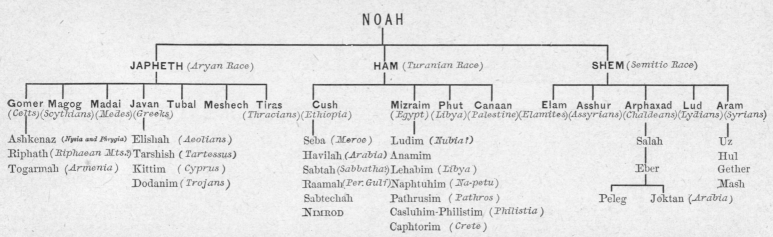

NOAH

JAPHETH (*Aryan Race*)   **HAM** (*Turanian Race*)   **SHEM** (*Semitic Race*)

Gomer Magog Madai Javan Tubal Meshech Tiras   **Cush**   **Mizraim Phut Canaan**   **Elam Asshur Arphaxad Lud Aram**
(*Celts*)(*Scythians*)(*Medes*)(*Greeks*)   (*Thracians*)   (*Ethiopia*)   (*Egypt*) (*Libya*)(*Palestine*)   (*Elamites*)(*Assyrians*)(*Chaldeans*)(*Lydians*)(*Syrians*)

Ashkenaz (*Nysia and Phrygia*) Elishah (*Aeolians*)   Seba (*Meroe*)   Ludim (*Nubia?*)   Salah   Uz
Riphath (*Riphaean Mts.?*) Tarshish (*Tartessus*)   Havilah (*Arabia*) Anamim   Hul
Togarmah (*Armenia*) Kittim (*Cyprus*)   Sabtah (*Sabbatha?*) Lehabim (*Libya*)   Eber   Gether
                      Dodanim (*Trojans*)   Raamah(*Per. Gulf*)Naphtuhim (*Na-petu*)   Mash
                                            Sabtechah   Pathrusim (*Pathros*)   Peleg   Joktan (*Arabia*)
                                            Nimrod   Casluhim-Philistim (*Philistia*)
                                                            Caphtorim (*Crete*)

THE JEWS' WAILING PLACE, AT JERUSALEM.

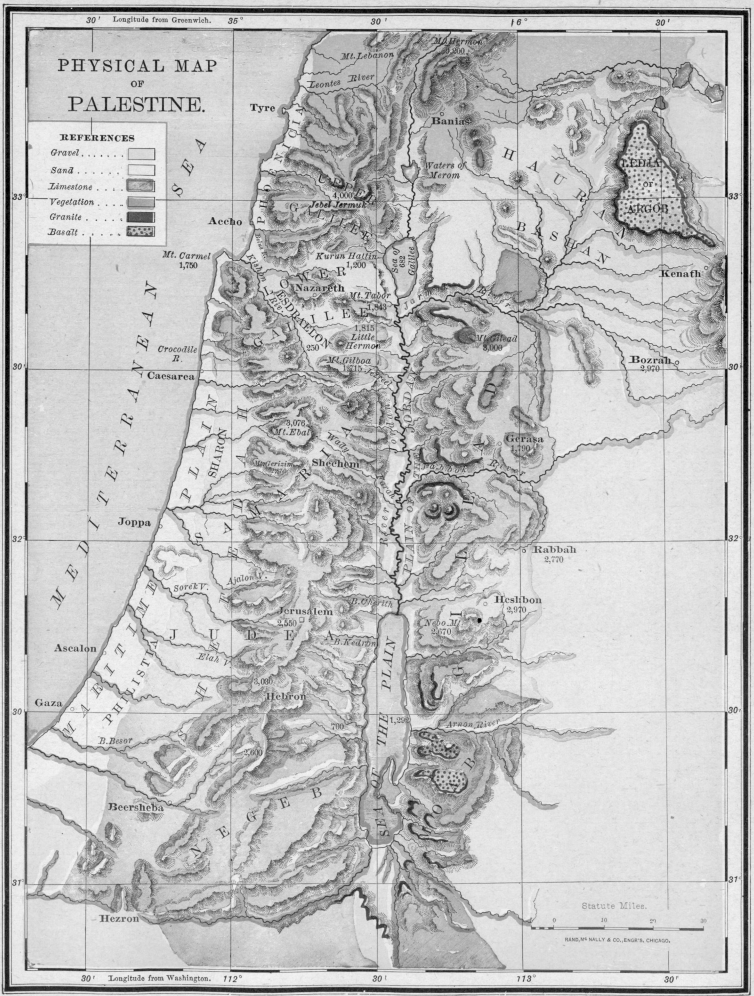

PHYSICAL MAP
OF
PALESTINE.

REFERENCES

Gravel . . . .
Sand . . . .
Limestone . . . .
Vegetation . . . .
Granite . . . . .
Basalt . . . . . .

RAND, McNALLY & CO., ENGR'S, CHICAGO.

PHYSICAL PALESTINE.

I. DIMENSIONS.

THE terms Canaan, Palestine and the Holy Land are used with various meanings. The first is the original name, taken from the ancestor of its early inhabitants; the second is a modernized form of the word "Philistine," a race occupying its southwest portion; the third is the name applied to it as the land where the Saviour of the world lived and died. In either one of these three names we may also find three different limitations of meaning. 1. Strictly speaking, the word "Canaan" refers to the country between the Jordan and the Mediterranean; bounded on the north by Mount Lebanon, and on the south by the desert. The name "Palestine" is often given to this section only. This region includes about 6,600 square miles, a territory

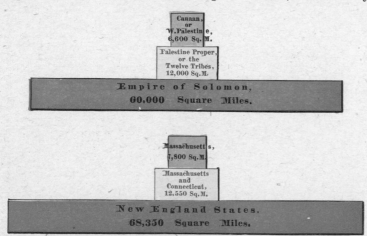

COMPARATIVE AREAS OF PALESTINE AND NEW ENGLAND.

smaller than the State of Massachusetts by 1,200 square miles. 2. Palestine Proper, the Land of the Twelve Tribes, embraces both Canaan and the region east of the Jordan, loosely called Gilead, though that name strictly belongs to but one section of it. Palestine Proper is bounded on the north by the river Leontes, Mount Lebanon and Mount Hermon; east by the Syrian desert, south by the Arabian desert, and west by the Mediterranean; and forms a sort of parallelogram, embracing an area of about 12,000 miles, about the size of Massachusetts and Connecticut. 3. The Land of Promise (Num. 34), in its largest meaning, extended from the "Entrance of Hamath," on the north, to Mount Hor, Kadesh-barnea, and the "River of Egypt" (*Wady el Arish*); and from the Euphrates to the Mediterranean; including an area of 60,000 square miles, a little less than that of the five New England States. This was realized only during a part of the reigns of David and Solomon. Not all of even Palestine Proper was possessed by Israel during most of its history; for the

plain along the sea-shore was held by the Philistines on the south, and by the Phœnicians on the north.

II. NATURAL DIVISIONS.

The divisions of Palestine made by the natural features of the country are four, generally parallel to each other: 1. The Maritime Plain. 2. The Mountain Region. 3. The Jordan Valley. 4. The Eastern Table-Land.

1. **The Maritime Plain** lies along the coast of the Mediterranean for the entire length of the country, broken only by Mount Carmel, north of which it is quite narrow; but immediately south of the mountain it is 8 miles wide, thence widening to 20 miles at the southern boundary of the country. It is an undulating surface of low hillocks of sandy soil, from 100 to 200 feet above the sea-level, and very fertile. In the Old Testament period it was but little occupied by the Israelites, whose home was on the mountains. It is divided into four portions. North of Mount Carmel a narrow strip is called Phœnicia. Directly east of Mount Carmel the level country is pressed inward, and lies between the mountains, forming the remarkable Plain of Esdraelon, physically belonging to the Maritime Plain, but geographically to the Mountain Region. South of Mount Carmel lay Sharon; and further southward was Philistia, a land whose people, the Philistines, were long the enemies of Israel, and have since given the name PALESTINE to the whole land.

2. **The Mountain Region,** between the Jordan Valley and the Plain, is the backbone of the country, and was the principal home of the Israelites. It is a continuation of the Lebanon range of mountains, and extends southward to the desert. It is divided into five sections, by natural rather than political lines of boundary. (1.) In Upper Galilee the mountains average a height of 2,800 feet above the sea, and *Jebel Jermuk*, the highest peak, is 4,000 feet high. (2.) In Lower Galilee the hills are about 1,800 feet high, their southeastern slopes precipitous, the northern and northwestern gentle. In this section lies the Plain of Esdraelon, about 250 feet above the sea, 9 miles across, and 14 miles north and south. (3.) The Hill Country of Samaria and Judæa, called in the Old Testament "Mount Ephraim," and "the mountains of Judah," is from 2,000 to 3,000 feet high, consisting of mountain and valley, with the watershed midway between the Jordan and the sea. Near the Dead Sea is the Wilderness of Judæa, an uninhabitable region, without verdure, and penetrated with ravines and caves; sometimes called Jeshimon. (4.) The *Shefelah*, or "low hills," are the foot-hills of the Mountain Region, forming a natural

terrace 500 feet above the sea-level, on the western side of the mountains, between them and the Plain. This extends along both Samaria and Judæa. (5.) The Negeb, a word meaning "dry," translated "South Country" in the Bible, begins just south of Hebron, and slopes southward to the Arabian desert, in a series of hills much lower than those in the northern section.

3. **The Jordan Valley** is a remarkable depression, beginning at the sources of the river, and plowing a gorge which grows deeper as it goes southward. At the springs of the Jordan it is 1,700 feet above the sea, with lofty mountains on each side, Hermon and Lebanon. At Lake Merom

pasturage. On the north is Bashan, now called "the Hauran," in the centre lies Gilead, and south was the land of Moab.

III. THE WATERS OF PALESTINE.

These may be noticed under three heads : 1. The River Jordan. 2. The Three Lakes. 3. The Brooks, or mountain torrents.

1. **The River Jordan** has three sources. (1.) The most northerly is at *Hasbeiya*, on Hermon. (2.) The largest stream proceeds from a great spring at the ancient Dan, now *Tell el Kady*. (3.) The one recognized as the source by

THE RIVER JORDAN.

it is 7 feet above the level of the sea. Below Merom it descends by a fall of 60 feet to the mile, and at the Sea of Galilee is 682 feet below the Mediterranean. Here begins the *Ghor* (its Arab name, meaning "hollow"), a gorge 65 miles long to the Dead Sea, and descending 610 feet further in its depth, with a barrier of cliffs on either side, from 2 to 8 miles apart, except at the "Plain of Jordan," or "Plain of Jericho," just north of the Dead Sea, which is 14 miles wide. This plain lies 400 feet above the level of the Dead Sea, and is encompassed by mountains which rise above it about 4,000 feet.

4. **The Eastern Table-Land** is a lofty plateau, east of the Jordan. The mountains on this side are higher and more steep than are those on the west; and from their summit a plain stretches away to the great Syrian desert. It is mostly fertile, and especially adapted to

the Jews is at Banias, near the ancient Cæsarea Philippi. It may be divided into three sections : from Hasbeiya to Lake Merom, about 40 miles; from its entrance into Merom to the Sea of Galilee, 15 miles; and from the northern end of that lake to the Dead Sea, 79 miles, — making its direct length 134 miles, though by its windings the channel is about 200 miles long. In its progress it falls over 3,000 feet, an average fall of over 22 feet to the mile. It varies in width from 80 to 180 feet, and in depth from 5 to 12 feet.

2. **The Three Lakes** are: (1.) Merom, now called *Huleh*, a triangular sheet of water three miles across, located in a swamp in Northern Galilee. (2.) The Sea of Galilee, called Chinnereth in the Old Testament, a pear-shaped lake, 14 miles long, and 9 wide. (3.) The Dead Sea, 46 miles long, its surface 1,290 feet below the level

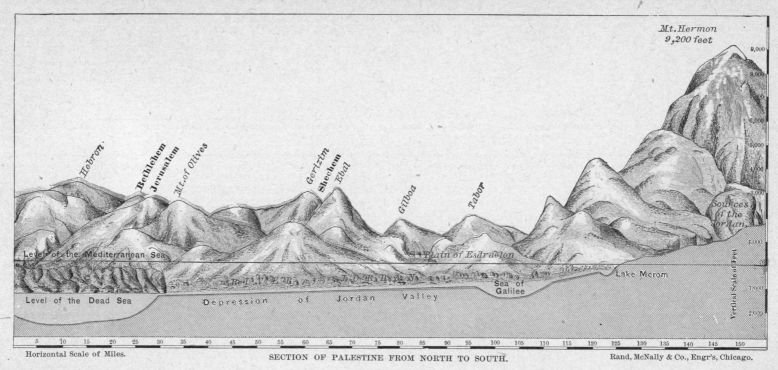

Mt. Hermon 9,200 feet

Hebron. Bethlehem Jerusalem Mt. of Olives Gerizim Shechem Ebal Gilboa Tabor Sources of the Jordan

Level of the Mediterranean Sea Plain of Esdraelon Lake Merom

RIVER JORDAN Sea of Galilee

Level of the Dead Sea Depression of Jordan Valley

Vertical Scale of Feet

Horizontal Scale of Miles. SECTION OF PALESTINE FROM NORTH TO SOUTH. Rand, McNally & Co., Engr's, Chicago.

of the Mediterranean, and in some places 1,300 feet deep, though the great lagoon on its southern end is not more than 20 feet deep.

3. **The Brooks,** or mountain torrents, are an important feature in the country. They are dry for most of the year, but during the winter are large and rapid. (1.) On the east of the Jordan Valley are : (*a*) the Hieromax (now called the *Jarmuk*), flowing from the highlands of Bashan into the Jordan, south of the Sea of Galilee ; (*b*) the Jabbok (now *Zerka*), descending from the table-land, and entering the Jordan a little south of midway between the Sea of Galilee and the Dead Sea ; (*c*) the Arnon (now *Mojeb*), entering the Dead Sea about the middle of its eastern shore. (2.) Flowing from the Mountain Region eastward are : (*a*) the *Farah*, "the

waters of Enon" (John 3:23); (*b*) the brook Cherith (1 Kings 17:3), perhaps *Wady Kelt*, near Jericho ; (*c*) the brook Kedron, running past Jerusalem, eastward, into the Dead Sea, probably the *Wady en Nar*. (3.) Flowing into the Mediterranean are : (*a*) the Leontes (now *Litany*), the northern boundary of Palestine, a stream almost as long as the Jordan ; (*b*) the Kishon, "that ancient river" (Judg. 5:21), watering the plain of Esdraelon ; (*c*) the brook Besor (*Wady es Sheriah*), near the southern frontier. Others might be named, but these are the most important, though not in all cases the largest.

IV. THE MOUNTAINS OF PALESTINE.

These may be considered either in order of height or of location. The diagram groups the principal mount-

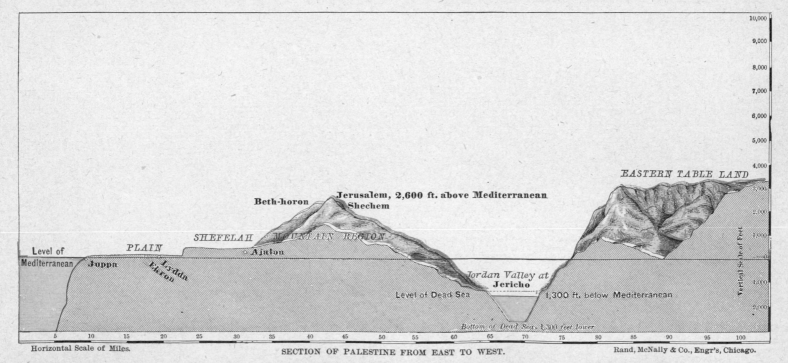

EASTERN TABLE LAND

Jerusalem, 2,600 ft. above Mediterranean
Beth-horon Shechem

SHEFELAH MOUNTAIN REGION

Level of PLAIN Ajalon
Mediterranean Joppa Lydda Ekron

Jordan Valley at Jericho
Level of Dead Sea 1,300 ft. below Mediterranean

Bottom of Dead Sea 1,300 feet lower

Vertical Scale of Feet

Horizontal Scale of Miles. SECTION OF PALESTINE FROM EAST TO WEST. Rand, McNally & Co., Engr's, Chicago.

ains in the relation of their comparative height above the sea-level; we may notice them in their order of location. They naturally divide into two sections: 1. Those of the Mountain Region west of Jordan. 2. Those of the Eastern Table-Land.

Beginning at the northern boundary of Palestine, we find: 1. Mount Lebanon, "the white mountain," a range of lofty mountains stretching northward, parallel with the sea, generally about 5,000 feet high, but at its highest point, *Jebel Mukhmeel*, 10,200 feet high. 2. The highest point in Galilee is *Jebel Jermuk*, northwest of the Sea of Galilee, 4,000 feet high. 3. West of the Sea of Galilee is *Kurûn Hattin*, "the horns of Hattin," the traditional "Mount of the Beatitudes," 1,200 feet high.

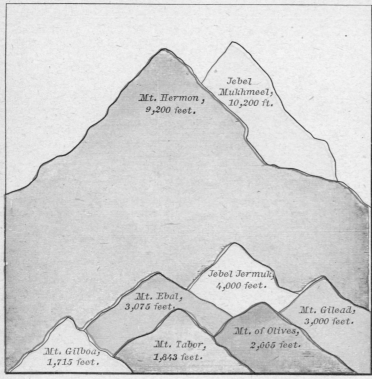

COMPARATIVE HEIGHT OF MOUNTAINS IN PALESTINE.

4. At the northeastern corner of the Plain of Esdraelon is Mount Tabor, a symmetrical cone, the battle-field of Deborah and Barak, 1,843 feet high. 5. A short distance to the south stands Little Hermon, "the Hill of Moreh," now *Jebel el Duhy*, 1,815 feet high. 6. Southward still is Mount Gilboa, the place of Gideon's victory and of King Saul's defeat, 1,715 feet high. 7. Sweeping around the southern border of the Plain of Esdraelon to the Mediterranean Sea is Mount Carmel, at its highest point

1,750 feet, but 500 as it meets the sea. These last four mountains form the boundary of the Plain of Esdraelon. In the land of Samaria, which we now enter, are but two important elevations: 8. Ebal, the mountain of the curses, 3,075 feet; 9. Directly opposite, Gerizim, the mountain of the blessings, 2,850 feet. The principal peaks in Judæa are the following: 10. Mount Zion, the seat of David's castle, 2,550 feet; 11. Across the valley of the Kedron eastward, the Mount of Olives, 2,665 feet; 12. Mount Hebron, 3,030 feet. South of Hebron the land slopes away to the level of the desert.

The Eastern Table-Land has fewer elevations, and is generally less noticed in the Scriptures. 1. On the north rises Mount Hermon, 9,000 feet high, the southern end of the range known as Anti-Lebanon, or "Lebanon toward the sun-rising." 2. South of the river Hieromax is Mount Gilead, about 3,000 feet high. 3. Near the northern end of the Dead Sea is Mount Nebo, 2,670 feet high, on a "shoulder" of which, Mount Pisgah, Moses beheld the Promised Land, and died.

V. THE PLAINS OF PALESTINE.

These have been already noticed, to some extent, but may be named together. Upon the Maritime Plain, we notice: 1. Phœnicia, a very narrow strip along the Mediterranean, north of Mount Carmel, never possessed by the Israelites, and having Tyre and Sidon as its principal cities. 2. Directly south of Mount Carmel, Sharon, having Cæsarea and Joppa as its most important places. 3. Still further south, Philistia, the land of Israel's ancient enemies, containing several cities, of which Gaza and Ashkelon (afterward Ascalon) were chief. Upon the Mountain Region we find imbedded, 4. The Plain of Esdraelon, a Y-shaped region, 250 feet above the sea-level, surrounded by mountains, and situated between Mounts Carmel, Tabor and Gilboa. 5. The Negeb, or South Country, between Hebron and the desert, in Southern Judæa, may be regarded as a plain, though of rolling character, as its hills are not so high as those on the north. 6. In the Jordan Valley, just north of the Dead Sea, is a place called "the Plain of Jordan," or "the Plain of Jericho," the site of the destroyed "cities of the plain." 7. In the northern section of the Eastern Table-Land is the vast highland known as "the Hauran," anciently called Bashan, watered by the streams which form the Hieromax river.

OUTLINE FOR REVIEW.

I. *Dimensions.* 1. Canaan. 2. Palestine (Twelve Tribes). 3. Land of Promise.

II. *Natural Divisions.* 1. Maritime Plain. 2. Mountain Region (Upper Galilee, Lower Galilee, Hill Country, Shefelah, Negeb). 3. Jordan Valley (Merom, Galilee, Dead Sea). 4. Eastern Table-Land (Bashan, Gilead, Moab).

III. *Waters.* 1. Jordan (sources, sections). 2. Lakes (Merom, Galilee, Dead Sea). 3. Brooks. (1.) East: Hieromax, Jabbok, Arnon. (2.) Mount-

ain Region: Farah, Cherith, Kedron. (3.) Maritime Plain: Leontes, Kishon, Besor.

IV. *Mountains.* 1. West of Jordan: Lebanon, Jermuk, Hattin, Tabor, Little Hermon, Gilboa, Carmel, Ebal, Gerizim, Zion, Olives, Hebron. 2. East of Jordan: Hermon, Gilead, Nebo.

V. *Plains.* 1. Phœnicia. 2. Sharon. 3. Philistia. 4. Esdraelon. 5. Negeb. 6. Jordan. 7. Hauran.

THE JOURNEYS OF THE PATRIARCHS.

AT the close of the eleventh chapter of Genesis a change is made in the subject of the Bible story. Thus far it has been a history of the entire race; but from this point to the close of Genesis a single family is brought into prominent notice, and the rest of the tribes of men are referred to only incidentally. The family of Abraham, of Semitic origin, deserve all their prominence in sacred history, since through them the true religion was perpetuated until the world was ready for its wider dissemination in the gospel period.

I. THE JOURNEYS OF ABRAHAM.

These extend over nearly all the lands of the Old Testament, from Chaldea to Egypt. They represent the separation of a Semitic clan from the great body of the race, which was then ruled by an Elamite dynasty; and they bring to our notice the political relations of the world about two thousand years before Christ, in the early Chaldean period of the East.

1. **From Ur to Haran.** (Gen. 11: 27–32.) The family of Abraham (then called Abram) lived at Ur of the Chaldees, probably *Mugheir*, south of the Euphrates, and an early seat of empire. Thence, at God's call, they migrated, moving up the Euphrates to Haran, in Mesopotamia, probably the Roman Carrhæ, and the modern *Haran*, on the river Belik, 50 miles above its entrance into the Euphrates. Here the family remained until the death of Terah, Abraham's aged father, whose traditional tomb is still shown.

2. **From Haran to Canaan.** (Gen. 12:1–9.) A branch of the family, the descendants of Abraham's brother Nahor, settled in Haran; but Abraham and his nephew Lot moved on southward, past Damascus, to the land of Canaan. They paused first at Shechem, and afterward at Bethel, at each place building an altar; but after a time removed further southward, impelled by the dearth of food in the land.

MUGHEIR, SUPPOSED TO BE UR OF THE CHALDEES.

3. **The Visit to Egypt.** (Gen. 12:10–20.) The famine caused a removal of the entire clan to Egypt, where the beauty of Sarah was the occasion of Abraham's deception, of Pharaoh's wrong, and of Abraham's expulsion from the land. He returned to his former abode at Bethel. (Gen. 13:3, 4.)

4. **The Removal to Hebron.** (Gen. 13:5–18.) This was occasioned by the scarcity of pasture for the immense flocks and herds of Abraham and Lot. The two chieftains made a division of the land, Lot choosing the Jordan Valley, north of the Dead Sea, near the city of Sodom, and Abraham the highlands around Hebron, anciently Kirjath-arba, now known by Abraham's title, *el Khalil*, "The Friend," *i. e.*, of God.

5. **Pursuit of the Elamites.** (Gen. 14.) At that period the early Babylonian empire, under Amraphel or Hammurabi (see p. 91), was at the height of its power. Its king governed Elam, Chaldea, Assyria, Mesopotamia, and most of Palestine. Chedorlaomer, the head of the united peoples, led his armies against the aboriginal races east of the Jordan. (See Map of Palestine Before the Conquest, and description, on page 37.) After subduing them he passed around south of the Dead Sea, smote the Amorites in the mountains near Hazezontamar, afterward En-gedi, and poured his host down upon the Jordan Valley. The cities on the north of the Dead Sea, Sodom and Gomorrah, with their dependent villages, being unable to stay his progress, were ravaged, and their inhabitants (including Abraham's nephew Lot) carried away captive, up the valley. News of the invasion came to Abraham, and he instantly gathered his servants and allies, and pursued the marauders. He overtook them near Laish, afterward Dan, now *Tell el Kady*, attacked them by night, pursued them as far as Hobah, near Damascus, and brought back the booty and

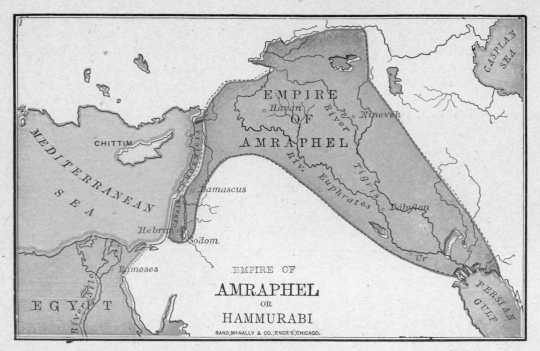

EMPIRE OF
AMRAPHEL
OR
HAMMURABI

RAND, McNALLY & CO.,'ENGR'S,'CHICAGO.

the prisoners. On the return took place the remarkable interview with Melchizedek, a priest-king over the city of Salem, perhaps the place afterward Jerusalem. After the return to Hebron the following events occurred: 1. The covenant of God with Abraham. (Gen. 15.) 2. The birth of Ishmael. (Gen. 16.) 3. The destruction of Sodom and Gomorrah. (Gen. 18, 19.) These cities were probably located on the plain of Jordan, north of the Dead Sea, and not on the south, as formerly supposed; but all traces of them have entirely disappeared

6. **The Settlement at Beersheba.** (Gen. 20–25.) After the destruction of the cities of the plain, Abraham moved southward, and made his home at Beersheba, on the desert border, now *Bir es Seba*. Here he spent most of his later years, as after various journeys we find him each time encamped at Beersheba.

7. **The Offering of Isaac.** (Gen. 22.) From Beersheba Abraham took his son Isaac, at God's command, to offer him as a burnt offering in "the land of Moriah." Some authorities accept the Samaritan tradition, that this place was Mount Gerizim; but we see no sufficient reason to dissent from the general view, that it was Mount Moriah, at Jerusalem, ten centuries afterward the site of the Temple. After this sublime token of his faith in God, the patriarch returned to his tent at Beersheba.

8. **The Burial of Sarah.** (Gen. 23.) We find Abraham again at Hebron, in his old age. Here Sarah died and was buried in the cave of Machpelah. This is undoubtedly covered by the Mohammedan mosque so sacredly guarded against the intrusion of travelers. The after events of Abraham's history may have taken place at Hebron or at Beersheba, as neither place is named as his residence at the time of Isaac's marriage or his own death. He was buried in the family sepulchre at Hebron, beside the body of Sarah.

II. THE JOURNEYS OF ISAAC.

The life of Isaac, though longer than the lives of Abraham and Jacob, was spent in a comparatively small range of territory, and with comparatively few events. We have not noted upon the map the lines of his journeyings; but the localities may be seen, as far as they are identified, upon the map of Palestine, on page 58.

The homes of Isaac were as follows: 1. Beer-lahai-roi, "Well of the Life of Vision," *i. e.*, where life remained after seeing God; an unknown locality in the south of Canaan, between Bered and Kadesh. It was so named by Hagar, after meeting an angel, before the birth of Ishmael. (Gen. 16:13.) 2. Gerar. (Gen. 26:1.) This was the chief city of the Philistines in that age; and is now called *Kirbet el Gerar*. The wells dug by Isaac, and seized by the Philistines, were probably in the region near this city. 3. Rehoboth (Gen. 26:22) is probably at the *Wady* (Valley) *er Ruhaibeh*, south of Beersheba. 4. Beersheba. (Gen. 26:23–35.) Here he made a treaty of peace with the Philistine king, and remained for many years. It was his home during the strife of Jacob and Esau, and from this place Jacob departed on his long visit to Haran. (Gen. 28:10.) 5. Hebron. (Gen. 35:27.) Here, beside the tomb of his parents, Isaac at last met his son Jacob, and here he died and was buried, at the age of 180 years.

III. THE JOURNEYS OF JACOB.

The life of Jacob is related with more of detail than that of any other person in Old Testament history; yet there is great uncertainty concerning the division of its periods. His first sixty years were passed near Beersheba; then twenty years in Haran, and fifty years in

COMPARATIVE AGE OF THE PATRIARCHS BEFORE AND AFTER THE DELUGE.		
Name		*Age*
Adam,		930.
Seth,		912.
Methuselah,		969.
Noah,		950.
Shem,		600.
Arphaxad,		438.
Eber,		464.
Terah,		205.
Abraham.		175.
Isaac,		180.
Jacob,		147.
Joseph,		110.

Canaan (though some of the best chronologers allow *forty* years in Haran, and *thirty* years in Canaan); and seventeen years in Egypt. The principal places named in Jacob's journeys are: 1. Beersheba, now *Bir es Seba*, a well-known place in the south of Palestine. 2. Bethel, now *Beitin*, 10 miles north of Jerusalem. 3. Haran, now bearing the same name. (See under Abraham's life, Journey No. 1.) 4. Mizpah, called also Jegar-sahadutha, "the heap of witness," perhaps the important place afterward known as Ramoth-gilead, now *es Salt*, 13 miles south of the Jabbok. But this seems too far south to represent the event, and we are inclined to place it at some unknown mountain between the Jabbok and the Hieromax. 5. Mahanaim, probably at *Mahneh*, 10 miles north of the Jabbok. 6. Peniel, afterward Penuel, unknown, but somewhere on the brook Jabbok. 7. Succoth, "booths," recently identified as *Tell Darala*, a mile north of the Jabbok, in the Jordan Valley. 8. Shalem, "peace." If this refers to a place, it is *Salim*, 3 miles east of Shechem. But some read the sentence, "Jacob came in peace [*i. e.*, in safety] to Shechem." (Gen. 33:18.) 9. Ephrath, the place of Rachel's death and burial, near Bethlehem.

The Journeys of Jacob may be arranged as follows:

1. **The Flight to Haran.** (Gen. 28:10 – 29:14.) Fearing the vengeance of Esau after the stolen blessing, Jacob hastily left his home at Beersheba, and journeyed northward to Haran. At Bethel he saw the vision of the heavenly ladder, and arrived safely at Haran, distant 450 miles from Beersheba. Here he remained either 20 or 40 years, according to different views, and married his two wives.

2. **The Return to Canaan.** (Gen. 31–33.) At Mizpah he made a treaty with Laban; at Mahanaim was comforted by a vision of angels; at Peniel wrestled

with "the angel of God," and was reconciled to his brother Esau; and at Salim (if that be the name of a place), near Shechem, he rested in the Land of Promise.

3. **The Residence in Canaan.** (Gen. 34–45.) The slaughter of the Shechemites by Simeon and Levi, caused Jacob to move his increasing clan further south. At Bethel he renewed the covenant with God. (Gen. 35:1–15.) Near Ephrath, or Bethlehem, his beloved wife Rachel died and was buried. (Gen. 35:16–20.) At Hebron he met once more his aged father, and remained during most of his after-life in the land. (Gen. 35:27.) While Jacob was living at Hebron, Joseph was sold a slave to the Midianites, at Dothan, on the southern slopes of Mount Gilboa, and by them taken down to Egypt. (Gen. 37.)

4. **The Descent into Egypt.** (Gen. 45–50.) At the invitation of Joseph, then prince in Egypt, Jacob left Hebron to go down into Egypt. At Beersheba he offered sacrifices, and received divine guidance. His home was fixed in the Land of Goshen, a small but fertile district between the eastern channel of the Nile and the desert, the modern province of *es Shurkiyeh*, including the *Wady Tumilat*. Here the family of Jacob remained until they became "a great nation," a period variously estimated at from 200 to 400 years, or even longer.

5. **The Burial Procession.** (Gen. 50.) After the death of Jacob, his embalmed body was borne from Egypt to Hebron. The direct route was not taken, probably on account of the hostility of the Philistine and Amorite tribes; but the procession passed around the south of the Dead Sea, through the land of Moab, and crossed the Jordan at Abel-mizraim, near Jericho, a place afterward known as Beth-hoglah; and thence to Hebron, where the last of the three fathers of the chosen people was laid to rest in the ancestral sepulchre.

OUTLINE FOR REVIEW.

I. *Journeys of Abraham.* 1. Ur to Haran. 2. Haran to Canaan. (Shechem, Bethel.) 3. Visit to Egypt. (Return to Bethel.) 4. Removal to Hebron. 5. Pursuit of Elamites. (Dan, Hobah, Salem.) 6. Settlement at Beersheba. 7. Offering of Isaac. (Moriah.) 7. Burial of Sarah. (Hebron.)

II. *Journeys of Isaac.* 1. Beer-lahai-roi. 2. Gerar. 3. Rehoboth. 4. Beersheba. 5. Hebron.

III. *Journeys of Jacob.* 1. Flight to Haran. (Beersheba, Bethel, Haran.) 2. Return to Canaan. (Mizpah, Mahanaim, Peniel, Shechem.) 3. Residence in Canaan. (Bethel, Bethlehem, Hebron, Dothan.) 4. Descent into Egypt. (Beersheba, Goshen.) 5. Burial Procession. (Abel-mizraim, Hebron.)

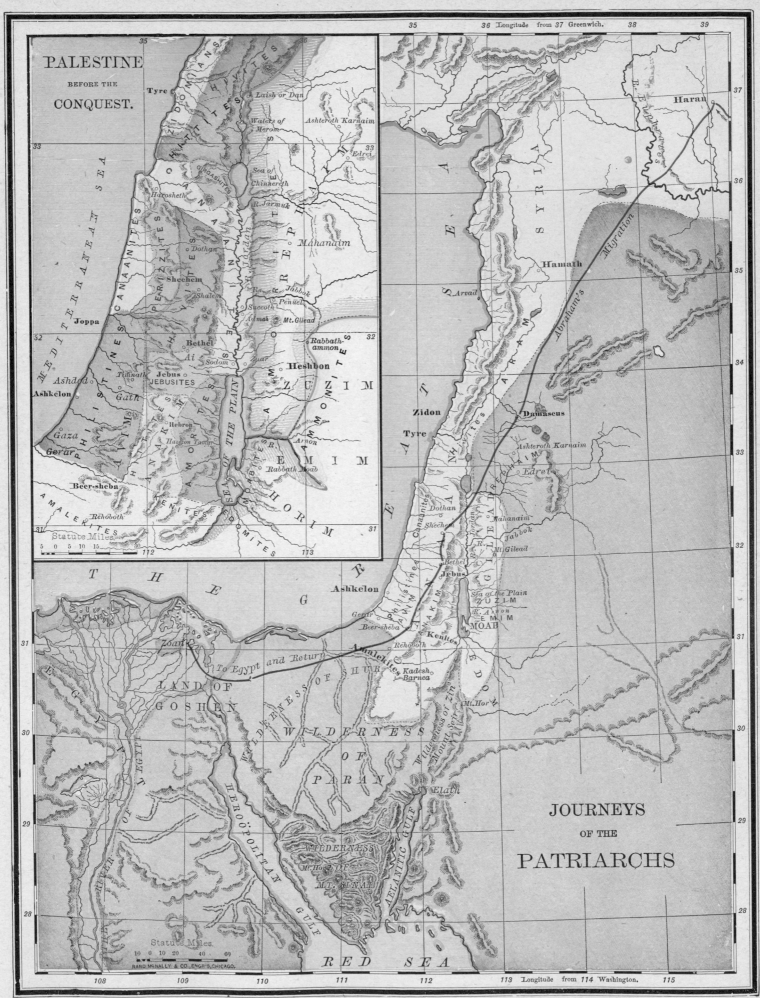

PALESTINE

BEFORE THE

CONQUEST.

Tyre

HITTITES
ZIDONIANS

Laish or Dan

Ashteroth Karnaim

Waters of
Merom

Edrei

GIRGASHITES

Sea of
Chinnereth

REPHAIM

MEDITERRANEAN SEA

Harosheth

R. Jarmuk

CANAANITES

HITTITES

PERIZZITES

Mahanaim

CANAAN

AMORITES

Dothan

Shechem

Shalem

R.

Tabbok

Succoth

Penuel

Joppa

Admah

Mt. Gilead

Bethel

Rabbath-
ammon

Ai

Sodom

Heshbon

Zoar

Ashdod

Jebus
JEBUSITES

ZUZIM

AMMONITES

Ashkelon

Gath

HIVITES

Timnath

AMORITES

HORIM

Hebron

Gaza

Hazon Tamar

Arnon

Gerar

R.

EMIM

Rabbath Moab

Beer-sheba

AMALEKITES

KENITES

Rehoboth

EDOMITES

Statute Miles.
5 0 5 10 15

112   113

PHILISTINES

SEA OF THE PLAIN

MOABITES

AMORITES

31   31

THE   GR

Ashkelon

ZUZIM

Gerar

R. Arnon

EMIM

Beer-sheba

MOAB

Rehoboth

KENITES

Amalekites Kadesh
Barnea

Zoan

To Egypt and Return

LAND OF
GOSHEN

WILDERNESS OF SHUR

WILDERNESS

OF

PARAN

Wilderness of Zin

Mount Seir

Mt. Hor

EDOM

RIVER OF EGYPT

HEROÖPOLITAN GULF

Elath

JOURNEYS

OF THE

PATRIARCHS

WILDERNESS

OF

Mt. Horeb
MT. SINAI

AELANITIC GULF

RED   SEA

Statute Miles.
10 0 10   20   40   60

RAND McNALLY & CO., ENG'R'S, CHICAGO.

108   109   110   111   112   113 Longitude from 114 Washington.   115

Tyre

Ashteroth Karnaim

Damascus

Hamath

SYRIA

ARAM

Abraham's Migration

Haran

R. Euphrates

SEA

GREAT

Arvad

HIVITES

Zidon

Tyre

Canaanites

Dothan

Shechem

GILEAD

REPHAIM

Edrei

Jordan

Mahanaim

Jabbok

Mt. Gilead

Bethel

Jebus

Sea of the Plain

NAKIM

Philistines

35   36 Longitude from 37 Greenwich.   38   39

36

PALESTINE BEFORE THE CONQUEST.

THE knowledge which we possess of the inhabitants of Palestine before the 13th century B. C. is quite scanty. The names of tribes, more or less settled, are given; but we know very little of their language, customs or origin. The description of Palestine during the first eight hundred years after the Deluge may be arranged as follows: 1. The Earliest Inhabitants. 2. The Tribes of the Patriarchal Era. 3. The Nations at the Time of the Conquest. 4. The Surrounding Nations.

I. THE EARLIEST INHABITANTS.

In most lands the earliest people have been of an unknown race, as the mound builders of America and the

JERICHO AND THE JORDAN.

cave dwellers of Europe. Very early in the history of the race a people entered Palestine, and settled upon both sides of the Jordan, generally among the mountains. They were remembered by different names in various parts of the country, but the names show the dread inspired by them among the later tribes. They were doubtless of one race, but whether of Hamitic or Semitic stock is uncertain; and their history is as unknown as their origin. They were already in their decline in the times of Abraham, when the Canaanite races, the second series of inhabitants, were in possession

of the land. They belonged to six tribes or divisions, each having a different name and location, but all bearing the same characteristics, and all regarded as giants by those who came after them. Our principal authorities concerning these archaic peoples are Gen. 14:5–7, and Deut. 2:10–23.

1. The **Rephaim,** "lofty men," are frequently named in the Old Testament, the word being generally translated "giants." In the age of Abraham they were living in the highlands of Bashan, where their capital, Ashteroth Karnaim, "the two-horned Ashtaroth," was taken by the Elamite king, Chedorlaomer, the earliest conqueror in Bible history. By degrees they lost their nationality and were merged with the Amorites, over whom one of their race, the gigantic Og, king of Bashan, ruled at the time of the conquest. They may have settled also west of the Jordan, near what was afterward Jerusalem, since a locality in that vicinity (see map on page 82.) was long afterward known as "the Valley of the Rephaim." (2 Sam. 5:18.)

2. The **Zuzim,** "tall ones," are supposed to be the same people with those who in Deut. 2:20 are called **Zamzummim.** They occupied the eastern table-land, south of Bashan and Gilead. Their capital was Ham, a city not yet identified, unless it was (as some suppose) the place afterward known as Rabbath Ammon. These people were also giants, like the Rephaim (Deut. 2:21), were also overswept in the raid of Chedorlaomer (Gen. 14·5), and during the time of the Israelites' sojourn in

Egypt, were dispossessed by the Ammonites, who occupied their country afterward, until in turn driven out by the Amorites.

3. The **Emim,** "terrible ones," were south of the Zuzim, and therefore directly east of the Dead Sea. They were overcome by Chedorlaomer at Shaveh Kiriathaim, "the dale of the two cities," and their land was afterward occupied by the Moabites.

4. The **Horim,** "cave dwellers," or Horites, occupied Mount Seir, south of the Dead Sea. Their genealogy is given in Gen. 36:20–30, and 1 Chron. 1:38–42. They lived in caves, which are still found in great numbers through that region. They were beaten by Chedorlaomer, and subsequently dispossessed by the descendants of Esau, the Edomites.

5. The **Avim,** "ruins," or "dwellers in ruins," lived in the Shefelah, or foot-hills, between the Philistine plain and the mountains of Judah. (Deut. 2:23; Josh. 13:2, 3.) They were early conquered by the Caphtorim, a Philistine race, and were in a depressed condition at the time of the entrance of the Israelites. The word Hazerim (Deut. 2:23) means "villages," or "nomad encampments," showing that they were not a settled, but a wandering people.

6. The **Anakim,** "long-necked ones." The name may refer either to their size, or their strength (which in Hebrew comes from a word similar to *neck*). They were descendants of Arba, and divided into three clans, named Sheshai, Ahiman and Talmai. (Josh. 14:15; 15:14.) Their principal home was at Hebron, called by them Kirjath-arba; but they also occupied a city near it, called Kirjath-sepher, or "book-town," a name which is suggestive of a national literature. Unlike the other races, they seem to have maintained a foothold in the presence of the incoming Canaanite races, and their gigantic appearance struck terror to the Israelite spies during the wandering. (Num. 13.) But they were conquered by Caleb (Josh. 14), and their remnant, driven from the mountains, mingled with the Philistines of the sea-coast plain. One family of this race remained as late as the days of David, that of Goliath and his brothers. (1 Sam. 17:4; 2 Sam. 21:15–22.)

II. THE TRIBES OF THE PATRIARCHAL ERA.

The chosen family came to Palestine about 1921 B. C., according to the common chronology, but probably from two to four hundred years earlier. At this time these earliest races were already superseded in nearly all the land by later tribes, of Hamitic origin, with which the patriarchs were often brought into contact. These tribes were often called Canaanites, because the nation of that name was both the original stock and in possession of the richest and best portion of the land.

We notice these tribes, as far as practicable, in the order of their location in the four great natural divisions of the country: the tribes of the maritime plain, those of the mountain region, those of the Jordan Valley, and those of the eastern table-land.

1. Beginning at the north, on the narrow plain by the Mediterranean Sea, we find the **Zidonians,** with their two great cities, Zidon the earlier, and Tyre the later. Perhaps the latter city was not yet founded in the patriarchal age. These people were early famous as the traders of the Mediterranean world, having commercial relations as far as Spain. They occupied a narrow strip of territory between Mount Lebanon and the sea, north of Mount Carmel. Their country was never possessed by the Israelites, and most of the time the relations between the two races were peaceful.

2. Next in order of location we come to the **Canaanites** proper, or that branch of the descendants of Canaan which retained the family name. While *all* the tribes of Palestine are often called Canaanites, as descended from one stock, the name strictly belongs only to people who lived in two sections of the country. The word means "lowlanders," and was applied particularly to those dwelling on the maritime plain, on both sides of Mount Carmel, the plain of Esdraelon and that of Sharon; and to those in the Jordan Valley. These together constituted "the Canaanites on the east and on the west." (Josh. 11:3.) They occupied the richest and most valuable portions of the land. The only city on the coast belonging to the Canaanites existing during the patriarchal age was Joppa, still standing. The Canaanite cities in the Jordan Valley were the "five cities of the plain," Sodom, Gomorrah, Admah, Zeboim and Zoar, of which all except the last were destroyed by the visitation of God. (Gen. 19.) Their location was in the plain on the north of the Dead Sea, and there is no reason to suppose that they are covered by its waters. In the time immediately before the conquest we find Jericho has arisen in the place of the destroyed cities, and not far from their site, as the most important city of the Jordan Valley.

3. South of the Canaanites, on the maritime plain, were the **Philistines.** "Emigrants" is the meaning of the word, supporting the view that they came from Caphtor, or Crete, which is but little more than a surmise. They were related to the Egyptians, and hence were of Hamitic stock. They came to the land before the time of Abraham, drove out and subdued the earlier Avim (Deut. 2:23), or Avites, and had frequent dealings with Abraham and Isaac. In the patriarchal age their principal cities were Gaza and Gerar; but before the conquest they had moved northward, and were a powerful confederacy of five cities: Gaza, Ashkelon, Ashdod, Gath and Ekron. (Josh. 13:3.) Their territory, if taken at all during the campaigns of Joshua, was soon reconquered, and the Philistines were the most dangerous enemies of Israel during all the period of the Judges. In David's time they were subjected; but not until the Maccabean age were they fully conquered, and their land made a part of Israel.

4. We turn now to the tribes of the mountain region, beginning, as before, at the north. As these northern regions are not alluded to in patriarchal history, and

only very briefly named in the annals of the conquest, it is not easy to determine which of the tribes occupied them. But, from allusions in Josh. 1:4 and 11:3, and from frequent mention on the monuments of Egypt, we incline to the opinion that the **Hittites** were the possessors of this country. They have left their name in *Hattin*, the Caphar Hittai of the Talmud, near the Sea of Galilee. Another branch, more frequently mentioned, were in the south, at and around Hebron (Gen. 23), perhaps extending as far south as Beersheba. (Gen. 27:46.) With these people the relations of the patriarchs were ever peaceful, and of them Abraham purchased his family sepulchre.

5. The position of the **Girgashites** is uncertain, from the infrequent mention of them. But the slight indications point to the region west of the Sea of Galilee, where we locate them conjecturally. They may have been absorbed by the surrounding tribes.

6. South of Mount Carmel, and extending to what was afterward the border of Benjamin, we find the **Hivites,** having Shechem as their principal city in the time of Jacob. (Gen.34:2.) Afterward, they occupied several towns immediately north of Jerusalem, four of which formed the "Gibeonite league," and made a treaty of peace with Joshua. (Josh. 9: 3–15.) They were a quiet people, averse to war, and submitting readily to foreign domination.

7. The **Perizzites,** "villagers" are always named in connection with the Canaanites. From the allusions in Gen. 34: 30, Josh. 17: 15, and other places, we locate them between the Hivites and the western Canaanites, in the northern portion of the Shefelah, or foothills, where villages would more readily cluster than among the mountains. They remained in the land as late as the time of the restoration from Babylonian captivity. (Ezra 9: 1.)

8. The **Jebusites** lived in the mountains around their city Jebus, afterward Jerusalem. They were of Canaanitish origin, a small but warlike tribe. Their king was slain by Joshua; but the city, though burned by the Israelites (Judges 1:8), was still held by its own people, and remained in their possession, a foreign fortress in the midst of the land, until finally taken by David, and made his capital. (2 Sam. 5.) South of the Jebusites were the southern branch of the Hittites, already referred to.

9. One more nation of the Canaanite stock remains, perhaps the most powerful of all, the **Amorites,** or "mountaineers." They occupied, originally, the wilderness between Hebron and the Dead Sea, having Hazezontamar (afterward En-gedi) as their capital; were smitten by Chedorlaomer, but aided Abraham in his pursuit and battle. (Gen. 14.) Afterward they pushed northward, crossed the Jordan, and possessed all the eastern table-

land north of the Dead Sea, dispossessing the Ammonites of its southern portion, and the Rephaim of its northern. This great country was the "land of the Amorites" at the time of the conquest, ruled by two kings, Sihon and Og.

It is probable, that, during the patriarchal era, while Abraham and his family lived as wanderers in their Land of Promise, the lands east of the Jordan were occupied by their primeval inhabitants, the Rephaim in the north, the Zuzim between the Jabbok and the Arnon, and the Emim in the south.

HEBRON.

III. THE NATIONS AT THE TIME OF THE CONQUEST.

What changes may have taken place among the tribes of Western Palestine during the four centuries while the Israelites were in Egypt, is not known; but, as the land became more thickly settled, the strifes of the Canaanite tribes and their roving traits would result in many alterations of boundary lines. But east of the Jordan the changes may be more distinctly marked.

1. The **Amorites,** already named, probably conquered the eastern table-land, north of the Jabbok, during the period of the sojourn (*i. e.*, the stay of the Israelites in Egypt), and dispossessed its early inhabitants. Many of these, however, remained among the conquerors, and one of this race, Og, the King of Bashan, ruled over the northern Amorites when the Israelites entered the land, and was slain by them.

2. Two new tribes, closely related, made their appearance during this epoch, the **Moabites** and **Ammonites.** They were descended from Lot, the nephew of Abraham, and their origin is related in Gen. 19. They arose during the period of the sojourn, and conquered the primitive Emim and Zuzim (Deut. 2:19–23), probably

as far north as the Jabbok. But the Amorites on the north wrested their conquests from them and drove them back south of the Arnon, which was thenceforward their northern boundary. The Moabites were the settled portion of the tribe, dwelling in cities; while the Ammonites were the predatory, wandering element, living mostly in the east, and without permanent dwelling places. During the period of the Judges they were among the oppressors of Israel (Judges 3 and 10), were defeated by Saul, (1 Sam. 11), and conquered by David. (2 Sam. 8:2.)

IV. THE SURROUNDING NATIONS.

The principal nations bordering upon the land of Canaan before the conquest were the following:

1. On the north were the **Hivites,** "that dwelt in Mount Lebanon, from Mount Baal-hermon unto the entering in of Hamath." (Judges 3:3.) This is supposed to have been the original home of the race, from which they journeyed to their seat in Central Palestine. Still further north were the **Arkites,** the **Sinites,** the **Arvadites** and the **Hamathites.**

2. On the northeast lay the desert, and on the southeast roamed the **Ammonites,** already mentioned.

3. On the south were several tribes, not all of which can be located with certainty. In the west, south of the Philistine country, were the **Amalekites,** a people of unknown origin and predatory habits. South of Judah were the **Kenites;** and southeast of the Dead Sea, were, in early times, the Horim (already mentioned), succeeded during the time of the sojourn by the **Edomites,** a race descended from Esau, who will be described hereafter. (See explanations to map on page 44.)

With regard to these early inhabitants of Palestine, the following facts may be noteworthy: 1. In respect to **race,** most of them belonged to the Hamitic stock; though the origin of the six earliest peoples remains unknown, and the two latest, the Moabites and Ammonites, were Semites, and closely related to Israel. 2. As to **language,** they probably spoke the Hebrew tongue, or one closely allied to it. In Isa. 19:18, the Hebrew is evidently "the language of Canaan," i. e., of the Canaanites. Whether this language was the one originally spoken by Abraham's ancestors or not, we have no means of knowing; but it is possible that it was gained, during the period of the journeyings, from the Canaanites. 3. In **government,** each village or tribe had its own ruler, who was called a "king"; but his authority was limited by the "elders," a body having influence partly from birth, and partly by force of character of its members. 4. Their **religion** was widely different from that of the Hebrews, who, from the age of Abraham, worshiped one invisible, self-existent, spiritual God. The Canaanites deified nature under various forms, especially as Baal, the giver of life, and Ashtoreth (Greek, Astarte), the corresponding female divinity. Their rites of worship were abominable, cruel and licentious. They sacrificed not only captured enemies, but their own children, to their idols, and performed acts of the grossest wickedness at their idolatrous service. 5. Their **history** is unwritten, save in its tragical close, the conquest of their land by the Israelites under Joshua, and the annihilation of many of their races. Still, many lived as a separate people through all Jewish history; and some of the best scholars are of opinion that the native population of Palestine at the present time mainly belongs to this old Canaanite stock.

OUTLINE FOR REVIEW.

I. *Earliest Inhabitants.* Rephaim, Zuzim, Emim, Horim, Avim, Anakim.

II. *Tribes of the Patriarchal Era.* 1. Maritime Plain: Zidonians, Canaanites, Philistines. 2. Mountain Region: Hittites (north), Girgashites, Hivites, Perizzites, Jebusites, Hittites (south), Amorites. 3. Jordan Valley: Canaanites. 4. Eastern Table-Land: Rephaim, Zuzim, Emim.

III. *Nations at the Time of the Conquest.* East of Jordan: Amorites, Moabites, Ammonites.

IV. *Surrounding Nations.* 1. North: Hivites, Arkites, Sinites, Arvadites, Hamathites. 2. Southeast: Ammonites. 3. South: Amalekites, Kenites, Edomites.

LANDS OF THE SOJOURN AND WANDERING.

THE LAND OF EGYPT.

I. **Names.** The present name, "Egypt," was given by the Greeks, and was never used by the inhabitants in ancient times. On the monuments it is generally called KEM. In the Old Testament the most frequent name is "Mizraim," in plural form. The poetical books of the Bible contain the name "Rahab," "the proud, or insolent," and "Land of Ham."

II. **Boundaries and Dimensions.** On the north, Egypt is bounded by the Mediterranean Sea; on the east, by Palestine, the Arabian Desert, and the Red Sea; on the south, by Nubia; and on the west, by the great African Desert. Its limits have been the same in nearly all ages. In a geographical sense, it embraces 115,000 square miles; but of this more than nine-tenths consists of uninhabitable deserts. The true Egypt, the home of its people, is simply the Valley of the Nile and the space between its mouths, an area of 9,600 square miles, a little larger than the State of New Hampshire. Deducting from this the area covered by the Nile and its branches, the land of Egypt which may be occupied or cultivated includes about 5,600 square miles, or less than the united area of Connecticut and Rhode Island.

III. **Divisions.** There have always been two Egypts, Northern and Southern. Northern or Lower Egypt comprises the Delta of the Nile, triangular in shape, a plain between the eastern or Pelusiac branch of the Nile and its western or Canopic branch. This is a vast garden, with soil the richest in the Old World, and the grain field of the Roman empire. Southeast of the Pelusiac branch lay the Land of Goshen (now *Esh Shurkiyeh*), the home of the Israelites during the Sojourn. Southern or Upper Egypt is a narrow valley, winding with the course of the Nile, varying in width from two to ten miles; a strip of fertile soil between two barren hills, beyond which the desert lies on either side. The two sections were always regarded as separate, and each was represented in the double crown worn by the kings. There was another division, made in very early times, into *nomes*, or provinces, each having its own ruler, and

its own object of worship. Of these nomes there were from 36 to 50 at different times.

IV. **The Nile.** This has been in every age the most important feature in the topography of the country, and the cause of its surpassing fertility. Its sources, long unknown, are in the great lakes of Central Africa, whence it flows in a northerly direction. The main stream, called the White Nile, receives in Nubia its prin-

AN EGYPTIAN TEMPLE.

cipal tributary, the Blue Nile, which rises in Abyssinia. During the last 1,500 miles of its course it is not increased by any other stream, and flows through a torrid desert. Yet, as it enters the Mediterranean, its current is still that of a mighty river. Its mouths are at present three in number, though formerly seven; and, from their resemblance on the map to the Greek letter $\triangle$, that portion of Egypt is called the Delta. Its annual overflow begins, in Lower Egypt, about the 25th of June, attains its height in three months, and remains stationary twelve days, at a height of about 36 feet above its ordinary level at Thebes, 25 feet at Cairo, and 4 feet at its mouth. This overflow is due to the rains in Central Africa, and as it brings down new soil, keeps the land always fertile. But for the Nile, Egypt would only be a part of the Great Desert.

V. **The People of Egypt** were of the Hamitic stock, a race of high capacity, forming the earliest civilization known in history. They were religious, but worshiping animals, and even the lowest forms of life; contemplative and studious, attaining to considerable knowledge, though on narrow lines of research; patriotic, but not fond of war, and therefore rarely conquerors of other nations. Their language was "agglutinative monosyllabic," with mingled Nigritic and Semitic characteristics.

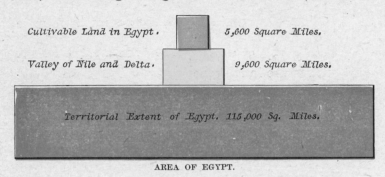

AREA OF EGYPT.

Their government was most thoroughly organized, and took cognizance of even the minute matters of life. Their art was massive and sombre, imposing from its vastness, but not varied, and therefore giving but little play to genius. The Egyptians were slender of frame,

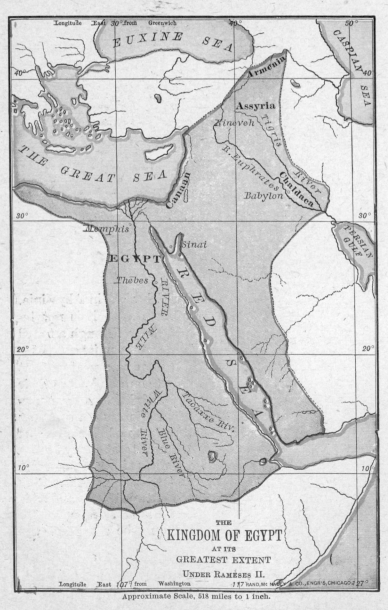

but strong. Their faces were oval and olive-colored; their hair long, crisp and jet-black. They are supposed to be represented at the present time by the Copts.

VI. The History of Egypt begins at a time undated, but long after the flood. It is divided into three periods, those of the Old, Middle, and New Empires. The Old Empire was founded by Menes, and had its capital at Memphis. During the fourth dynasty of this period the Pyramids were built. The Middle Empire arose at Thebes, and lasted until 1570 B. C. The Twelfth dynasty was most powerful during this epoch, conquering Ethiopia and Arabia. About 2000 B. C. the land was conquered by foreign princes, who ruled 400 years, and were known as the Hyksos, or Shepherd Kings. The New Empire arose in 1570 B. C., after the expulsion of the Hyksos, and lasted for a thousand years. Its greatest monarch was Rameses II., who has been supposed to be the "Pharaoh of the Oppression" (not of the Exodus), and ruled as far east as Chaldea and Assyria. The above dates are all uncertain. Concerning the chronology, see page 13. The land was conquered by the Persians, B. C. 527, and annexed to the Persian empire.

VII. The principal **Places** were, in Lower Egypt, Memphis, the ancient capital; Heliopolis, called in the Bible On, near the eastern branch of the Delta; Rameses, in the Land of Goshen; Pelusium, at the eastern mouth of the Nile; and Alexandria, in later history the metropolis of Egypt, near the Canopic mouth of the Nile. In Upper Egypt, Thebes was the most important place, and long the capital.

OUTLINE FOR REVIEW.

1. *Names.* Egypt, Kem, Mizraim, Rahab, Land of Ham.
2. *Boundaries and Dimensions.* North (Mediterranean Sea); East (Palestine, Arabia, Red Sea); South (Nubia); West (African Desert). Area, 115,000 square miles. Inhabitable, 9,600 square miles. Land, 5,600 square miles.
3. *Divisions.* Lower (Delta); Upper (Valley).
4. *Nile.* White Nile, Blue Nile; Sources; Delta; Overflow.
5. *People.* Hamitic Origin; Civilization, Language; Art; Physical Traits.
6. *History.* Old Empire (Memphis, Pyramids); Middle Empire (Thebes, Dynasty XII., Hyksos); New Empire (Rameses II., Persians).

THE WILDERNESS OF THE WANDERING.

I. Situation. This region lies between Egypt and Edom, a great triangle, having for its three points the border of *Lake Menzaleh*, the southern extremity of the Dead Sea, and *Ras Mohammed*, the southern end of the peninsula. Its northern boundary is the Mediterranean Sea, the land of the Philistines, and the *Negeb*, or South Country. Its southeastern line is the depression of the *Arabah*, and the Gulf of Akaba, or Ælanitic Gulf. Its southwestern line is the Isthmus of Suez and the Gulf of Suez. From Egypt, in a line due east, to the Dead Sea, is about 200 miles; from the Mediterranean, at the *Wady el Arish* ("the River of Egypt"), to Ras Mohammed, a line a little east of south, is about 225 miles, thus making the entire area of the triangle about 22,500 square miles, or less than the aggregate area of New Hampshire, Vermont and Massachusetts, though larger than any two of those States.

II. **Natural Features.** This region has two general divisions, and three others closely connected with them. 1. The Table-Land. 2. The Sinaitic Mountains. 3. The narrow plain by the western arm of the Red Sea. 4. The Arabah, or valley between the Ælanitic Gulf and the Dead Sea. 5. The Negeb, or South Country.

1. The northern and central portion of the triangle is a sterile table-land of limestone, from 2,000 to 2,500 feet high, and consisting of rolling plains with a gravelly surface; with few springs, and these mostly of impure water; and watered only by the streams of the *Wady el Arish* ("the River of Egypt"), a torrent which is dry during most of the year. This was the Wilderness of Paran, "the great and terrible wilderness" (Deut. 1:19) in which the Israelites wandered for 38 years. It is now called *et Tih*, "the wandering," and is traversed from east to west by two caravan routes, marked by the bleached bones of camels that have perished by the way. On the north it slopes away to a plain of white sand reaching to the Mediterranean, which was generally called the Wilderness of Shur. On the other three sides it is bounded by a chain of mountains, 4,000 feet high, called *Jebel et Tih.* It was in this wilderness country that the children of Israel were doomed to wander until all the generation that came out of Egypt died, except Caleb and Joshua. Even Moses was not permitted to more than see the Promised Land from the top of Pisgah.

2. Beyond the desert, and separated from it by the chain of mountains above named, and also by a narrow strip of sand south of the mountains, is the group of the Sinaitic Mountains. This group is triangular in form, and consists of ranges radiating from a centre. The names Horeb and Sinai seem to have been used inter-changeably, though some consider the former the name of the group, and Sinai a single peak. There has been much discussion as to which is the "Mountain of the Law," from which the Ten Commandments were given. Three peaks have been most prominently presented by different explorers. *Jebel Musa,* "the Mountain of Moses," which is supported by local tradition, and by the authority of Ritter, Kurtz, Keil and Kalisch; *Jebel Serbal,* claimed by Lepsius; and *Râs es Sufsafeh,* supported by Robinson, Dean Stanley, and the most of recent travelers. This is a granite cliff standing above the plain so boldly that one may walk up and lay a hand upon its wall, which rises 1,500 feet above the plain, and 6,500 feet above the sea. The plain in front of it is called *er Rahah,* and is 2,300 yards long and 900 yards wide, sufficiently large for the presence of all the Israelites before the mount, without including another plain on the northeast, branching from *er Rahah,* and called *Wady esh Sheikh.* It is situated in a vast and dreary desert, occupied for the most part by hordes of Arabs, who subsist by plunder, and render the journey to Sinai impossible except to large and well defended caravans.

RÂS ES SUFSAFEH (MOUNT SINAI).

3. Between the mountains and the western arm of the Red Sea lies a narrow plain, following the line of the coast. On the northwestern section it was called the Wilderness of Etham; opposite the Sinaitic group of mountains, the Wilderness of Sin. This lower portion is now called *el Kaa.*

4. From the head of the Gulf of Akaba (Ælanitic Gulf) a gorge extends nearly north-ward to the Dead Sea, an extension of the Jordan Valley, the Arabah, called in the history the Wilderness of Zin. It lies between the mountain chain on the east of the Wilderness of Paran (*et Tih*) and Mount Seir, the home of the Edomites. The opinion held by many early writers, that the Jordan

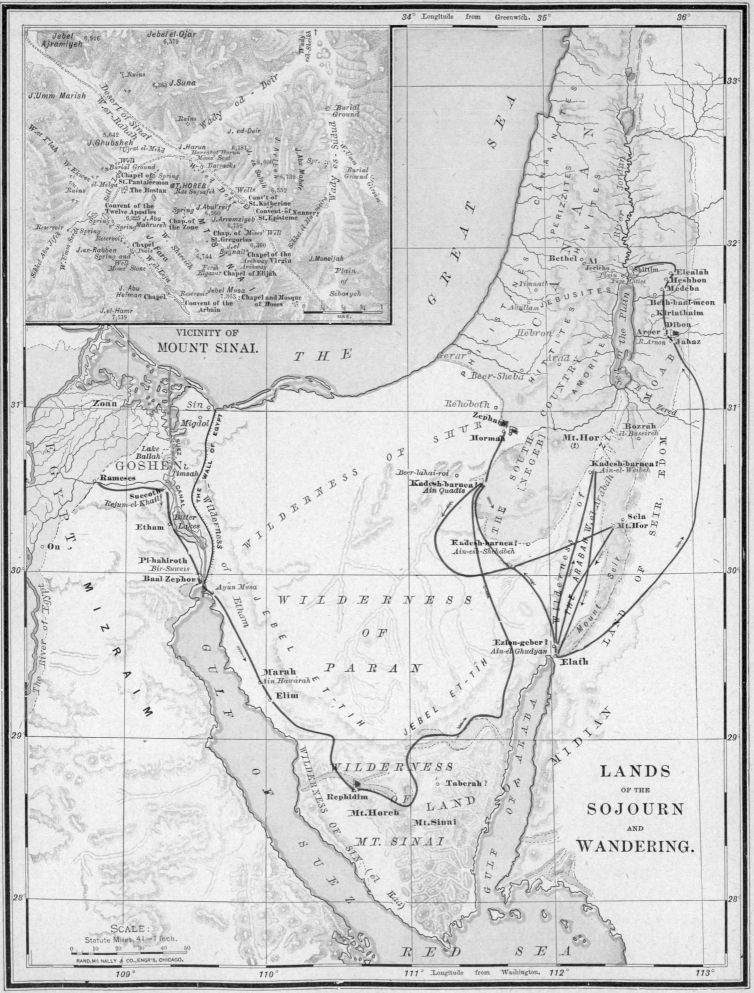

VICINITY OF MOUNT SINAI.

LANDS OF THE SOJOURN AND WANDERING.

SCALE: Statute Miles, 41 = 1 Inch.

RAND, McNALLY & CO., ENGR'S, CHICAGO.

once flowed through this depression into the Red Sea, may be correct as regards a past geologic period, but not as an historical fact; for it is evident that no great change has taken place in this region within the limit of historical time. Opposite the traditional Mount Hor the bed of the valley is about 500 feet above the sea-level; and from this point it slopes northward to the Dead Sea, 1,300 feet below the sea-level, and southward to the Gulf of Akaba.

5. The Negeb, or South Country, has already been described. (See p. 32.) The southern section of this region belongs to the Wilderness of the Wandering, from Mount Halak northward.

III. **Inhabitants.** The only inhabitants of this region at the time of the Israelite Wandering were the Amalekites, who roamed throughout the desert of Paran. Their origin is uncertain; and they may have belonged to the same stock with the earliest inhabitants of Canaan, as they were a distinct tribe in the times of Abraham. (Gen. 14.) They were the bitter enemies of Israel during all the period of the Wandering, attacking their rear, and destroying detached companies of them on their march. (Deut. 25:18.) The only pitched battle with them took place at Rephidim, near Mount Sinai, when they were defeated by Israel; but they attacked the Israelites again at Hormah, and inflicted serious injury. Long afterward their power was broken by Saul (1 Sam. 15), and their destruction was completed by David. (1 Sam. 27 and 30.)

OUTLINE FOR REVIEW.

I. *Situation.* Triangle (Menzaleh, Dead Sea, Ras Mohammed). Boundaries. North (Mediterranean Sea, Philistines, Negeb); Southeast (Arabah, Akaba); Southwest (Isthmus and Gulf of Suez). 200 miles east and west; 225 north and south.

II. *Natural Features.* Table-Land (Paran, Shur); Sinaitic Mountains (Horeb and Sinai); Plain (Etham, Sin); Arabah (Zin); Negeb (Mount Halak).

III. *Inhabitants.* Amalekites (Rephidim, Hormah).

THE LAND OF EDOM.

I. **Boundaries.** The country of Edom, or of the Edomites, lay south of that of the Moabites, the boundary between them being the brook Zered (*Wady el Ahsy*), which flows into the southern lagoon of the Dead Sea. On the east it extended to the great Arabian desert, in that section supposed to be the "land of the Temanites." On the south its border was the country of the Midianites, and the head of the Gulf of Akaba. The western boundary was the Arabah, or sunken ravine running northward between the Red Sea and the Dead Sea. There is, however, an opinion gaining ground, that "the field of Edom" extended somewhat to the west of the Arabah, and south of Palestine.

II. **Names.** The earliest name of this country, and one often used throughout Bible history, was Mount Seir, "the rugged," from its rough, mountainous nature. This was the name of its earliest inhabitants, "the sons of Seir the Horite." (Gen. 36:20.) Afterward it was possessed by the descendants of Esau, and called Edom, "red," from the "red pottage" for which Esau sold his birthright. Probably the red color of its sandstone mountains also aided to fix the name. In the New Testament time the word received a Greek form, and became Idumea. Josephus called it Geballene, "mountainous." At present it is divided into two sections, each having a different name; north of Petra being called *Jebal*, and south, *esh Sherah*.

III. **Natural Features.** Edom is emphatically a land of mountains. On the west, along the side of the Arabah, is a line of low limestone hills. Back of these rise higher, igneous rocks, surmounted by variegated sandstone, of peculiar color, 2,000 feet high. The eastern side of the mountains slopes gently away into the Arabian desert. But, though rough, the land is rich, and the terraced hillsides have in all ages been bright with vegetation, and its people have been prosperous. So the blessing of Esau (Gen. 27:39, 40) has been fulfilled in a land of "the fatness of the earth, and of the dew of heaven." Its capital during the Old Testament period was Bozrah (now *Busireh*), near its northern border. Afterward, Sela, the *Petra* of remarkable rock-hewn buildings, arose to prominence. Ezion-geber, at the head of the Gulf of Akaba, was its sea-port.

IV. **History.** Mount Seir was first settled by the Horites, or Horim, like the inhabitants of Palestine a people of unknown origin. During the later patriarchal age it was conquered and possessed by Esau, the brother of Jacob, and ever after occupied by his descendants, the Edomites. The refusal of this people to allow the Israelites to journey through their territory compelled them to make a long detour around Edom on the south and east, and enter Palestine by the land of the Moabites. During the period of the Judges the Edomites are not mentioned; but they were beaten by Saul, and thoroughly conquered by David, after a severe struggle. At the division of the kingdom, B. C. 935, Edom was held by Judah. Its people rebelled in the time of Jehoram, the son of Jehoshaphat, and, although defeated by Judah, were able to maintain their independence. They joined the Chaldeans under Nebuchadnezzar in the destruction of Jerusalem, for which the later prophecies and psalms gave them bitter denunciations. About the time of the captivity, B. C. 587–536, the Edomites gained possession of most of the country south of Judah, extending even to the confines of Egypt. But they lost their own land, Mount Seir, which became the possession of the Nabatheans. These were a race, perhaps allied to the Arabians, who laid aside their nomad habits, and founded a kingdom, whose people grew rich by the caravan trade. The Edomites, or Idumeans, south of Palestine, were conquered by the Maccabean princes and incorporated with the Jews, B. C. 130, and the Nabathean kingdom was annexed to the Roman empire, A. D. 105.

V. **Peculiarities.** The Edomites, though descended from the stock of Abraham, adopted the idolatry of the Canaanites, with whom they had intermarried. But their most remarkable feature, as a nation, was that of dwelling in caves. The mountains of Idumea are of soft sandstone, easily wrought, and are penetrated with caves and grottoes, which were used, not like those of other nations, for burial places, but for residence. The rock-hewn temples, palaces and homes of Petra, so well known to travelers, are magnificent in appearance. The custom probably arose from the fear of robbers, and from the ease with which the caves could be excavated in the sandstone rock.

OUTLINE FOR REVIEW.

1. *Boundaries.* Moab; Desert: Midianites; Arabah.
2. *Names.* Seir, Edom, Idumea, Geballene, Jebal and esh Sherah.
3. *Natural Features.* Mountains; Soil; Capitals (Bozrah, Petra).
4. *History.* Horites; Esau; Edomites; Israelite Supremacy; Chaldeans; Nabatheans; Maccabeans; Romans.
5. *Peculiarities.* Religion; Rock Houses.

THE WANDERING IN THE WILDERNESS.

There are great difficulties in fixing the location of the places and the order of events in the history of the forty years which intervened between the exodus, or "going out," from Egypt, and the entrance into the Promised Land (B. C. 1250–1210). These difficulties arise from various causes: the antiquity of the events, the fragmentary character of the history, the extent of the country, our scanty knowledge of the region, and especially the changes which have taken place in the sea-coast during the 3,000 years past. While the general course of the journey can be easily defined, the particular localities are, in many instances, exceedingly uncertain. For the convenience of the student, we divide the entire journey from Egypt to Canaan into sections.

I. **From Rameses to the Red Sea.** (Exod. 12–14; Num. 33:5–8.) The sojourn of the Israelites was passed in the Land of Goshen, between the Nile and the Isthmus of Suez. The court of the reigning Pharaoh during the time while Moses was negotiating for the departure of the Israelites, was at Zoan, or Tanis (Psa. 78:12), the royal city of the Delta. Rameses, the place of meeting for the Israelites, was probably a district rather than a city (Gen. 47:8), but may have been at *Abu Kesheib.* Pithom (Exod. 1:11) has been discovered at *Tell Maskutor,* ten miles west of Lake Timsah. Succoth, "booths" or "tents," was probably not a city but a camp, and its location is unknown. Etham, "wall" (Exod. 13:20), may indicate a place near the great wall which extended across the isthmus. Pi-hahiroth may be at *Agrud,* near Suez. Baal-zephon may be the mountain *Jebel Alaka.* The Israelites crossed the sea at the narrow Strait of Suez, where the distance from shore to shore is about two-thirds of a mile. At that time the gulf probably extended several miles north of its present position. The northeast wind drove out the waters, leaving a path across the gulf, with pools on either side, as a "wall" or defense to the crossing Israelites.

II. **From the Red Sea to Mount Sinai.** (Exod. 15–19; Num. 33:8–15.) The general direction can be traced with certainty, but the precise places of encampment are only conjectural. It is probable that so vast a body of people, about two millions, must have occupied a large extent of territory, and the "stations" were the various headquarters of the camp. This section of the journey was mostly spent in the two narrow plains along the coast, the Wilderness (or desert) of Etham, and that of Sin. At Marah (*Ain Hawarah*) the bitter waters were healed; at Elim (*Wady Ghurundel*) they were refreshed by the "twelve wells and three-score and ten palm trees." At the next station, No. 9, "the encampment at the Red Sea," they saw for the last time the waters of the western gulf, and the land of Egypt beyond them. Here they turned eastward, and, passing the mountain barrier, entered the Wilderness of Sin. (This is to be distinguished from the Wilderness of Zin, or the Arabah, on the eastern side of the peninsula.) In this wild and barren country, food failed them, and the manna began to be supplied (Exod. 16), to last for forty years. Their general course was now eastward, through the *wadies,* or dry beds of winter torrents. At Rephidim (station 13) two events are recorded as occurring. The want of water led to a miraculous supply from the smitten rock (Exod. 17:2–7); and the Israelites fought the first battle in their history, with the wandering Amalekites, who attacked the rear of the scattered host. Under Joshua, who here appears for the first time, they were defeated, and devoted to complete destruction. (Exod. 17:8–16; Deut. 25:18.) The next station was Mount Sinai, in front of which they encamped, probably on the plain *er Rahah.* Their journey thus far had occupied two months and a half, and here they remained for a year. The principal events at Mount Sinai were: 1. The giving of the law. (Exod. 19–31.) 2. The worship of the golden calf, and its punishment. (Exod. 32.) 3. The building and consecration of the Tabernacle. (Exod. 35–40.) 4. The numbering and organization of the people. (Num. 1–2.)

III. **From Mount Sinai to Kadesh-barnea.** After a year spent at and around Mount Sinai, the camp was taken up, and the host, led by the Ark of the Covenant, entered once more upon its march. The direction of the journey was northeast, and the route was probably through the *Wady Saal.* At Taberah (station 15), the "fire of the Lord" consumed some on the verge of the camp who murmured against God's commands. (Num. 11:1–3.) At Kibroth-hattaavah (station 16), (perhaps the same place with the preceding), a dislike of the manna and a lust for flesh-meat seized the crowd of people, and for a month they fed upon quails, but were punished by a plague, which destroyed multitudes, and gave a name to the place, "the graves of lust." (Num. 11:4–35.) At Hazeroth (probably *Ain Hudherah*), Miriam instigated Aaron to a rebellion against Moses, but was smitten with leprosy, though healed at the prayer of Moses. (Num. 12:1–16.) The Israelites followed the mountain chain by the Red Sea, keeping upon the western side of the hills, and, passing through the edge of the Wilderness of

Paran and along the Arabah, followed up the line of the "Mount of the Amorites" (which appears to have been a general name for the mountains in the southern portion of the Negeb, or South Country), until they came to Kadesh-barnea. The location of this place is the great difficulty in the geography of the period. The name appears to be used with reference to a region, and more definitely referring to a place. Three localities have been claimed, all on the border of the "Mount of the Amorites," or the South Country. The most southerly location is that now known as *Ain esh Shehabeh*, on the *Wady Jerafeh;* the most westerly, at *Ain Gadis*, or *Quadis*, directly south of the land of Judah; the one farthest to the north and east, at *Ain el Weibeh*, in the edge of the Arabah, south of the Dead Sea. The latter has been regarded by most explorers since Dr. Robinson, as the correct site, and as it appears on the older maps. But the Rev. J. Rowlands, on a journey through the entire region, identified *Ain Quadis* as the true Kadesh-barnea, and his conclusion was confirmed by Dr. H. C. Trumbull after a thorough investigation of all the three places. It is now accepted by most writers. We have therefore regarded *Ain Quadis* as Kadesh-barnea, and have made it the center of Israelite journeying during the thirty-eight years of the wandering. The change in the location of Kadesh-barnea may necessitate a change in the location of Mount Hor, which Trumbull places at *Jebel Maderah*, but we have retained the old locality on the edge of Edom. Twice the Israelites were encamped at Kadesh, which marked the beginning and end of the thirty-eight years' wandering in the Wilderness of Paran. From Kadesh the twelve spies were sent northward into the Land of Canaan, and the adverse report of ten of them caused such terror and rebellion in the host, that God declared that they should not enter the Promised Land until all that generation should have passed away. (Num. 13, 14.) They were ordered to turn back into the wilderness, but disobeyed, and, against their leaders' advice, undertook to force a passage to Canaan, probably up the pass *es Sufa*. But the inhabitants of the mountains (Amorites, Canaanites, and Amalekites in alliance) attacked them to their utter defeat at Hormah, and effectually barred their entrance to the land through the South Country, as the warlike Philistines had closed it against them by the way of the plain by the sea. (Exod. 13:17.) Discouraged and despairing, the host of Israel again turned their faces once more toward the terrible Wilderness of Paran.

IV., V., VI. **From Kadesh-barnea to Mount Hor, Ezion-geber, and Return.** The period of the next thirty-eight years remains in shadow. Scarcely an event is named which certainly belongs to this division, the longest by far in the journey. In the history at Num. 14:45, there is a break in the record, and other topics are referred to until we find the people at Kadesh once more, at the end of the 38 years, in chapter 20; and

the list of stations in Num. 33:18–36, is only a barren catalogue of 18 places, in which not one is clearly recognized, and only two or three can be even guessed at. Some have thought that the entire period was spent in the Arabah, wandering up and down, as two of the stations plainly belong there. But it is more probable that the people wandered over the borders between the Negeb (South Country) and the Wilderness of Paran. For convenience we may subdivide this period of wandering into its three journeys. From Kadesh, through 12 unknown stations, to Moseroth, which is afterward named in the account of Aaron's death (Deut. 10:6), showing that it was near Mount Hor. This is indicated on the Map as Journey IV. Journey V. was from Mount Hor down the Arabah southward to Ezion-geber, at the head of the Ælanitic Gulf. Journey VI. was once more through the Arabah, northward to Kadesh-barnea, completing the period of the punishment for the rebellion of 38 years before. Here three events took place. 1. The rock was

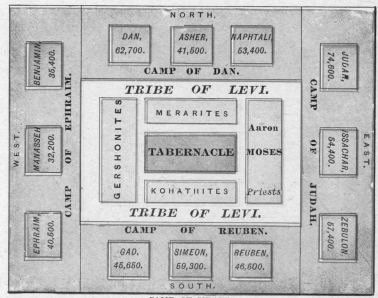

CAMP OF ISRAEL.

smitten by Moses, when God had bidden him speak to it, in order to bring forth water; and, as a penalty, he was not permitted to enter Canaan. (Num. 20:1–13.) 2. The Israelites asked of the Edomites (on whose western border they were encamped at Kadesh), the privilege of crossing their territory on their journey to Canaan, but their request was denied. 3. Soon after this, the king of the Canaanite city of Arad, in the Negeb, or South Country, 20 miles south of Hebron, hearing of Israel's approach by the same route as that of the spies, 38 years before, went out to meet the invading host. He was repulsed near the same place where Israel had suffered a defeat before, and which was thenceforth called Hormah, "destruction." (Num. 21:1–3.)

VII., VIII. **From Kadesh-barnea to Elath and Jordan.** The Israelites were now ready to enter their Land of Promise. But, as the entrance by the south was found impracticable, and the Edomites would not permit them to cross their mountains, a long detour became necessary; so for a third time they took their journey through the Arabah. This we have indicated on the map as No. VII. They paused before Mount Hor, while Aaron left them, to ascend the mountain and to die. The peak still bears his name, *Jebel Haroun.* So according to most travelers; but Trumbull locates Mount Hor in the Negeb. At Ezion-geber and Elath (stations 43 and 44), they saw once more the Red Sea, at its eastern arm. On this journey, too, but whether before or after passing the Red Sea, is uncertain, they were plagued by serpents, and "the brazen serpent" was lifted up by Moses. (Num. 21:4–9.) At last the southern point of Mount Seir was reached and passed, and now for the last time (Journey VIII.) the Israelites turned their faces northward. They traveled through the land of Teman, between Edom and the

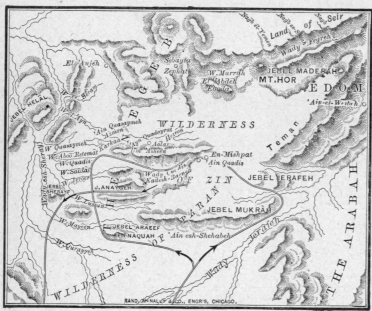

KADESH-BARNEA AND VICINITY.
(According to Dr. Trumbull.)

Arabian desert. At the brook Zered (*Wady el Ahsy*), station 49, they entered the land of Moab, which they crossed in safety (Num. 21:11); and at the brook Arnon they came into the country of Sihon, the king of the Amorites, who came against them, and was defeated and slain at Jahaz. (Num. 21:12–31.) The Amorites of Bashan on the north were ruled by the giant Og, a descendant of the ancient Rephaim. (See page 37.) His land was conquered and himself slain in a decisive battle at Edrei. From the heights of Abarim (station 57) they descended to the Jordan Valley, and encamped at their last station (No. 58) before entering the Land of Promise, on the eastern bank of the Jordan, opposite Jericho. Here occurred: 1. The episode of Balaam's prophecy. (Num. 22–24.) 2. The iniquity of Israel with the women of Moab, and the plague on the people as a result. (Num. 25:1–18.) 3. The numbering of Israel. (Num. 26.) 4. The campaigns against the Moabites and Midianites. (Num. 31.) 5. The allotment to the tribes of Reuben and Gad, and half the tribe of Manasseh. (Num. 32.) 6. The repetition of the law and the recapitulation of the journeys, in the book of Deuteronomy.

7. Last of all, the ascent of Moses up the height of Nebo, his prophetic view of the Promised Land, and his lonely death. (Deut. 34.)

STATIONS OF THE ISRAELITES
DURING THEIR JOURNEY FROM EGYPT TO CANAAN.

I. FROM RAMESES TO THE RED SEA.

STATION.	IDENTIFICATION.	EXOD.	NUM.	DEUT.
1. Rameses	Abu Kesheib	12: 37	33: 3	......
2. Succoth	Unknown	12: 37	33: 5	......
3. Etham	Unknown	13: 20	33: 6	......
4. Pi-hahiroth	Bir Suweis	14: 2	33: 7	......
5. Red Sea		14: 22	33: 8	......

II. FROM THE RED SEA TO MOUNT SINAI.

STATION.	IDENTIFICATION.	EXOD.	NUM.	DEUT.
6. Desert of Shur, or of Etham	Shore of the Red Sea	15: 22	33: 8	......
7. Marah	Ain Hawârah	15: 23	33: 8	... .
8. Elim	Wady Ghurundel	15: 27	33: 9	......
9. Red Sea	Wady Taiyibeh		33: 10	......
10. Desert of Sin	El Murkiyeh (?)	16: 1	33: 11	......
11. Dophkah	Ain Markhâ (?)		33: 12	......
12. Alush	Uncertain		33: 13	......
13. Rephidim	Wady Feiran	17: 1	33: 14	......
14. Sinai	Plain er Râhah	19: 1	33: 15	......

III. FROM MOUNT SINAI TO KADESH-BARNEA.

STATION.	IDENTIFICATION.	NUM.	NUM.	DEUT.
15. Taberah	Wady Sâal (?)	11: 3	......	9: 22
16. Kibroth-hattaavah	Erweis el Ebeirig	11: 34	33: 16	......
17. Hazeroth	Ain Hudherah	11: 35	33: 17	......
18. Mount of the Amorites	Jebel Magrah (?)			1: 19
19. Kadesh-barnea	Ain el Weibeh (?)	13: 26		1: 19

IV. FROM KADESH-BARNEA TO MOUNT HOR.

STATION.	IDENTIFICATION.	NUM.	NUM.	DEUT.
20. Rithmah	Uncertain		33: 18	......
21. Rimmon-parez	Uncertain		33: 19	......
22. Libnah	Uncertain		33: 20	......
23. Rissah	Uncertain		33: 21	......
24. Kehelathah	Uncertain		33: 22	......
25. Mount Shapher	Jebel Araif (?)		33: 23	......
26. Haradah	Uncertain		33: 24	......
27. Makheloth	Uncertain		33: 25	......
28. Tahath	Uncertain		33: 26	......
29. Tarah	Uncertain		33: 27	......
30. Mithcah	Uncertain		33: 28	......
31. Hashmonah	Uncertain		33: 29	......
32. Moseroth	Mount Hor		33: 30	......

V. FROM MOUNT HOR TO EZION-GEBER.

STATION.	IDENTIFICATION.	NUM.	NUM.	DEUT.
33. Bene-jaakan	Arabah		33: 31	......
34. Hor-hagidgad	Wady Ghudhaghidh		33: 32	.....
35. Jotbathah	Emshâsh (?)		33: 33	......
36. Ebronah	Uncertain		33: 34	......
37. Ezion-geber	Gulf of Akabah		33: 35	......

STATIONS OF THE ISRAELITES — CONTINUED.

VI. FROM EZION-GEBER TO KADESH-BARNEA.

STATION.	IDENTIFICATION.	NUM.	NUM.	DEUT.
38. Kadesh barnea	Ain Quadis	20: 1	33: 36	

VII. FROM KADESH-BARNEA TO ELATH.

STATION.	IDENTIFICATION.	NUM.	NUM.	DEUT.
39. Bene-jaakan	Arabah			10: 6
40. Mosera	Mount Hor	20: 22	33: 37	10: 6
41. Gudgodah	Wady Ghudhaghidh			10: 7
42. Jotbath	Uncertain			10: 7
43. Ezion-geber	Gulf of Akaba	21. 4		2: 8
44. Elath	Akabah			2: 8

STATIONS OF THE ISRAELITES — CONTINUED.

VIII. FROM ELATH TO JORDAN.

STATION.	IDENTIFICATION.	NUM.	NUM.	DEUT.
45. Zalmonah	Wady Amran (?)		33: 41	
46. Punon	Uncertain		33: 42	
47. Oboth	Uncertain	21: 10	33: 43	
48. Ije-abarim	Uncertain	21: 11	33: 44	
49. Zered	Wady el Ahsy	21: 12		10: 13
50. Arnon	Wady Môjeb	21: 13		10: 24
51. Dibon-gad	Dhibân		33: 45	
52. Almon-diblathaim	Uncertain		33: 46	
53. Beer	Uncertain	21: 16		
54. Mattanah	Uncertain	21: 18		
55. Nahaliel	Uncertain	21: 19		
56. Bamoth	Uncertain	21: 19		
57. Abarim, Nebo, or Pisgah	Jebel Neba	21: 20	33: 47	
58. Plains of Moab, or Jordan	Ghôr en Nimrîn	22: 1	33: 48	

GARDEN OF GETHSEMANE.

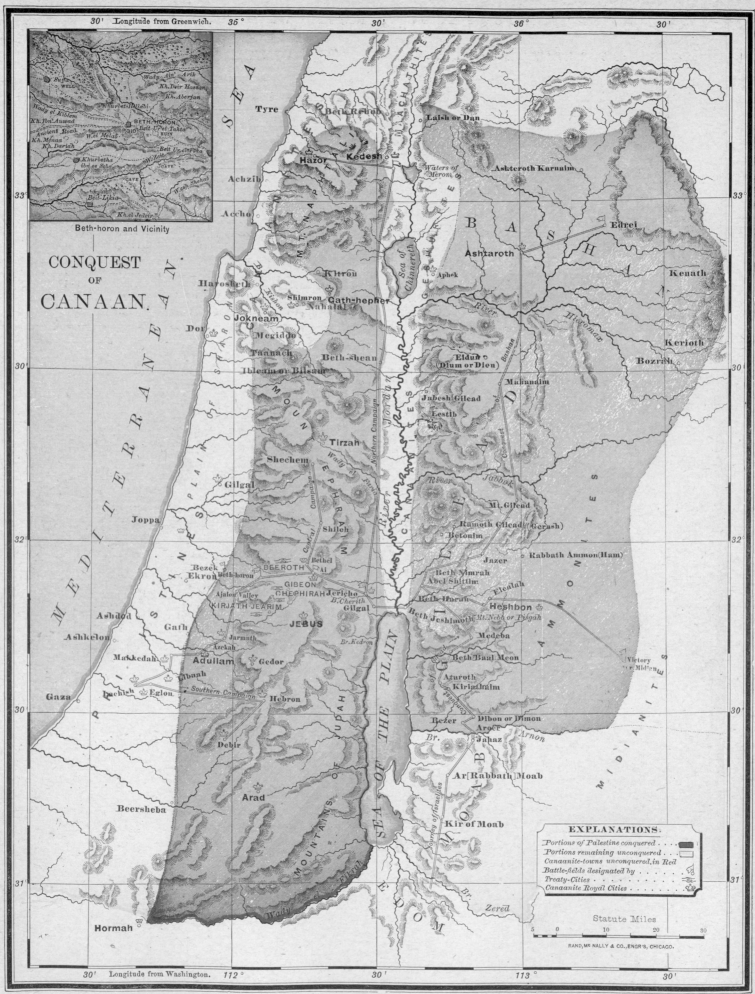

CONQUEST
OF
CANAAN.

Beth-horon and Vicinity

EXPLANATIONS.

Portions of Palestine conquered . . . . .
Portions remaining unconquered . . . .
Canaanite-towns unconquered, in Red
Battle-fields designated by
Treaty-Cities
Canaanite Royal Cities . . . .

Statute Miles

RAND, McNALLY & CO., ENGR'S, CHICAGO.

THE CONQUEST OF CANAAN.

AFTER the forty years of the Wandering came the seven years of the Conquest. Yet it is true, that in the complete sense the conquest began before the Israelites crossed the Jordan under Joshua, and was not finished until long after the period of the Judges. As Dean Stanley says: "The conquest began from the passage of the brook Zered, under Moses; it was not finally closed till the capture of Jerusalem by David. But in a more limited sense it may be confined to the period during which the territory, afterward known by the name of Palestine, was definitively occupied as their own by the Israelites." The map on page 36 shows us the territorial divisions of the land before the conquest; the one which we are now studying presents the campaigns by which it was won. These may be divided into three sections. 1. The conquest of the territory on the east of the Jordan, in three campaigns, during the rule of Moses. 2. The conquest of that on the west of the Jordan, under the leadership of Joshua, in three campaigns. 3. A series of supplementary conquests completing the work of subjugation.

SHECHEM.

in battle at Jahaz, near their border, at the brook Arnon. They were defeated, and their whole land was conquered, including their own territory north of the Jabbok, as well as their Moabite possessions south of it. Thus the Israelites obtained, as their first foothold, the rich region of the eastern table-land, from the Arnon to the Hieromax.

I. THE CONQUEST OF EASTERN PALESTINE.

This region was occupied, at the time of the arrival of the Israelites, by the Moabites between the brooks Zered and Arnon, and by the Amorites north of the Arnon. The latter people were divided into two kingdoms. The land of Gilead was ruled by King Sihon, whose capital was at Heshbon; and the table-land of Bashan by Og, a remnant of the old race of the Rephaim. Tributary to Sihon, and on the border of the Arabian desert, were the Midianites (Josh. 13:21); and near the Moabites were their nomadic kinsmen, the Ammonites.

1. **The Conquest of Gilead.** (Num. 21:21–31.) The Amorites, under Sihon, had wrested from the Moabites the land between the Arnon and the Jabbok, a short time before the coming of Israel. Moses sent messengers, requesting the privilege of journeying through their land; but they refused to permit the passage of such a vast host, and came out to meet the Israelites

2. **The Conquest of Bashan.** (Num. 21:32–35.) The success of the war with one nation of the Amorites encouraged the Israelites to cross the Hieromax and undertake the conquest of the rich pasture fields of Bashan, the kingdom of Og, whose capital was at the ancient city of his race, Ashteroth Karnaim. There is some evidence to indicate that the leader in this campaign was Nobah, of the tribe of Manasseh. (Num. 32:42.) A decisive battle was fought at Edrei, at the entrance to the *Ledja*, or mountainous district; and Og was slain, and his kingdom possessed by Israel. Its western portion, including Kenath and its vicinity, was given to Nobah, who named the region after himself. (Num. 32:42; Judges 8:11.)

3. **The Conquest of Midian.** (Num. 25 and 31.) While the Israelites were encamped on the plain of Jordan, opposite Jericho, their last station, called Shittim (Num. 25:1), a league was formed by the Moabites and Midianites to resist their advance. Balaam, the Mesopotamian seer, was summoned to aid them by his curses

against Israel; but his words were turned to blessing. (Num. 22–24.) Fearing the result of open war, the allied nations now undertook to corrupt Israel by their friendship and the seductions of their women; and they succeeded to such an extent that multitudes of the people perished by a plague which fell upon the nation as a penalty. The Moabites were punished by exclusion for ten generations from the privileges of Israel (Deut. 23:3, 4), and by the loss of that portion of their territory already taken from the Amorites. The Midianites, evidently the guiltier nation, were doomed to utter destruction. The campaign against them was regarded as a sacred war, and Phinehas the priest took command of the army. The entire people were laid under the ban, and the portion of them east of the Jordan were thoroughly annihilated. This was, however, only a small section of the great tribe of Midian, whose principal home was on the eastern shore of the Red Sea, south of the Edomites; and their former home near Moab was again repopulated, and, some centuries afterward, gave new trouble to Israel.

The entire country east of the Jordan and north of the brook Arnon was thus conquered by the Israelites before the death of Moses. It was assigned to the tribes of Reuben and Gad, and half the tribe of Manasseh, as their home, upon condition that their warriors should accompany the rest of the tribes in the conquest of Western Palestine. (Num. 32.) Their boundaries will be noticed in connection with the map of Israel, as divided among the Twelve Tribes.

II. THE CONQUEST OF WESTERN PALESTINE.

This was undertaken by Joshua after the death of Moses, and, as far as can be ascertained from the record, was accomplished in three campaigns. The war began with the passage of the Jordan, B. C. 1210, and, so far as active hostilities were concerned, was finished in seven years. But the great mass of the native population remained upon the soil, to plague the Chosen People by the influence of their wickedness, so that the conquest was never thoroughly completed. Indeed, some writers think that the inhabitants of Palestine at the present time belong mainly to the old Canaanite stock, which has perpetuated itself under all the changes of government.

1. **The Conquest of Central Palestine.** (Josh. 3–8.) According to the account in the book of Joshua, this was a brief campaign; but the Samaritan records relate a series of supplementary sieges and battles, which would indicate that the war may have been longer than appears. Still, there are evidences that the Hivites and Perizzites, who occupied most of this district, were peaceful peoples, readily yielding to the conquerors, so that the resistance was less stubborn than in other sections. The war began with the passage of the Jordan, an event ever kept in mind as the entrance of the people upon their own land. They pitched their camp at Gilgal, in the Jordan Valley, and fortified the place as a permanent headquarters during the entire period of conquest. (Josh. 5.) Jericho was first taken, by supernatural aid, and devoted to God as the first fruits of conquest. (Josh. 6.) An act of trespass against God by Achan, caused a defeat at Ai (near Bethel), the next place attacked; but the sin was punished, and, by a stratagem and ambush, Ai was taken. They then marched northward to Shechem, an ancient Hivite city, of which the last previous account is its destruction by the sons of Jacob. (Gen. 34.) It may not have been rebuilt, as we find at this time the Hivites occupying a number of towns at a distance from it (Gibeon and others, Josh. 9); or it may have submitted to the overwhelming power of Israel. In the Vale of Shechem, between the mountains Ebal and Gerizim, all the Israelites were assembled, the law was read in their hearing, and memorial stones were erected. After this, the Hivites of four villages, of which Gibeon was the most important, by means of a deception made a treaty of peace with the Israelites, and obtained a pledge of protection; being the only nation in all the land formally spared from destruction. Their deceit was soon discovered; but the word of Israel was kept, though the people of the four villages were reduced to the condition of "servants of the sanctuary," i. e., employed in the menial duties of the Tabernacle. The central portion of the land was now possessed by Israel, from Jericho and Gibeon northward to the Carmel range of mountains, and the army returned to the fortified camp at Gilgal. (Josh. 9.)

2. **The Conquest of Southern Palestine.** (Josh. 10.) The conquest had thus far been easy; mainly because there was no union among the native tribes, but each city and village was ruled by its own "king," or sheikh, and all were jealous of one another, so that they were readily conquered in detail. Warned by the fate of Jericho and Ai, and alarmed at the defection of Gibeon, the kings of five cities formed a league to resist the invading host. The head of the confederation was Adoni-zedek, the king of Jerusalem, and associated with him were the rulers of Hebron, Jarmuth, Lachish and Eglon, and perhaps other subordinate chiefs. They began by an attack on the city of Gibeon, as a tributary of Israel. Joshua at once called forth his warriors, left the camp at Gilgal, made a swift night march through the mountain passes, and came suddenly upon the enemy near Beth-horon. Here was fought perhaps the most important battle in all human history, and one at which "the sun and moon" might well "stand still," since the religious destiny of all the world was at stake in its result. In this one battle the conquest of Canaan was made certain, though it was not fully accomplished until long afterward. The flying host were pursued to Makkedah, on the border of the plain, where the five kings were captured and slain. Then in succession, the strongholds of Libnah, Lachish, Eglon, Hebron, and, last of all, Debir, were taken by storm. From the list of the kings captured (Josh. 12:9–24), it would appear

that Joshua carried his conquests through the South Country, as far as Arad and Hormah, places where the Israelites had suffered defeat during the period of the wandering (Num. 21:1–3); though these kings may have been captured at Hebron or Debir. But, though all may not have been ravaged by the Israelites, all was certainly conquered, from Jerusalem to the great desert on the south. The conquest was afterward made complete by the aged Caleb, who with his nephew Othniel took possession of the very cities of which the name had filled the Israelites with terror a generation before. (Num. 13.)

3. **The Conquest of Northern Palestine.** (Josh. 11.) This region was also occupied by a number of

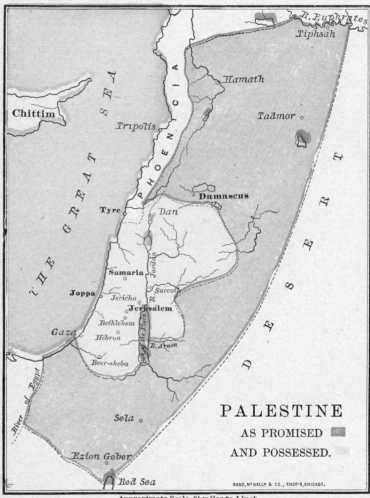

PALESTINE

AS PROMISED

AND POSSESSED.

RAND, McNALLY & CO., ENGR'S, CHICAGO.

Approximate Scale, 94 miles to 1 inch.

independent chiefs, of whom the most powerful was Jabin, the king of Hazor, a title which afterward reappears in the history. (Judges 4, 2.) They ruled over small tribes of various races, from Mount Hermon to Mount Carmel, especially on the Plain of Esdraelon. The king of Hazor called together the associated tribes, and their camp was pitched near Lake Merom. Joshua made one of his characteristic swift marches, up the Jordan Valley, attacked them suddenly, and utterly defeated and scattered them. He burned the many war chariots, and so cut the sinews of their horses as to make them useless; since these animals were never used by the Israelites. After the battle he marched through

6

the northern regions, capturing the cities and slaying their rulers, a number of whom are mentioned in the catalogue of Josh. 12:9–24 This campaign closed the active operations, so that "the land rested from war" (Josh. 11:23); but for many years the strife was feebly continued, and it was not entirely finished until the reign of David.

III. SUPPLEMENTARY CONQUESTS.

Although the struggle of the conquest was over, yet in most of the land the task of expulsion or destruction was yet to be accomplished, and in many places was never entirely wrought. The entire section of the maritime plain remained in the hands of the Philistines; in almost every tribe were fortresses, which long resisted the Israelites, and formed centres of rebellion, and sometimes of oppression. And many of the cities taken by Joshua were soon reoccupied by their original inhabitants, and once more fortified. The book of the Judges relates briefly three campaigns after the conquest.

1. **The Campaign of the Judaites and Simeonites.** (Judges 1:1–8.) This was undertaken against Adoni-bezek, the king of Bezek, a place in or near the tribe of Judah, not positively identified. Adoni-bezek was a petty chieftain, who had cruelly mutilated no less than 70 local chiefs whom he had taken in battle. He was surprised by the allied forces of Judah and Simeon, and ten thousand of his warriors were slain. He was taken prisoner, and treated as he had treated other captive kings; his thumbs and great toes being cut off, thus making him helpless. After this, the allied tribes marched down upon the maritime plain, and took the Philistine cities of Gaza, Ashkelon and Ekron. But their conquests were not permanent; they withdrew to the mountains, and the Philistines were soon in possession of their cities, which long stood as a menace to Israel. Another campaign was directed against the cities of the Negeb, or South Country, and resulted in the destruction of Zephath and Hormah, both south of Hebron.

2. **The Campaign of Caleb and Othniel.** Caleb was the oldest man in Israel, having accompanied Joshua and the other spies, thirty-eight years before the entrance of Israel into the Promised Land. (Num. 13–14.) For his faithfulness when so many were overcome with terror, he received a promise of inheritance in the land. At least 45 years afterward, Hebron, in the south of Judah, was allotted to him. It had been taken by Joshua (Josh. 10:36, 37), but afterward reoccupied by the Anakim (see page 38), and the Amorites, its original possessors. Caleb led an army against it, once more won the city, and made it his own. He promised his daughter, Achsah, to the warrior who should take Debir, or Kirjath-sepher, south of Hebron, which had also been reoccupied by the enemy. His younger brother (perhaps nephew) Othniel, won the city and his bride. (Josh. 14:1–15; 15:13–19; Judges 1:10–15.) This campaign was probably about the same time with the one narrated above, and may have been in connection with it.

3. **The Danite Campaign.** (Judges 18.) The tribe of Dan found themselves unable to overcome their Philistine neighbors, and were straitened for room in their narrow possessions. They sent out a body of men to search for a new home. These spies traversed the country as far to the north as Laish, or Leshem, a Phœnician city, near one of the sources of the Jordan. The Danite spies returned to their people at Zorah and Eshtaol, and made their report. A part of the tribe agreed to migrate to this northern region. Their first encampment on the journey, near Kirjath-jearim, in Judah, long bore the name of "the camp of Dan." At a village in Mount Ephraim they plundered Micah of his idols and carried away their priest, who was a degenerate grandson of Moses the prophet. At Laish they fell suddenly upon the defenseless Phœnicians, destroyed their city, and built in its place one which they called Dan. It was the northern landmark of the land, as Beersheba was its southern, giving rise to the term "from Dan to Beersheba." Dan remained an idol sanctuary, and a place of corrupting influence during all the after history of Israel.

Upon the map are noted: 1. The six campaigns of the conquest, three on each side of the Jordan. The precise route of travel cannot be identified, but the general direction is shown by a red line. The "supplementary conquests" are not indicated, in order to avoid confusion, but can be easily traced. 2. The important battle-fields are indicated by flags. These were at (1) Jahaz, (2) Edrei, (3) the land of Midian, (4) Jericho, (5) Ai, (6) Beth-horon, (7) Hazor. Besides these were many cities captured by Joshua during his campaign in Southern Canaan. 3. The royal cities captured by Moses and Joshua are each indicated on the map by a crown. These were, on the east of Jordan: Heshbon, the capital of Sihon's kingdom, and Ashtaroth, the capital of Og's kingdom; and on the west of Jordan, 31 cities, whose kings were taken and slain by Joshua. (Josh. 12:9-24.) The places identified are the only ones marked upon the map. 4. The four cities of the Hivite league, which alone made a treaty with Israel, are shown by clasped hands, the token of peace. 5. At the close of the conquest a large part of the country was left in the possession of the native races. This region is indicated by the yellow color. 6. Many towns remained in the hands of the Canaanite and Philistine races. Some were taken by Israel, but afterward reoccupied by their original inhabitants; others held out against the Israelites, and were a constant source of danger, both by their opposition, and still more by their friendship. The ceasing of the war before the native races were either utterly exterminated or driven away, was a mistaken mercy, which cost Israel centuries of strife, the infection from their idolatry, and the corrupt influence of their morals. The sparing of the Canaanites imperiled and well nigh thwarted the destiny of Israel as the depositary of religious truth for all the world.

OUTLINE FOR REVIEW.

I. *Conquest of Eastern Palestine.* 1. Gilead. (Amorites, Sihon, Jahaz.) 2. Bashan. (Amorites, Og, Edrei; Nobah, Kenath.) 3. Midian. (Phinchas.)

II. *Conquest of Western Palestine.* 1. Central. (Gilgal, Jericho, Ai, Shechem, Gibeon.) 2. Southern. (Beth-horon, Makkedah, Libnah, Lachish, Eglon, Hebron, Debir.) 3. Northern. (Hazor.)

III. *Supplementary Conquests.* 1. Judah and Simeon. (Adoni-bezek, Bezek; Gaza, Ashkelon, Ekron; Zephath, Hormah.) 2. Caleb and Othniel. (Hebron, Debir.) 3. Dan. (Laish.)

CHURCH OF THE ASCENSION.

PALESTINE AMONG THE TWELVE TRIBES.

THE division of the land among the Twelve Tribes took place in three stages. 1. After the conquest of Eastern Palestine, during the lifetime of Moses, the two tribes of Reuben and Gad and half the tribe of Manasseh received their portion, on condition that their warriors should aid their kinsmen in the war for the rest of the land. (Num. 32.) 2. After the campaigns in Western Palestine (see last map and explanations), the two leading tribes of Judah and Ephraim and the remaining

upon the general position, but not upon the precise boundary lines. We follow the map of Dr. James Strong, in McClintock and Strong's Cyclopedia.

I. **The Tribe of Reuben** (Num. 32:1-38; Josh. 13: 15-23) had the river Arnon for its southern border, this river separating it from Moab. It was bounded on the east by the Syrian desert, and on the west by the Dead Sea and the lower end of the Jordan. Its northern line began at Beth-jeshimoth, and extended northeasterly to near Rabbath Ammon. Its territory consisted of a low region by the sea and the river, a precipitous mountain range, and a rolling plateau eastward, well adapted for pasture. Among its prominent localities were: Heshbon, the capital of the Amorite king, Sihon; Dibon, where recently the Moabite stone was discovered; Mount Nebo, where Moses died;

VIEW IN THE EASTERN TABLE-LAND—BASHAN.

half of Manasseh received their inheritance, and took possession of it, as far as conquered: Judah in the south, Ephraim a small but choice portion in the centre, and Manasseh immediately north of it. (Josh. 15-17.) 3. The remaining seven tribes delayed long in obtaining their portions in the land, but at last, after a rebuke from the aged Joshua for their slowness, made the division by lot, and entered upon their inheritance. (Josh. 18, 19.) The cities of refuge, and those for the priests and Levites, were last of all appointed, late in the life of Joshua, and then "the land had rest from war," and Israel entered upon its history in its own land.

It is not easy to fix the tribal boundary lines, since some tribes possessed cities within the domain of other tribes, and the boundaries, if not entirely indeterminate, varied greatly in different ages. Geographers are agreed

Bezer, a city of refuge; Aroer, Ataroth, Medeba, Kiriathaim, and Kedemoth.

II. **The Tribe of Gad** (Num. 32:34-36; Josh. 13: 24-28) was located north of Reuben. Its boundary on the west was the river Jordan, from the Sea of Chinnereth (Galilee) almost to its mouth. Its eastern border was the desert, from Rabbath Ammon to Mahanaim, from which point its line ran northwest to the Sea of Chinnereth. Like the land of Reuben, its territory embraced portions of the Jordan Valley; the eastern mountains, divided by the torrent Jabbok; and the table-land, a rich and well-watered district. The part in the Jordan Valley was, however, never possessed by the Israelites, but remained in the hands of the native Canaanites. In the valley, its cities were Beth-nimrah and Succoth. Among the mountains the places were: Jazer, near the border of Reuben; Ramoth-gilead, a famous fortress, often the scene of war; Penuel, the place of Jacob's wrestling with the angel (Gen. 32:24–32); Jabesh-gilead, whose warriors rescued the bodies of Saul and Jonathan (1 Sam. 31:11–13); Mahanaim, a place of refuge both for the son of Saul, and afterward for David (2 Sam. 2:8; 2 Sam. 17:24); and Gadara, a foreign city, on the northern frontier.

III. The Half Tribe of Manasseh, East (Num. 32:39–42; Josh. 13:29–31), occupied the northern portion of Eastern Palestine, generally known in the Old Testa-

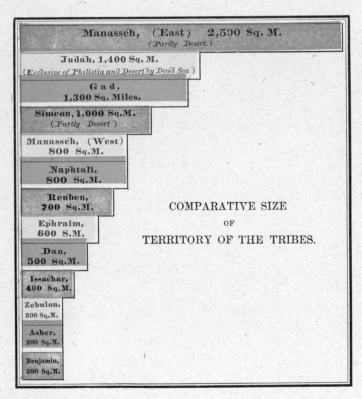

COMPARATIVE SIZE
OF
TERRITORY OF THE TRIBES.

Manasseh, (East) 2,590 Sq. M.
(Partly Desert.)
Judah, 1,400 Sq. M.
(Exclusive of Philistia and Desert by Dead Sea)
Gad, 1,300 Sq. Miles.
Simeon, 1,000 Sq.M. (Partly Desert)
Manasseh, (West) 800 Sq.M.
Naphtali, 800 Sq.M.
Reuben, 700 Sq.M.
Ephraim, 600 S.M.
Dan, 500 Sq.M.
Issachar, 400 Sq.M.
Zebulon, 300 Sq.M.
Asher, 300 Sq.M.
Benjamin, 300 Sq.M.

ment as Bashan, larger than the portion assigned to any one tribe. It extended from Mahanaim northward to Mount Hermon, and from the river Jordan and its two northern lakes eastward to the desert. Though some of this land is a desert, yet most of it is fertile, and even now it is called "the granary of Palestine." It consists of undulating plains between two masses of mountains; the one on the east, now known as *el Ledja*, and the other on the side of the Jordan Valley. On its western hills were Aphek, and Golan, a city of refuge; near its centre were Ashtaroth, the former capital of Og, who reigned over Bashan before the conquest, and Edrei. Kenath, taken by Nobah, was at the foot of *el Ledja*, east of the line of the map. Its people never conquered the Geshurites on the east, and were separated from their brethren by the Canaanites in the Jordan Valley (see map on page 50), so that they were not closely iden-

tified with the history of Israel, and were the first to be carried away captive. (2 Kings 10:32, 33.)

IV. The Tribe of Simeon (Josh. 19:1–9) received a portion of the land previously given to Judah. Its location was on the extreme south, and its boundaries were indeterminate, being indicated only by the list of eighteen towns belonging to it. It was the strip of grazing land between the mountains and the desert of the wandering, where Abraham and Isaac spent most of their lives. Its most important place was the historic Beersheba; but it included also Gerar, on the Philistine border; Arad, whose king twice resisted the Israelites' progress during the wandering; Hormah, in the South Country; and Ziklag, at one time the home of David. Nothing is known of this tribe's history. From its frontier position it probably lost its individuality, a part of its people becoming merged with the wandering races of the desert, and a part with its more powerful neighbor, Judah. Most of its cities were held by the Philistines until the reign of David.

V. The Tribe of Judah (Josh. 15:1–63) occupied the most valuable portion of the land, and for three centuries was the rival of Ephraim in the leadership of the nation. Its boundary line on the north is described with great minuteness, but was changed after the building of the Temple to include a part of the city of Jerusalem. It ran from the northern end of the Dead Sea, south of Jerusalem, in a direction generally east, though with many turnings, from the Jordan to the Mediterranean. The region embraced five sections. 1. The Philistine plain, by the sea, never conquered. 2. The Shefelah, or low hills, a boundary disputed with the Philistines. 3. The "hill country," the home of the tribe. 4. The Negeb, or South Country, extending from Hebron southward. 5. The wild, uninhabitable Jeshimon, called in later history "the wilderness of Judæa," on the western shore of the Dead Sea. Omitting the Philistine cities by the Mediterranean, its most important cities were: Hebron, the inheritance of Caleb; Debir, the conquest of Othniel; Bethlehem, the birthplace of David, and, in after ages, of his greater Son; Maon, Carmel; En-gedi, a haunt of David during his exile; Lachish and Libnah, on the Shefelah; and Kirjath-jearim, at one time the abode of the ark.

VI. The Tribe of Benjamin (Josh. 18:11–28) was located between Judah and Ephraim, having the Jordan on the east, and Dan on the west. It was a small country, 25 miles long by 12 wide, yet rich in natural advantages; and many events of Bible history took place within its borders. It included 26 cities, of which the most important were: Gilgal, the military capital during the conquest; Jericho, the first town taken on the west of the Jordan; Jerusalem, long held by the Jebusites, but from the time of David the capital of the country; Bethel, connected with many events; Ramah, the home of Samuel; Gibeah, the residence of King Saul; Michmash, Gibeon and Mizpeh, the places of famous battles. No portion of the land contains more of Jew-

ish history than Benjamin, the smallest of all the tribes of Israel.

VII. **The Tribe of Dan** (Josh. 19:40–48; Judges 18) was situated between Benjamin and the sea, and, though apparently large, was in reality very small, since nearly all its territory was held by the original inhabitants, the Canaanites. Its southernmost town was Timnath, a small village not on the map, but two miles west of Beth-shemesh; its northern limit was a brook just north of Joppa. The original inhabitants proved too strong for the Danites, who were compelled to maintain a sort of forti-fied camp in and between the villages of Zorah and Esh-taol, called "the camp of Dan." (Judges 13:25.) A part of the tribe migrated northward, as related in the interest-ing account in Judges 17, 18; and, by a surprise, seized the Phœnician village of Laish, or Leshem, in the far north of Palestine, changed its name to Dan, and made it a new rallying centre for the tribe. This place, with Beersheba on the south, was named, in the expression "from Dan to Beersheba," as one of the limits of the land. It re-mained for centuries the place of an idolatrous worship, perpetuated under all the changes of government, down to the final captivity of the land.

VIII. **The Tribe of Ephraim** (Josh. 16) was located on the north of Benjamin and Dan, and extended from the Jordan to the Mediterranean, in the centre of the country. But inasmuch as the Canaanites were able to resist the power of the Ephraimites on both sides of the mountain, toward the river Jordan and toward the sea, the haughty tribe deemed its possession too small for its needs, and asked a larger space of Joshua. They were answered in a half-jesting, half-rebuking manner by the leader, and urged to drive out the enemy and make for themselves more room, a counsel which they followed only in part. (Josh. 17:14–18; Judges 1:22–26.) The principal places in "Mount Ephraim" (as the district of this tribe was generally called) were: Shechem, between the twin mountains of Ebal and Gerizim; Shiloh, the place of the ark, and the religious centre of the land; Beth-horon, the field where the decisive victory of the conquest was won; Timnath, the burial place of Joshua; and Samaria, built during the kingdom as the capital of the Ten Tribes.

IX. **The Half Tribe of Manasseh, West** (Josh.17), was located north of Ephraim, and extended from the Jordan to the Mediterranean. Its boundary followed the northern slope of Mount Carmel, except by the sea, where the mountain was given to Asher. The lowlands on the Jordan, the Plain of Esdraelon, and the Mediter-ranean, were held by the Canaanites, in the cities of Dor, Megiddo, Taanach and Beth-shean, a chain of fortresses which gave control of the larger portion of the province, so that the Manassites were restricted to the mountains, where they occupied Geba, Dothan and Jarmuth.

X. **The Tribe of Issachar** (Josh. 19:17–23) was allotted the Plain of Esdraelon (which it was never able to possess), and the mountains of Tabor and Little Her-mon ("Hill of Moreh"), extending to the Jordan south

of the Sea of Chinnereth (Galilee). Both the plain and the Jordan Valley were held by the Canaanites, but the tribe occupied the mountains. Its cities were En-gan-nim, Shunem, Haphraim, Daberath, and Beth-shemesh. The towns of Cana, Nain and Nazareth, in New Testa-ment history, were located in this tribe.

XI. **The Tribe of Asher** (Josh. 19:24–31) lay along the sea-coast, and extended from Mount Carmel to Zi-don. Nearly all its cities were controlled by the Canaan-ites and Phœnicians, and the people soon entered into friendly relations with them, and lost their power. A part of the tribe, however, occupied the mountain range, and retained their relationship with the rest of the Israelites.

XII. **The Tribe of Zebulon** (Josh. 19:10–16) occu-pied a triangle between Mount Carmel, the Sea of Chin-nereth (afterward the Sea of Galilee), and the village of Aijalon; having as its base the mountain border north

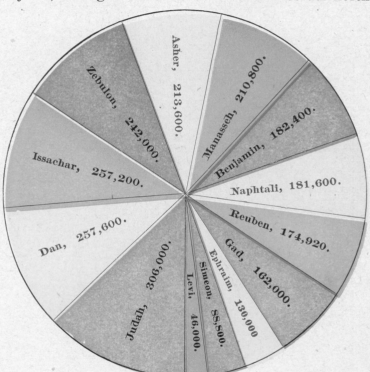

COMPARATIVE POPULATION OF THE TWELVE TRIBES
AT THE ENTRANCE INTO CANAAN.

of the Plain of Esdraelon, and its western line the mountain chain following the Mediterranean. As this belonged to the mountain region, it was controlled mainly by the Israelites, though the Canaanites held two towns, Kitron and Nahalol. (Judges 1:30.) Its principal places were: Gath-hepher, the home of the prophet Jonah; Bethlehem (to be distinguished from the town of the same name in Judah); and, in later times, most of the cities of Galilee visited by our Lord.

XIII. **The Tribe of Naphtali** (Josh. 19:32–39) was the farthest to the north in all Israel. It occupied a sec-tion running north and south, between the Jordan and the Sea of Chinnereth on one side, and the Phœnician border on the other. Its central city was Kedesh, a city of refuge. Other towns were Hazor, Abel-beth-maa-chah, Beth-rehob (the extreme point visited by the spies,

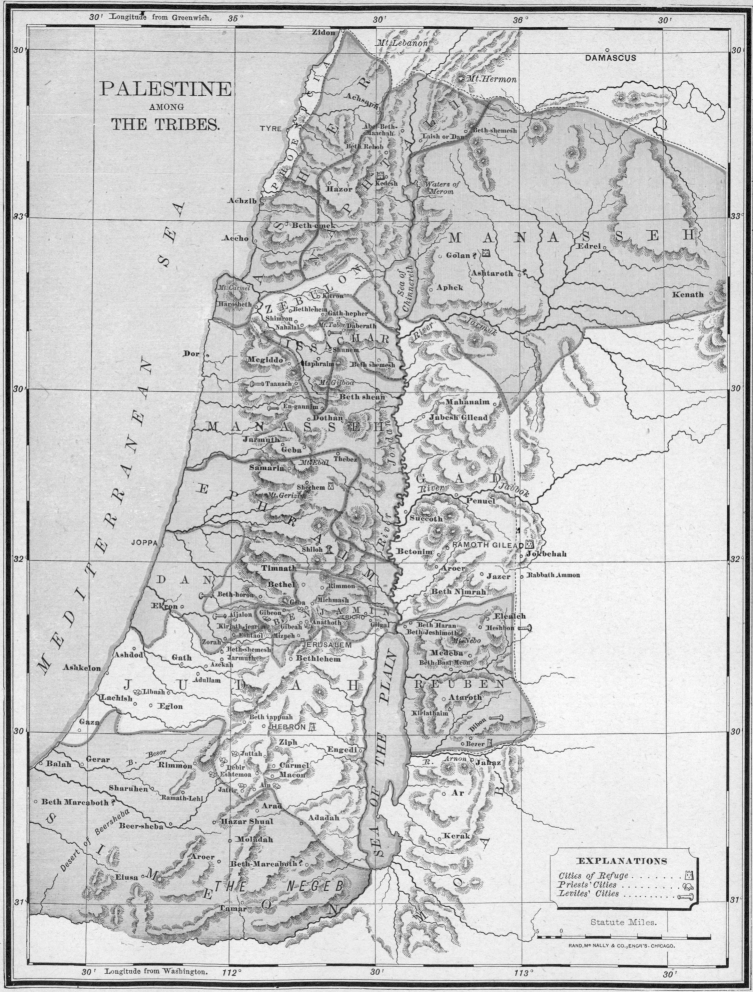

PALESTINE
AMONG
THE TRIBES.

DAMASCUS

Zidon
Mt. Lebanon
Mt. Hermon
TYRE
Achsaph
Abel-Beth-maachah
Beth-Rehob
Laish or Dan
Beth-shemesh
Kedesh
Hazor
Waters of Merom
Achzib
MANASSEH
Beth-emek
Accho
Golan ?
Edrei
Ashtaroth
Aphek
Mt. Carmel
Kenath
Harosheth
ZEBULON
Kitron
Bethlehem
Gath-hepher
Shimron
Nahalal
Mt. Tabor Daberath
ISSACHAR
Shunem
Dor
Megiddo
Haphraim
Beth-shemesh
Taanach
Mt. Gilboa
Beth-shean
En-gannim
Mahanaim
Dothan
Jabesh Gilead
MANASSEH
Jarmuth
Geba
Samaria
Mt. Ebal
Thebez
GAD
EPHRAIM
Shechem
River Jabbok
Mt. Gerizim
Penuel
Succoth
JOPPA
Betonim
RAMOTH GILEAD
Shiloh
Jokbehah
Timnath
Aroer
Jazer
Rabbath Ammon
DAN
Bethel
Rimmon
Beth Nimrah
Beth-horon
Geba
Michmash
Ekron
Aijalon
Gibeon
BENJAMIN
JERICHO
Elealeh
Kirjath-jearim
Gibeah
Anathoth
Gilgal
Heshbon
Zorah
Eshtaol
Mizpeh
JERUSALEM
Beth Haran
Beth-shemesh
Beth-Jeshimoth
Ashdod
Gath
Jarmuth
Bethlehem
Mt. Nebo
Ashkelon
Azekah
Medeba
Adullam
Beth-Baal Meon
JUDAH
REUBEN
Libnah
Ataroth
Lachish
Eglon
Kirjathaim
Gaza
Beth-tappuah
HEBRON
Dibon
Gerar
Ziph
Engedi
Bezer
Balah
Besor B.
Rimmon
Juttah
Carmel
Arnon R.
Jahaz
Sharuhen
Debir
Eshtemoa
Macon
Ramath-Lehi
Jattir
Ain
Ar
Beth Marcaboth ?
Arad
Adadah
Beer-sheba
Hazar Shual
Kerak
Moladah
Aroer
Beth-Marcaboth ?
NEGEB
Elusa
THE
Tamar

MEDITERRANEAN SEA

SEA OF THE PLAIN

Sea of Chinnereth

River Jordan

Desert of Beersheba

EXPLANATIONS
Cities of Refuge . . . . . .
Priests' Cities . . . .
Levites' Cities . . . .

Statute Miles.

RAND, McNALLY & CO., ENGR'S. CHICAGO.

Num. 13:21) and Beth-shemesh. Dan (see on Tribe of Dan) was also in the limits of this tribe.

XIV. **The Tribe of Levi** was the priestly caste, and received no separate province in the land, but was allotted certain cities throughout the tribes. These cities were given up to the Levites, either wholly or in part; though it is evident that they were not the only places occupied by the priests, and that others besides the Levites dwelt in them. These "Levitical cities" were divided into two classes: those for the priests proper, or descendants of Aaron, thirteen in number, and all in the tribes of Judah, Simeon and Benjamin (a remarkable arrangement, since the altar and the Tabernacle were in the tribe of Ephraim); and those for the Levites, or subordinate priests, thirty-five in number, divided among the other tribes. Thus there were in all forty-eight Levitical cities. These were so arranged that in each tribe four cities were assigned to the priests, except in Judah (which had more), and Simeon and Naphtali, the frontier tribes, which had less. As far as they have been identified and located, they are indicated upon the map: the priests' cities by the *tiara*, or head-dress, worn by the priests; the Levites' cities by a *trumpet*, as they formed the choral bands in the worship of the Temple. Six of these cities were assigned as "cities of refuge" for the innocent man-slayer. (Josh. 20.) Three cities were chosen on each side of the Jordan; in the south, the centre and the north of the land. These were: Bezer, in Reuben; Ramoth-gilead, in Gad; Golan, in Manasseh, East; Hebron, in Judah; Shechem, in Ephraim; and Kedesh, in Naphtali. Each of these is indicated on the map by a tower.

OUTLINE FOR TEACHING AND REVIEW.

SUGGESTIONS FOR TEACHING.

Draw a rough map of Palestine, omitting mountains and all other lines except the river and the seas. Do not attempt to make it accurate. In presence of the class, draw the boundary lines of the tribes, not attempting an accurate copy, but roughly indicating them. With each tribe indicate the most important places by their initial letters. Review all the places before beginning another tribe, and occasionally go back to the beginning and review all the work done. Let the class, on slate or paper, also draw the map, and locate the places. At the close, call upon the scholars to give the location and name the places of the tribes.

REVIEW.

I. *Reuben*. Heshbon, Dibon, Mount Nebo, Bezer, Aroer, Ataroth, Medeba, Kiriathaim, Kedemoth.

II. *Gad*. Beth-nimrah, Succoth, Jazer, Ramoth-gilead, Penuel, Jabesh-gilead, Mahanaim, Gadara.

III. *Manasseh, East*. Aphek, Golan, Ashtaroth, Edrei, Kenath.

IV. *Simeon*. Beersheba, Gerar, Arad, Hormah, Ziklag.

V. *Judah* (5 sections). Hebron, Debir, Bethlehem, Maon, Carmel, En-gedi, Lachish, Librah, Kirjath-jearim.

VI. *Benjamin*. Gilgal, Jericho, Jerusalem, Bethel, Ramah, Gibeah, Michmash, Gibeon, Mizpeh.

VII. *Dan*. Zorah, Eshtaol, Dan.

VIII. *Ephraim*. Shechem, Shiloh, Beth-horon, Timnath, Samaria.

IX. *Manasseh, West*. Dor, Megiddo, Taanach, Beth-shean, Geba, Dothan, Jarmuth.

X. *Issachar*. En-gannim, Shunem, Haphraim, Daberath, Beth-shemesh, Cana, Nain, Nazareth (in New Testament History).

XI. *Asher*.

XII. *Zebulon*. Gath-hepher, Bethlehem.

XIII. *Naphtali*. Kedesh, Hazor, Abel-beth-maachah, Beth-rehob, Beth-shemesh.

XIV. *Levi*. Forty-eight Levitical cities in all. Six of these were cities of refuge, as follows: Bezer, Ramoth-gilead, Golan, Hebron, Shechem, Kedesh.

ROUND ABOUT JERUSALEM.

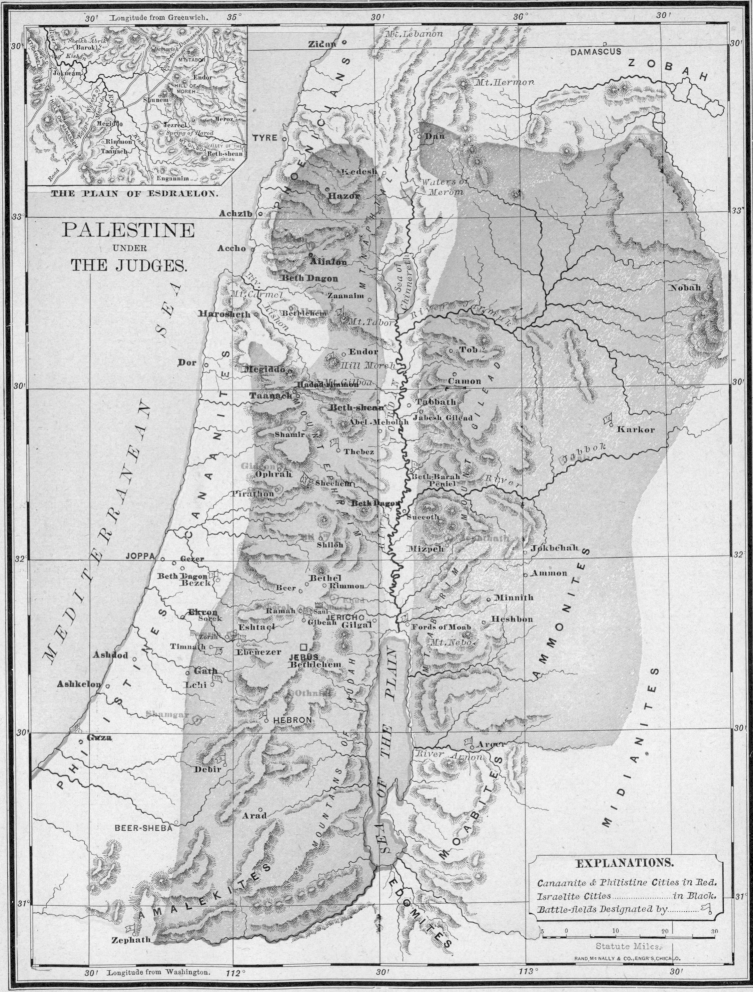

PALESTINE
UNDER
THE JUDGES.

THE PLAIN OF ESDRAELON.

EXPLANATIONS.

Canaanite & Philistine Cities in Red.
Israelite Cities..................in Black.
Battle-fields Designated by............

Statute Miles.
RAND, McNALLY & CO., ENGR'S, CHICAGO.

PALESTINE UNDER THE JUDGES.

THE map on page 60 is intended to illustrate the history of Palestine from the division of the land (about 1170 B. C.) to the accession of David (B. C. 1010.) This period may be noticed under three topics. 1. The movements among the tribes supplementary to the conquest. 2. The oppressions and the Judges. 3. The reign of the first king, Saul. (See The Kingdom of Saul, page 64.)

I. SUPPLEMENTARY TO THE CONQUEST.

1. **The Conquests of Judah and Simeon.** (Judges 1.) These were made by the two southern tribes in alliance, and were accompanied by decisive victories at Bezek, Hebron, Debir, and Zephath (afterward known as *Hormah*, "destruction"). These places are marked with flags upon the map. Jerusalem, Gaza, Ashkelon, and Ekron were also attacked and taken; but the conquest was not permanent, since these places were soon reoccupied by the native races.

2. **The Danite Migration,** related in Judges 17, 18, took place about the same time. The tribe of Dan was crowded by the Philistines into two towns, Zorah and Eshtaol. A part of the warriors went upon an expedition northward, and finding Laish, at one of the sources of the Jordan, undefended, slew its Zidonian inhabitants, and made it their home and a sanctuary of idols, under a new name, Dan. This formed the northern outpost of the land of Israel.

3. **The Civil War.** (Judges 19–21.) This was caused by a crime among the people of one city, Gibeah, whose part was taken by the entire tribe, according to the Oriental view of honor among members of a clan. It led to a war between Benjamin and the rest of the tribes, at the end of which, by the battle of Gibeah, the one tribe was almost annihilated.

II. THE OPPRESSIONS AND THE JUDGES.

From the times of Joshua to those of Saul, the Israelites were ruled by men raised up to meet the needs of the hour, not by succession or appointment, but by personal character and influence. Most of them ruled over a limited region, and more than one doubtless was in authority at the same time, in different parts of the land. They were called forth by a series of *oppressions*, which were sometimes invasions by foreign tribes, and sometimes the uprising of the native peoples against their Israelite conquerors, reversing the relation for a time. The judges were, in most instances, men who led the Israelites in throwing off the yoke of these foreign races. The oppressions are generally reckoned as seven, though the third was rather an invasion than an oppression; and the judges, as fifteen in number, though several were not judges, in the strict sense of the word.

1. **The Mesopotamian Oppression** (Judges 3:1–11) was the first, occurring soon after the death of Joshua.

MOUNT TABOR.

It resulted from the conquests of a king named Chushan-rishathaim, who reigned in Mesopotamia. From the two facts, that at this period the kings of Edom had Aramean names (Gen. 36), and that the deliverer of Israel was Othniel, of the tribe of Judah, the first judge, it has been concluded that the region of this oppression was the territory of that tribe, in the southern portion of Palestine.

2. **The Moabite Oppression.** (Judges 3:12–30.) The Moabites lived south of the torrent Arnon, on the east of the Dead Sea. In alliance with the wandering Ammonites, further eastward, and the Amalekites of the desert, under their king, Eglon, they took possession of Jericho (which stood as an unwalled town), and made it the centre of rule over the central portion of the land,

chiefly Benjamin and Judah. Ehud, the second judge, assassinated Eglon, and then called upon his countrymen to assemble at Mount Ephraim. A decisive battle was fought at the "Fords of Moab" (where the Israelites had crossed the Jordan on their first entrance to the land), resulting in the defeat of the Moabites and the freedom of Israel.

3. **The Early Philistine Oppression** (Judges 3:31) was perhaps no more than a raid of these people upon the mountain region of Judah. It was repelled by Shamgar, the third judge, whose army of farmers, hastily gathered, had no other weapons than their formidable ox-goads. The precise place of the victory is unknown, but it was on the frontier between Judah and Philistia.

4. **The Canaanite Oppression** (Judges 4, 5) was an uprising of the native people against the Israelite conquerors. They changed the relations of the two races, by becoming the dominant people in all the region north of the Carmel range of mountains. Their capital was at Hazor, and their chief military post at Harosheth, near the Plain of Esdraelon. A woman, Deborah, living between Ramah and Bethel, was then recognized as the fourth judge. She called upon Barak, of Naphtali, who aided her in gathering a little army, chiefly from the tribes of Issachar, Zebulon and Naphtali. They met at Mount Tabor, from which they poured down upon the Canaanites, who were encamped upon the plain. In the route that followed, the Israelites were aided by a sudden storm, and a rise in the torrent Kishon, which swept away many of their enemies. The power of the Canaanites was broken, and thenceforward the race made no attempt to regain its independence.

5. **The Midianite Oppression** (Judges 6–8) was the most severe, thus far, in the history of the judges. The Midianites, a migratory tribe on the east of Palestine, joined with the Amalekite Bedouins in an invasion which overran all the central portion of the land, plundering the inhabitants, and destroying the fruits of the field. So low were the Israelites reduced, that they were compelled to hide their crops, and themselves also, in the caves of the mountains. The deliverer of Israel at this period was Gideon, the fifth judge. At God's call he summoned his countrymen, and gathered an army on Mount Gilboa, while their enemies were encamped at the foot of the Hill Moreh (Little Hermon), an innumerable host. With three hundred chosen men Gideon made a night attack upon the Midianite host. They were defeated, and fled down the ravine to the Jordan Valley, past Beth-shean, Abel-meholah and Tabbath. Beth-barah, where they were intercepted by the men of Ephraim, was not the same with the Bethabara of the New Testament, but probably in the Jordan Valley, north of the Jabbok. At Succoth, near the junction of the Jabbok and the Jordan, and at Penuel, in the valley of the Jabbok, the pursuing Israelites under Gideon were inhospitably treated by the inhabitants, but avenged themselves on their return. The remains of

the routed Midianite army were found by Gideon at Karkor, a place not precisely known. He made a circuit, attacked them on the east, and utterly destroyed them. After this victory Gideon bore rule over Israel from his home in Ophrah, until his death.

After the death of Gideon arose his son Abimelech, the sixth judge, "the bramble king," who reigned over a small district around Shechem. (Judges 9.) He was not one of the divinely chosen deliverers, and strictly should not be reckoned in the list of judges. He was slain ignobly at Thebez, north of Shechem. The seventh judge was Tola, who ruled from Shamir, in Mount Ephraim. (Judges 10:1, 2.) The eighth was Jair, whose home was at Camon, in Mount Gilead, east of the Jordan. (Judges 10:3–5.)

6. **The Ammonite Oppression** (Judges 10:6–18; 11:1–40) was perhaps contemporaneous with the early part of the one named after it, the Philistine. It embraced the land of the tribes on the east of the Jordan, and lasted eighteen years. The Israelites rallied at Mizpeh of Gilead (the place where Jacob and Laban made their covenant, Gen. 31:49), and called to the command Jephthah, the ninth judge, who was living as a freebooter in the land of Tob, north of Gilead. He marched against the Ammonites, and fought them at Aroer, on the border of the torrent Arnon. He drove them in flight northward, and wasted their territory as far as Minnith, near Heshbon. On his return took place the fulfillment of his vow upon his daughter (Judges 11:40); and a civil strife with the haughty tribe of Ephraim (Judges 12:1–6), which attacked Gilead, but was beaten and put to flight. At the fords of Jordan many thousand Ephraimites were slain in attempting to cross. Probably this was the same place referred to already as Beth-barah. (Judges 7:24.)

After Jephthah, the tenth judge was Ibzan of Bethlehem, north of Mount Carmel; the eleventh, Elon of Aijalon, in the tribe of Zebulon; the twelfth, Abdon of Pirathon, in Ephraim. (Judges 12:8–15.)

7. **The Philistine Oppression** (Judges 13–16) began about the same time with the Ammonite, but lasted far longer. During all the judgeships of Eli, the thirteenth judge, of Samson the fourteenth, of Samuel the fifteenth and last, and the forty years of Saul's reign, Israel remained more or less under Philistine domination. In the reign of Saul we read of Philistine garrisons throughout the land, as at Bethel (1 Sam. 10:3–5) and at Geba (1 Sam. 13:3), and not until all Israel was consolidated under the strong sceptre of David, was the Philistine yoke entirely thrown off.

Eli, the thirteenth judge, was also high-priest, and ruled from Shiloh, the place of the ark. The history relates only the events at the close of his judgeship, when, by the loss of the ark at Ebenezer, and the death of Eli, on the same day, the Israelites were reduced to the lowest condition of trouble.

The exploits of Samson were all personal, and in a narrow district. He led no army, but wrought brave deeds singlehanded, in the "camp of Dan" and the country of the Philistines. Had he added the administrative powers of a Samuel to his courage and strength, the triumphs of David would have been anticipated by a century. He was born at Zorah, in the tribe of Dan (Judges 13:2), and won victories at Timnath (Judges 15:1-8); at Lehi ("the jaw," from the weapon used), a place whose precise location is uncertain (Judges 15:9-20); and in his death, at Gaza. (Judges 16.)

Samuel, the fifteenth judge, was born at Ramah (also called Ramathaim-zophim (1 Sam. 1:1), and ruled from the same place during his period of government, from the loss of the ark to the Anointing of Saul. The great event of his rule was the victory at Ebenezer (1 Sam. 7), which gave a name to the place of the former defeat. Other places connected with this period are Kirjath-jearim, where the ark was long kept; Mizpeh, the place where the active rule of Samuel both began and ended; Bethel and Gilgal, where also he exercised the functions of judge; and Beersheba, in the south of Judah, where his sons ruled for a time as deputies in his name.

Upon the map the names of the towns which remained during this period under the control of the native races, are printed in red. Some of these were Philistine, others Canaanite. Those on the maritime plain, west of Judah and Benjamin, were mainly Philistine, as Gaza, Ashkelon, Ashdod, Ekron and Gath. Those in the interior, as Aijalon and Jebus; around the Plain of Esdraelon, as Harosheth, Megiddo, Taanach and Hadad-rimmon; and in the Jordan Valley, as Bethshean and Jericho, were under the control of the Canaanite races.

We give the names of the fifteen judges, and their various centers of authority, as indicated in the books of Judges and First Samuel. Some of the locations are uncertain; but the places cannot be far from those assigned upon the map. The names and locations are: 1. Othniel, tribe of Judah. 2. Ehud, tribe of Benjamin. 3. Shamgar, tribe of Judah. 4. Deborah, between Ramah and Bethel, in Ephraim. 5. Gideon, Ophrah, in Manasseh, West. 6. Abimelech, "the bramble king," at Shechem, in Ephraim. 7. Tola, in Shamir, of Manasseh, East. 8. Jair, in Manasseh, East. 9. Jephthah, in the tribe of Gad. 10. Ibzan, in Bethlehem, north of Mount Carmel. 11. Elon, at Aijalon, of Zebulon. 12. Abdon, at Pirathon, in Ephraim. 13. Eli, at Shiloh, in Ephraim. 14. Samson, at Zorah, in Dan. 15. Samuel, at Ramah, in Benjamin.

The battles of this period are indicated upon the map by flags, and are as follows: 1. Bezek. 2. Hebron. 3. Debir. 4. Zephath. All these in the campaign of Judah and Simeon. (Judges 1.) 5. Laish (Dan), in the north, the Danite conquest. (Judges 18.) 6. Gibeah, the extermination of Benjamin. (Judges 20.) 7. Fords of Moab, Ehud's victory over the Moabites. (Judges 3.) 8. Mount Tabor, Deborah's victory over the Canaanites. (Judges 4.) 9. The Hill Moreh (Little Hermon), Gideon's victory over the Midianites. (Judges 7.) 10. Karkor, the capture of the chiefs of Midian. (Judges 8.) 11. Shechem, Abimelech's conquest. (Judges 9.) 12. Thebez, Abimelech's death. (Judges 9.) 13. Aroer, Jephthah's victory over the Ammonites. (Judges 11.) 14. Beth-barah, Jephthah's victory over Ephraim. (Judges 12.) 15. Timnath. 16. Lehi. 17. Gaza, Samson's three slaughters of the Philistines. (Judges 14-16.) 18. Ebenezer, the loss of the ark. (1 Sam. 4.) 19. Ebenezer, the victory of Samuel. (1 Sam. 7.)

OUTLINE FOR REVIEW.

I. SUPPLEMENTARY TO CONQUEST.

1. *Judah and Simeon.* Bezek, Hebron, Debir, Zephath.
2. *Danite Migration.* Zorah, Eshtaol; Laish (Dan).
3. *Civil War.* Benjamin, Gibeah.

II. OPPRESSIONS AND JUDGES.

1. *Mesopotamian.* (South.) Othniel, 1st Judge.
2. *Moabite.* (Central.) Jericho. Ehud, 2d Judge; Fords of Moab.
3. *Early Philistine.* (South.) Shamgar, 3d Judge.
4. *Canaanite.* (North.) Hazor, Harosheth. Mount Tabor; Deborah, 4th Judge, Ramah.
5. *Midianite.* (Central and North.) Hill Moreh, Karkor; Gideon, 5th Judge, Ophrah. Abimelech, 6th Judge; Shechem, Thebez. Tola, 7th Judge, Shamir. Jair, 8th Judge, Camon.

6. *Ammonite.* (East.) Aroer; Jephthah, 9th Judge; "Fords of Jordan." Ibzan, 10th Judge, Bethlehem. Elon, 11th Judge, Aijalon. Abdon, 12th Judge, Pirathon.

7. *Philistine.* (South and Central.) Eli, 13th Judge, Shiloh; Ebenezer. Samson, 14th Judge; Timnath, Lehi, Gaza. Samuel, 15th Judge, Ramah; Ebenezer.

Battles of the Period. 1. Bezek. 2. Hebron. 3. Debir. 4. Zephath. 5. Laish (Dan). 6. Gibeah. 7. Fords of Moab. 8. Mount Tabor. 9. Hill Moreh. 10. Karkor. 11. Shechem. 12. Thebez. 13. Aroer. 14. Fords of Jordan (Beth-barah?). 15. Timnath. 16. Lehi. 17. Gaza. 18. 19. Ebenezer.

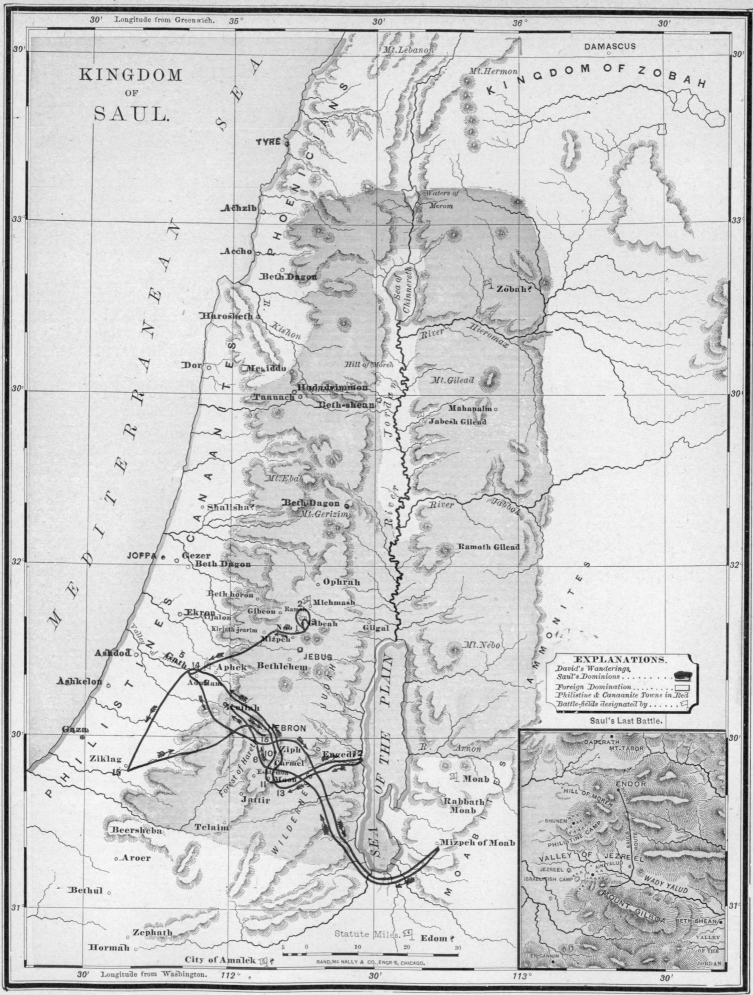

KINGDOM
OF
SAUL.

RAND, McNALLY & CO., ENGR'S, CHICAGO.

Statute Miles.

EXPLANATIONS.
David's Wanderings
Saul's Dominions
Foreign Domination
Philistine & Canaanite Towns in Red
Battle-fields designated by

Saul's Last Battle.

THE KINGDOM OF SAUL.

DURING the last century of the Judges, there was a growing tendency toward a more settled form of government; and the wise rule of Samuel inspired a still stronger desire for a better organization of the state. The rival tribes of Ephraim and Judah were conciliated by the choice of a king from the weak tribe of Benjamin, equally dependent upon both; and Saul, an obscure farmer of Gibeah, was called to the throne. The events of his reign are here related only so far as is necessary to present the localities referred to, which may be grouped under the following heads: 1. His Appointment. 2. His Wars. 3. His Pursuit of David. 4. His Death.

I. **Saul's Appointment as King.** (1 Sam. 9–12.) This is connected with four places. Ramah, the residence of Samuel (probably *Neby Samwil*, 3½ miles nearly north of Jerusalem), where Saul was privately crowned; Mizpeh, an unknown place, near by, and also north of Jerusalem, where he was introduced to the people as king; Gibeah (*Tuleil el Ful*, 4 miles north of Jerusalem), his home and capital; and Gilgal, in the Jordan Valley, where he was formally recognized as king, after his victory at Jabesh-gilead. The places named in the account of Saul's search for his father's stray asses, which led him to Samuel, are not known with certainty; but Shalisha may be *Sirisia*, 13 miles north of Lydda, and Zuph may be another name for Zophim, or Ramah, of which the name in full was Ramathaim-zophim.

II. **The Wars of Saul.** (1 Sam. 11–18.) These were as follows:

1. *The Ammonite War.* (1 Sam. 11.) The Ammonites were a roving, predatory, cruel people, ancient enemies of Israel, living east of the Moabites. Under their king, Nahash, they invaded the territory east of the Jordan, and besieged Jabesh-gilead (*ed Deir*). Word came to Saul, who instantly summoned the warriors of Israel. They met at Bezek (not the same with the Bezek of Judges 1:4, but probably the ruin *Ibzik*, a little north of Tirzah), marched against the Ammonites, and, under Saul's vigorous leadership, utterly discomfited them. The relief of Jabesh-gilead, Saul's first victory, greatly strengthened his authority as king, over the tribes.

2. *The First Philistine War.* (1 Sam. 13, 14.) At the time of Saul's accession, the Philistine outposts held Geba, Bethel, and other places in the mountain region. Saul undertook to free the land, and summoned the Israelites, who came tremblingly, being thoroughly cowed under their oppressors. Saul's son Jonathan struck the first blow, by attacking the Philistines at Geba (*Jeba*), near Gibeah, Saul's capital; and soon followed it up by a great victory at Michmash, across the valley from Geba. The Israelites now gained courage, and pursued the Philistines, even to their own borders. Nevertheless, the Philistines continued to hold their fortresses in Israel through all the reign of Saul, and wars were constant between the two races.

Three other wars of Saul are named in a single verse (1 Sam. 14:47), without mention of particular events. These are as follows:

3. *The Moabite War.* These people lived south of the brook Arnon, and east of the Dead Sea. The war with them may have taken place in connection with the Ammonite campaign, already referred to. No battle-fields are named, so that the places of the war cannot be given. It resulted in the defeat of the Moabites, but not in their subjection to Israel.

4. *The Edomite War* perhaps occurred at the same time, and may have been caused by an alliance of Edom Moab and Ammon against Israel, as all these tribes lived near each other, the Edomites south of the Dead Sea. Probably after the victory at Jabesh-gilead, Saul pursued the flying Ammonites, ravaged their territory, and then entered the lands of Moab and of Edom.

5. *The Syrian War.* This was against "the kings of Zobah." (1 Sam. 14:47.) Zobah was situated near Damascus, northeast of Palestine, and was the head of a kingdom until subjected in the reign of David. It is likely that Saul's campaign was a defensive one, protecting his border against a Syrian inroad, but no places or particulars are named.

6. *The Amalekite War.* (1 Sam. 14:48; 15:1–35.) This marked the turning point in Saul's career; for, though a signal victory, it was the occasion of his alienation from Samuel, the priests and the prophetic order, and the beginning of his decline. The Amalekites were wild Bedouins of the desert, whose presence made the southern border unsafe, and against whom an ancient ban had been pronounced. They were to be utterly destroyed, not merely conquered or despoiled. Saul assembled his army at Telaim, on the southern border (probably *el Kuseir*, between Beersheba and the Dead Sea), and marched into the land of the Amalekites, destroyed their principal city, laid waste their country, and brought away their king a prisoner. But the command had been, not to plunder, but to destroy; as the safety of Israel (and, we may add, the salvation of the world through Israel) was endangered by these nomad hordes; and Saul, after leading his host with their plunder over the mountains of Judah, met Samuel at Gilgal, and received a rebuke for his disobedience, and the warning of his own rejection as the theocratic king.

7. *The Second Philistine War.* (1 Sam. 17, 18.) War

was the normal condition between the Israelites and the Philistines, and there were doubtless many battles and campaigns of which no mention is made. But this was notable for the first appearance of DAVID, the destined king, who had been privately anointed by Samuel at Bethlehem. The Philistines were encamped at a place called Ephes-dammim, or Shochoh, and the Israelites across the Valley of Elah, where between the two hosts David met the gigantic Goliath of Gath, and killed him, in a deed of mingled skill and courage. As a result the Philistines fled, and were pursued by Israel even to the gates of Ekron and Gath. David was now brought prominently into notice, and became one of Saul's household at Gibeah, though soon an object of suspicion by the jealous king.

III. **Saul's Pursuit of David** (1 Sam. 19-28) is the principal subject of the history during the close of his reign. We have indicated upon the map, by a red line, the wanderings of David during this period, as nearly as the localities have been identified, and have marked each place by a number.

1. At *Gibeah*, the capital, David was more than once threatened with death, until at last he fled from Saul's wrath to Ramah.

2. At *Ramah*, David was with Samuel and the "sons of the prophets," in a neighborhood called Naioth, "pastures," or "dwellings." Here Saul came to slay him, but was overcome by the ardent worship of the prophetic band, and, forgetting his errand, joined in their devotions, while David escaped once more to Gibeah. (1 Sam. 19:18-24.)

3. At *Gibeah*, David found a place of hiding for a few days, and then met his friend Jonathan, in the farewell interview, when "the arrows" were shot as tokens. (1 Sam. 20.)

4. David's first stopping place, in his permanent exile, was at *Nob*, where stood the Tabernacle. Here he received food, and took the sword of Goliath, which he carried as his weapon during his wanderings. This act of hospitality afterward cost the high-priest and many of his order their lives, at the hand of Saul. (1 Sam. 21:1-9; 22:6-23.) Nob was probably about two miles north of Jerusalem.

5. From Nob, David made his way down the mountains to *Gath*, at that time the head of the Philistine league. Here he was suspected by the Philistines, and compelled to escape by a stratagem. (1 Sam. 21:10-15.)

6. He found a hiding place in the *Cave of Adullam*. This was in the Shefelah, or low country, perhaps at *Beit-jibrin*, where immense caverns are found. Here a force of men gathered around him, and his aged parents and brothers joined him, probably from a well-grounded fear, that Saul, who about this time slaughtered the priests for an act of kindness to David, would not scruple to kill the members of his family. (1 Sam. 22:1, 2.)

7. To find a safe refuge for his parents, David left Judah, and went into the land of Moab. Here he placed his parents in the care of the king of Moab, while David

and his men took up their abode at *Mizpeh of Moab*, in a place called "the hold." This may have been at *Kerak*. (1 Sam. 22:3-5.)

8. By the advice of the prophet Gad, who probably had been one of his companions at Samuel's "school of the prophets," in Ramah, David led his little army back to the land of Judah, and made his headquarters in the *Forest of Hareth* (perhaps *Kharas*, in the mountains near Hebron). Here he received news of the massacre of the priests, and was joined by Abiathar, bearing the ephod of the high-priest. (1 Sam. 22:5, 20-23.)

9. Next, he led his men to *Keilah* (*Kilah*, in the mountains northwest of Hebron), to repel an attack of the Philistines. But, learning that the ungrateful people were about to betray him to Saul, he removed in haste to the wilderness between Hebron and the Dead Sea, called Jeshimon, "waste." (1 Sam. 23:1-13.)

10. In this wilderness David remained for a time, at *Ziph* (*Tell Zif*, south of Hebron). Here he met his friend Jonathan for the last time. His followers scattered, and David was alone, except for the presence of a few faithful companions. The Ziphites were willing to betray him to Saul, and he was again compelled to flee. (1 Sam. 23:14-24.)

11. His next hiding place was a mountain in the wilderness of *Maon*, 7 miles south of Hebron. Here he was again in great danger from Saul, but was saved by an opportune foray of the Philistines, which called the king and his troops away. (1 Sam. 25:24-28.)

12. From Ziph he took refuge in the almost inaccessible mountains of *En-gedi* (*Ain-jedy*), overlooking the Dead Sea. Here David showed his generosity in sparing Saul, when it was in his power to slay him. (1 Sam. 24.)

13. About the time of Samuel's death, David returned into the south of Judah, to the neighborhood of *Maon*, 7 miles south of Hebron. (See above, Nos. 10, 11. The likeness of the account in the two visits, has suggested that but one event may be related in both.) Here the narrow-minded Nabal was saved from David's wrath by the wisdom and generosity of his wife, Abigail, who, after Nabal's death, became David's wife. (1 Sam. 25.) About this time, and while David was in or near this locality, occurred David's act of mercy in sparing Saul's life a second time, when by moonlight he penetrated to the very centre of Saul's camp. (1 Sam. 26.)

14. Despairing of safety in Saul's realm during his reign, David finally took refuge in *Gath* (*Tell es Safieh*), on the Shefelah, the capital of the Philistines. Here he was more kindly received than before (see No. 5), as his relations with Saul were better understood, and he was able to obtain from Achish, the king of Gath the grant of a city as his home. (1 Sam. 27:1-4.)

15. The place allotted to David, was *Ziklag*, on the south of Judah, which was at that time recognized as a possession of the Philistines. Its location is unknown, but we have followed Conder in placing it at *Zuheilikah*, 11 miles south of east from Gaza. Here David remained during the closing years of Saul's reign. He accom-

janied the Philistines as far as Aphek, in Mount Ephraim, but was sent back, from a fear lest he might desert to the Israelites. Returning, he found his home plundered by a roving band of Amalekites, pursued them, rescued his family and possessions, and also took a great quantity of booty, which he judiciously used in making presents to the leading people of various places in Judah, after the death of Saul. (1 Sam. 27, 29, 30.) These places are located upon the map as far as they are known.

16. From Ziklag David went up into the mountain region at *Hebron*, soon after the death of Saul. Here he was made king, first of the tribe of Judah, and afterward of all Israel. (2 Sam. 2:1–3.)

IV. **Saul's Death.** This took place B. C. 1010, when Saul had reigned 40 years. We have noticed two wars with the Philistines as prominent in the history of Saul's reign. We call the last campaign of Saul the *third* Philistine war, as no others are related, though their existence may be inferred. This marked the flood tide of Philistine power; for it left them at Saul's death in command not only of the Plain of Esdraelon and the Jordan Valley, but of all the centre of the country. Their armies met at Aphek, in the tribe of Benjamin (their old rallying place, 1 Sam. 4:1), and thence marched northward to the Plain of Esdraelon, at the foot of Mount Gilboa, on which the Israelites were encamped. Saul, full of fear, went around the Philistine camp to the village of Endor, where he sought the counsel of a "woman having a familiar spirit," and met the spirit of Samuel, which gave him warning that on the morrow he should die. The battle was fought on the next day. Saul and three of his sons, including the princely Jonathan, were slain; and Israel experienced the heaviest defeat thus far in its history. All the middle section of the land of Palestine was conquered by the Philistines, cutting the tribes in sunder in each direction, from north to south and from east to west. At such a low ebb were the fortunes of the Chosen People, when David ascended the throne. Saul's body was fastened up on the wall of the Canaanite city of Beth-shean, but was rescued by the warriors of Jabesh-gilead, in grateful remembrance of Saul's brave deed in behalf of their city, early in his reign. (1 Sam. 31.)

Upon the map the following are indicated: 1. The portions of the land under Philistine and Canaanite control are given in yellow, while the territory governed by Saul is shown in pink. The mountain region was held by Israel, and the lowlands, both by the sea and the Jordan, by the Philistines. 2. The names of Philistine cities are printed in red. Some of these were their own hereditary possessions; others (as Aphek, Geba and Bethel) were fortresses in the mountain region, garrisoned to hold Israel in subjection. 3. The battle-fields and wars of Saul are indicated by flags, and numbered. (1.) Jabesh-gilead, over the Ammonites. (1 Sam. 11.) (2.) Michmash, over the Philistines. (1 Sam. 14.) (3.) In Moab, at some unknown place. (1 Sam. 14:47.) (4.) In Edom, at a place also unknown. (1 Sam. 14:47.) (5.) Over the Syrians of Zobah. (1 Sam. 14:47.) This we have indicated as taking place in the half tribe of Manasseh, East; but its precise location is unknown. (6.) "A city of Amalek," place unknown. (1 Sam. 15:5.) (7.) Valley of Elah, over the Philistines. (1 Sam. 17:2.) (8.) Mount Gilboa. (1 Sam. 31.) 4. The various places named in Saul's pursuit of David are shown upon the map, with their most probable identifications. These places are: (1.) Gibeah. (2.) Ramah. (3.) Gibeah. (4.) Nob. (5.) Gath. (6.) Adullam. (7.) Mizpeh of Moab. (8.) Hareth. (9.) Keilah. (10.) Ziph. (11.) Maon. (12.) En-gedi. (13.) Maon. (14.) Gath. (15.) Ziklag. (16.) Hebron.

OUTLINE FOR REVIEW.

I. *Saul's Appointment.* Ramah, Gibeah, Gilgal, Shalisha, Zuph.

II. *Wars of Saul.* 1. Ammonite. (Jabesh-gilead, Bezek.) 2. First Philistine. (Geba, Michmash.) 3. Moabite. 4. Edomite. 5. Syrian. 6. Amalekite. (Telaim, Gilgal.) 7. Second Philistine. (Valley of Elah.)

III. *Pursuit of David.* 1. Gibeah. 2. Ramah. 3. Gibeah. 4. Nob. 5. Gath. 6. Adullam. 7. Mizpeh of Moab. 8. Hareth. 9. Keilah. 10. Ziph. 11. Maon. 12. En-gedi. 13. Maon. 14. Gath. 15. Ziklag. 16. Hebron.

IV. *Saul's Death.* Aphek, Gilboa, Beth-shean, Jabesh-gilead.

JERICHO

THE
EMPIRE
OF
DAVID AND SOLOMON.

THE EMPIRE OF DAVID AND SOLOMON.

THE greatness of David may be shown by a comparison of our last map with the present one, keeping in mind the difference of scale between them. David succeeded to the throne of Israel when it represented about 6,000 square miles of territory, more or less, under control; he left to his successor, Solomon, an empire embracing an area of 60,000 square miles. See the comparative diagram on page 70. The map now before us being upon a scale greatly reduced from that of Saul's kingdom, it will be impossible to represent upon it all the localities mentioned in the history of David and Solomon. Those in the neighborhood of Jerusalem will be found on the map of the Environs of Jerusalem, page 83, and those of minor importance in the land of Israel may be found on the map of Palestine Among the Tribes, page 58.

We present the events and localities under the following outline: 1. David's Reign over Judah. 2. The Union of Palestine. 3. David's Foreign Conquests. 4. David's Calamities. 5. The Closing Events. 6. The Reign of Solomon.

I. David's Reign over Judah. (2 Sam. 1–4.) After the death of Saul, David went from Ziklag to Hebron, and was there accepted as king over the tribe of Judah. His reign lasted for seven years, from 1010 to 1003 B. C. During a part of this time, Ishbosheth, the only remaining son of Saul, was also nominally reigning over a large part of the land, the real power being held by Abner, Saul's general, and the ablest man of his time. War naturally arose, and many battles were doubtless fought, of which but one, at Gibeon, is related. At last, Abner and Ishbosheth were both murdered, though not by David's desire nor with his approbation; and, with one consent, David was accepted as king over all the Twelve Tribes.

TOWER OF DAVID.

II. The Union of Palestine. (2 Sam. 5–7.) David was now ruler over the mountain region only, as Saul had been before him, and in various places were garrisons of the Philistines, and cities held by the Canaanite races. He began by a siege of Jebus, or Jebusi, a fortress of the Jebusites, on the border of Judah and Benjamin. Though deemed impregnable by the natives, it was taken by storm, and, under its new name, JERUSALEM, became the capital of the kingdom. The Philistines had been friendly with David in the past, and were perhaps recognized as the "lords paramount" during his reign over Judah; but now they were jealous of his growing power, and, as of old, entered the mountain region with their armies. But in David they met an enemy of a different character from either Samson or Saul. Two battles were fought, both near Jerusalem, at a place called "the Valley [or plain] of the Rephaim"; and in each the Philistines were utterly routed.

David followed up his advantage, after the second victory, by marching down upon the Shefelah and the plain. He took Gath (called Metheg-ammah, "the bridle of the metropolis," in 2 Sam. 8:1), and subjugated the entire Philistine confederacy so completely that thenceforward they ceased to trouble Israel for centuries.

The land was now united, and David turned his attention to the religious reformation of the people, brought the ark from Baale, or Kirjathjearim, to Jerusalem, planned for the Temple to be built by his successor, and organized the worship on a magnificent scale. (2 Sam. 6, 7.)

III. David's Foreign Conquests. These were not

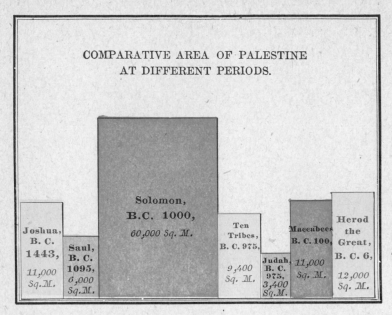

COMPARATIVE AREA OF PALESTINE
AT DIFFERENT PERIODS.

Joshua, B.C. 1443, 11,000 Sq. M.

Saul, B.C. 1095, 6,000 Sq. M.

Solomon, B.C. 1000, 60,000 Sq. M.

Ten Tribes, B.C. 975, 9,400 Sq. M.

Judah, B.C. 975, 3,400 Sq. M.

Maccabees B.C. 100, 11,000 Sq. M.

Herod the Great, B.C. 6, 12,000 Sq. M.

4. *Edom* (2 Sam. 8:13, 14), south of the Dead Sea. The word "Syrians," in verse 13, should undoubtedly be "Edomites." The battle was fought at the "valley of salt," an unknown place, but probably near Sela, or Petra, the capital of Edom.

5. *Ammon.* (2 Sam. 10-13.) This was the longest of David's wars, and was waged not against the Ammonites only, but against the allied forces of several small Syrian kingdoms, as Zobah (already conquered, but not subjugated), Maachah, Rehob and Tob, districts on the north and east of Israel. Three great battles were fought; the first near Medeba; the second at Helam, an uncertain locality (if it be the name of a place, which is questioned, as the word means "host," or "army"); and the third, the siege and capture of Rabbah, the capital of the Ammonites, which ended the war. During this war occurred the crime of David with Bathsheba, and the murder of Uriah. (2 Sam. 11.) This completed the series of conquests, and made the throne of David supreme from the Red Sea to the Euphrates. One fact which made these conquests possible, was, that the tribes around Israel were not united into strong nations, as afterward in the cases of Syria and Assyria, but were independent principalities, easily overcome in turn by the trained warriors of David.

altogether inspired by ambition, but were necessary for the safety of Israel, and to keep its people from the contamination of the idolatry of the surrounding nations. These conquests are indicated by flags on the map, though the precise locations of the battles are not known in all cases. The lands conquered by David were as follows:

1. *Moab.* (2 Sam. 8:2.) It is stated by Josephus, that the cruel treatment of the Moabites (though fully in accord with the customs of Oriental war in that day) was in revenge for the slaughter of David's parents by the king of Moab, an event not mentioned in the Bible.

2. *Zobah* (2 Sam. 8:3, 4), at that time the principal state between Damascus and the Euphrates.

3. *Damascus* (2 Sam. 8:5-12), in alliance with Zobah, and the largest city in Syria.

As a result of these wars the kingdom of David, which he transmitted to his son Solomon, was the largest in the Oriental world at that time. The Assyrian empire had not arisen, the great kings of Egypt had passed away, and the East was broken up into small principalities, among which Israel easily rose to power.

IV. The Calamities of David's Reign. (2 Sam. 12-20, 24.) Three great troubles befell David and his kingdom as the result of his sins.

1. The first and greatest was the *Rebellion of Absalom.* We can only mention the places referred to in the history, not relate its events. Geshur, where Absalom was in exile, was a small kingdom under the rule of Absalom's maternal grandfather. Tekoa, whence came the "wise woman," was near Bethlehem. The places near Jerusalem named in David's flight, may be seen on the map of the Environs of Jerusalem, page 83. David's resting place was at Mahanaim, east of the Jordan, and south of the Hieromax. Absalom was defeated and killed at

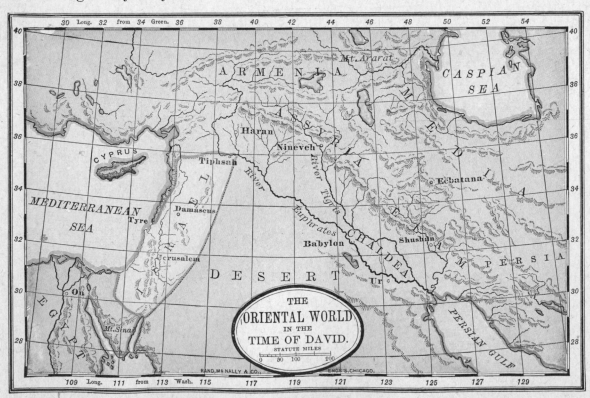

THE ORIENTAL WORLD IN THE TIME OF DAVID.
STATUTE MILES
0   50   100   200
RAND, McNALLY & CO.   ENGR'S, CHICAGO.

"the wood of Ephraim," a locality not in the tribe of that name, but east of the Jordan, perhaps where the Ephraimites sustained a great defeat from Jephthah. (Judges 12.)

2. The second calamity was the *Rebellion of Sheba*, following soon after Absalom's, and arising from the same disaffection. It was ended at Abel-beth-maachah, in the extreme north, by the death of Sheba. (2 Sam. 20.)

3. The third calamity was the *Pestilence*, after the numbering of the people, an enumeration with a view either to heavy levies of assessment, or to foreign conquest; either of which was contrary to the spirit of the Hebrew constitution. (2 Sam. 24.) The places named will be found upon the map, except the inexplicable Tahtim-hodshi, which may mean "the land newly inhabited," but whose location is unknown. The sacrifice of David at Araunah's threshing-floor gave the location to the great altar of the Temple, probably the rude rock which now rises from the floor of the Mosque of Omar, in Jerusalem.

V. The Close of David's Reign (1 Kings 1, 2; 1 Chron. 22–29) was occupied in the organization of his empire, and in preparation for the building of the Temple. There are but few localities named with this period, and they may be easily found upon the maps, those near Jerusalem being upon the map of its Environs.

VI. The Reign of Solomon was a period of peace, with few incidents to mark its even tenor. Its principal event was the building of the Temple. We insert here a plan of Solomon's Temple, largely conjectural, as neither of the descriptions is sufficiently exact for a complete knowledge. The Temple, as it afterward stood in the time of Christ, may be found described on page 139.

Upon the map are noted most of the battle-fields, which may be enumerated as follows: 1. At Gibeon,

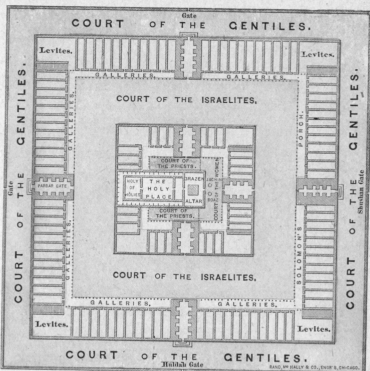

PLAN OF SOLOMON'S TEMPLE.

the victory over Abner and the adherents of Ishbosheth. 2. At Jerusalem, its capture from the Jebusites. 3, 4. Near Jerusalem, not indicated upon the map; two decisive victories over the Philistines. 5. Gath, the capture of the Philistine capital. 6. The victory over the Moabites, probably near Ar. 7. The conquest of Zobah, north of Damascus. 8. The conquest of Damascus and its dependent places. 9. The conquest of Edom, near Sela. 10. The victory at Medeba, over the Ammonites. 11. The victory at Helam, near the Euphrates, over the Syrian allies of the Ammonites. 12. The siege and capture of Rabbah. 13. The defeat of Absalom's army in the wood of Ephraim, east of the Jordan.

OUTLINE FOR TEACHING AND REVIEW.

I. Draw a rough map of the country from the Red Sea to the Euphrates, as in the map of the kingdom of David and Solomon, and locate upon it the land of Israel proper, showing the dominion of Saul.

II. Draw the boundary line to show the kingdom of David at Hebron, and that of Ishbosheth at Mahanaim; mention and locate the battle of Gibeon.

III. Show in order the conquests of David, writing upon the board the names of the lands conquered in order, and indicating the battles by flags.

IV. Show the dimensions of David's kingdom, by another map of the Oriental World in the time of David. Locate and drill upon the leading lands and capitals.

V. Give an account of the calamities in David's reign, show the flight of David, and locate the battle with Absalom.

CHURCH OF NATIVITY, BETHLEHEM.

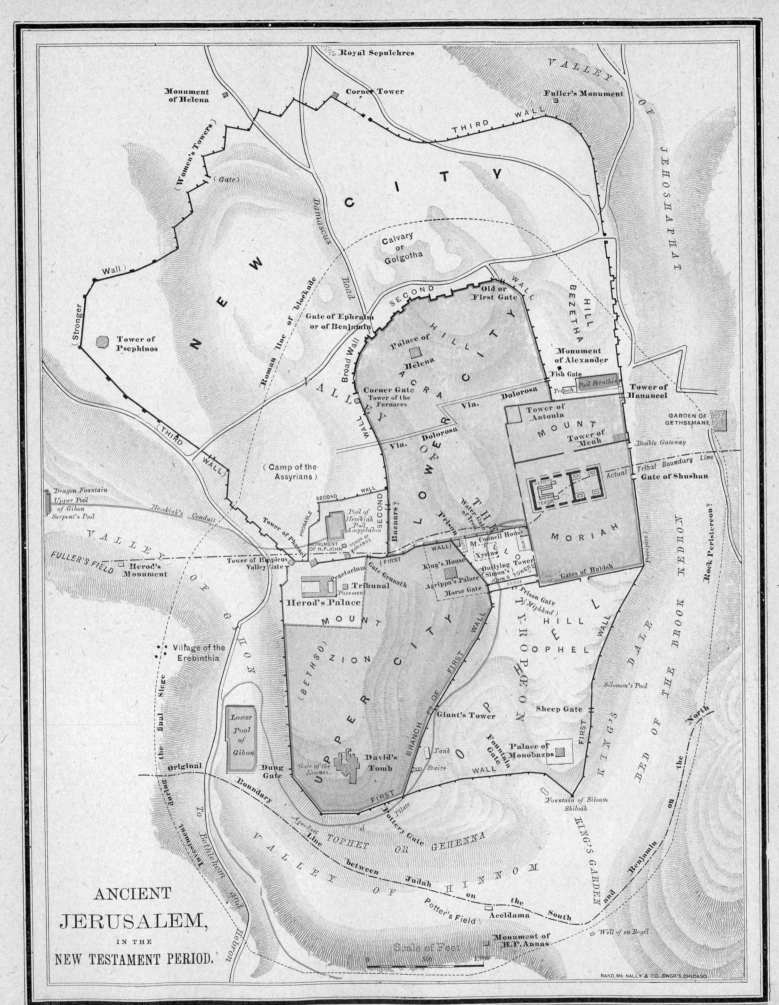

ANCIENT
JERUSALEM,
IN THE
NEW TESTAMENT PERIOD.

ANCIENT JERUSALEM.

I. **Names.** The city of Jerusalem has been known by a different name during each of the most important periods of its varied history. 1. In the patriarchal age it was the seat of Melchizedek's priestly kingdom, and was known as SALEM, properly pronounced *Shalem*. (Gen. 14:18; Psa. 76:2.) 2. During the Jebusite period it was known as JEBUS. (Judges 19:10.) Probably at this time the full name was *Jebus-shalem*. 3. After the capture by David it received the name JERUSALEM, properly *Jeru-shalaim*. The earliest instance of this name is in Judges 1:7, 8, where it may have been used by anticipation; or there may have been a change, for euphony, from Jebus-shalem to *Jeru-shalem*. The word means "possession of peace." The Greek form of this word is Hierosolyma. 4. It is called by the prophets by the poetical name of ARIEL, "the lion of God." (Isa. 29:1.)

DAVID'S TOMB.

5. More than once in the Bible it is called "the holy city." (Matt. 4:5; 27:53.) 6. After its destruction by Titus. it was rebuilt by the emperor Ælius Hadrianus, A. D. 135, and named ÆLIA, or, in full, ÆLIA CAPITOLINA, a name that it held until the year 536, A. D., when the ancient name Jerusalem again became prevalent. 7. It is now known to the Arabs as EL KHUDS, "the holy."

II. **Location.** The city of Jerusalem stands in latitude 31° 46′ 45″ north, and longitude 35° 13′ 25″ east of Greenwich, the observations being taken from the dome of the Church of the Holy Sepulchre. This may have been outside the ancient wall, but was certainly near it. The city is 32 miles from the Mediterranean, 18 from the Dead Sea, 20 from Hebron, and 36 from Samaria; and its general elevation is about 2,500 feet above the level of the ocean.

III. **Geologic Formation.** "The vicinity of Jerusalem consists of strata of the Eocene and chalk formations, having a general dip down the watershed of about 10° east-southeast. The action of denudation has left patches of the various strata; but, generally speaking, the oldest are on the west. The upper part of the Olivet chain consists of a soft white limestone, with fossils and flint bands belonging to the Upper Chalk; beneath this are,—first, a hard silicious chalk, with flint bands; second, a soft white limestone, much used in the ancient buildings of the city; third, a hard chalk, often pink and white in color, and then known as Santa Croce marble. The underlying beds belonging to the period of the Greensand are not visible, the lowest strata in the Kedron precipices belonging to the Lower Chalk epoch." (*Encyclo. Britan.*)

IV. **Valleys.** The peculiar natural features of Jerusalem, and much of its history, are due to the arrangement of its three valleys. These unite near the southeastern corner of the city. 1. *The Valley of the Kedron*, called also "the Valley of Jehoshaphat" (perhaps referred to in Joel 3:2, 12); and "the king's dale" (Gen. 14:17; 2 Sam. 18:18). This lies on the east of the city, between Mount Moriah and the Mount of Olives. During the summer it is dry; but in the rainy season it is the bed of a brook, from which it receives its name. 2. *The Valley of the Tyropæon* (a word supposed to mean "cheesemongers," though the meaning and derivation are questioned) branches from the Kedron Valley at the southern end of Mount Moriah, and extends in a northwesterly direction. The principal ravine curves in crescent form around Mount Zion, but a shallower and less noticeable branch extends further to the north. This valley is now almost obliterated by the accumulation of debris, but its ancient course has been established by recent soundings. 3. *The Valley of Hinnom*, called also, "the valley of the son of Hinnom" (Josh. 15:8), forms the western and southern border of the city, and unites with the Kedron Valley near its junction with the

Tyropœon. Its lower portion, near the Kedron, was called Tophet, or "place of fire" (Jer. 7:31), and Gehenna (Ge-Hinnom). It was at one time the seat of idolatrous worship to Molech, and afterward became a cesspool, and place where the offal of the city was burned. Gihon (1 Kings 1:33) is located by most in the upper portion of this valley; but, by Conder and a few others, in the lower portion of the Kedron Valley, at the spring en Rogel.

V. **Mountains.** Jerusalem is and has ever been emphatically a place of mountains; as it stood anciently upon four distinct hills, with others around its walls on every side. The names of these hills are well known, but the identification of them is neither easy nor unanimous among investigators. We name the locations as given by the largest number of leading scholars.

1. *Mount Zion* is the largest and highest of the four hills within the city. It lies on the southwestern section, between the Valleys of the Tyropœon on the east and north, and Hinnom on the south and west. Its crown is 2,540 feet high. Upon it, probably, stood the Jebusite fortress which so long defied the Israelites, but was finally taken by David.

2. *Acra* is a little east of north from Zion, and is an irregularly shaped eminence, now 2,490 feet high, but anciently higher, as its crest was cut down by the Maccabean princes, in order to bring it nearer to the level of the Temple-hill. It is surrounded upon the south, east and north by the two arms of the Tyropœon Valley. On this may have stood the castle, or Millo. (2 Sam. 5:9.)

3. On the eastern side of the city is *Mount Moriah*, the place once occupied by the Temple, and now by the Dome of the Rock, mistakenly called the Mosque of Omar. It lies between the two valleys of the Kedron on the east and the Tyropœon on the west, and is 2,432 feet high. Its southern end is a steep declivity, called Ophel (in Josephus, Ophlas), running southward to the junction of the valleys.

4. *Bezetha* is a little west of north from Mount Moriah, and separated from it by a slight depression. It lies between the Kedron Valley and the northern branch of the Tyropœon. Only in the later age of New Testament history was it within the walls of the city. Its height is a little over 2,500 feet.

These four mountains are all that are named as within the ancient walls. Calvary was not a mountain, but merely a place outside the city where the crucifixion of Jesus took place; so that it is not to be counted in the list. But we must notice, in addition, the most important of the "mountains round about Jerusalem."

5. *The Mount of Olives* lies east of the Kedron Valley, and is a range of hills having several summits, which are a little under 3,000 feet in height. (1.) The northern peak, called *Scopus*, lies northeast of the wall, and is supposed to be the point from which Titus obtained his first view of the doomed city. (2.) The second is called *Viri Galilœi*, "men of Galilee," from a tradition that the angels, at the time of Christ's ascension, appeared upon

it. (Acts 1:11.) (3.) The central summit is the *Mount of Ascension*, 2,665 feet high, and directly east of the Temple. It is probable that the true place of the ascension is to be found on the eastern slope of this hill, near Bethany, and not in sight of Jerusalem. (4.) The next peak southward is called "*The Prophets*," from a tradition that some of the prophets were buried upon its side near the Kedron. (5.) The southern peak is called the *Mount of Offense*, from the idol worship which Solomon established upon it. (1 Kings 11:7.)

6. South of the Valley of Hinnom, and directly opposite to Mount Zion, is an eminence known as the *Hill of Evil Counsel*, where Judas is said to have bargained for the betrayal of his Lord. Upon the slope of this hill is the traditional Aceldama, "the field of blood." (Matt. 27:7, 8.)

VI. **Walls.** Of these, three are named by the early historians and mentioned in the Bible. 1. The first wall was built by David and Solomon, and surrounded what was known as "the city of David." It included Zion, Moriah, Ophel, and the southern portion of the Tyropœon Valley. The lines of this wall may still be traced and the ancient foundations shown in various places. 2. The second wall, including Acra, extended in a curved line from the tower Antonia, north of the Temple, to a point not yet marked with certainty, on the northern border of Mount Zion. The location of Calvary and the place of the Saviour's burial depend upon the question, whether this wall ran outside or inside of the place where now stands the Church of the Holy Sepulchre. For, as these were "outside the gate," if the wall include the traditional localities, they are wrongly located, and the true places must be sought elsewhere, perhaps near the so-called Grotto of Jeremiah, north of the city. We indicate both localities, but regard the northern as preferable. 3. The third wall was not built until after the time of Christ, but was begun by Herod Agrippa, and was completed not long before the Roman siege. This section was called "the new city," and included Mount Bezetha, and the region north and northwest of Mount Zion. Only a small portion of the wall can be located with certainty.

VII. **History of Jerusalem.** This may be briefly noticed under seven periods.

1. *The Patriarchal Period* (B. C. 2000–1300). The earliest mention of Jerusalem is that in Gen. 14:18, which, taken with Psa. 76:2, seems to indicate the place, though the identity is questioned by some scholars. In the time of Abraham, B. C. 1918, according to the common chronology, Jerusalem was the seat of a kingdom under the priest Melchizedek, who received homage and tithes, as God's representative, from the patriarch. At that time it was a centre, not only of political power, but of a religious worship which was recognized by Abraham as divine and spiritual.

2. *The Jebusite Period* (B. C. 1300–1003). The next reference to Jerusalem (and the earliest *certain* account) is at the time of the conquest, B. C. 1210. At that

period it was held by the Jebusites, a race of Canaanite origin, small in numbers, but of indomitable courage and resolution, since they were able to hold their city for four centuries against all the power of Israel. Their king, Adoni-zedek (Josh. 10:1), may have been a descendant of the pious Melchi-zedek, as the names are similar; but the ancient purity of the people's worship had been lost in the idolatry of the surrounding races. The little city of Jebus, as it was then called, formed a confederation with the other clans of the south to resist Joshua's invading host. But in the decisive battle of Beth-horon the Canaanites were routed, their five kings were slain (among them the king of Jerusalem), and the alliance was broken up. For the present, Jerusalem was not attacked, but its territory was assigned to the tribe of Benjamin. (Josh. 18:28.) Soon after the death of Joshua, however, it was besieged by the united tribes of Judah and Simeon, as dangerous to the northern frontier of the former. From Judges 1:8, and the history of Josephus, we learn that the lower city (perhaps on Acra) was taken and burned; but the fortress was found impregnable "by reason of its walls and also of the nature of the place." (Josephus.) The city was soon rebuilt (Judges 19:11), and remained in Jebusite hands through all the age of the Judges and the reign of Saul.

3. *The Royal Period* (B. C. 1003–587). With the accession of David a new era began in Israel, and every part of the kingdom soon felt the strong hand of its new master. He was not one to brook a foreign fortress in the centre of his realm, and in the first year of his reign over united Israel he marched against it, and demanded its surrender. Trusting to their strong situation, the Jebusites refused, and, as an insult, placed "the blind and the lame" on its walls in mockery of his attempt. But, under the valiant Joab, the height was scaled, the fortress was taken, and Jerusalem was thenceforth "the city of David." (2 Sam. 5.) David made it his capital, brought thither the ark of the covenant, and surrounded it with a new wall. Solomon enriched it with treasures, and with its greatest glory, the Temple on Mount Moriah. After the division it remained the capital of Judah, though close to the border of the Ten Tribes. It was taken without resistance from Rehoboam, by Shishak, the king of Egypt, and robbed of its wealth, 930 B. C. In the reign of Jehoshaphat it was restored to something like its former prosperity; but under his son Jehoram, B. C. 840, it was taken by a sudden attack of the Philistines and Arabians, and again plundered. Under Athaliah it became a shrine of abominable Baal worship, but was reformed by Jehoiada in the earlier days of the reign of Joash. Joash, however, in his later years allowed the people to relapse into idolatry, with the usual result; for, about B. C. 800, the powerful Hazael, king of Syria, overran the Shefelah, defeated the Judaites, and was only kept from entering the city by a gift of its treasures. Amaziah, the next king, elated by a victory, offered battle at Beth-shemesh to Joash, king of Israel, then the most powerful state

between Egypt and Assyria. He was defeated; and, as a result, Jerusalem was entered by the Israelites, its wall was thrown down, and it was again plundered. The city suffered during the wicked reign of Ahaz, but was restored and divinely protected from its Assyrian besiegers in the good reign of Hezekiah. After the death of Josiah it was entered by the Egyptians under Necho; but its final destruction was wrought by Nebuchadnezzar, of the Babylonian empire. Twice he visited it with a heavy hand, setting up one king after another; and, when his vassal Zedekiah again rebelled, he besieged it for more than a year, with some intermissions, and at last, in B. C. 587, made a breach in its walls and took it by storm. Then, for the first time, the city was absolutely

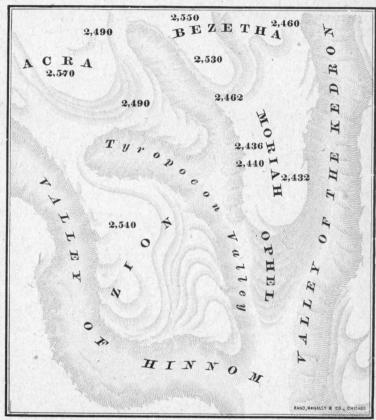

NATURAL FEATURES OF JERUSALEM.

destroyed, and made a heap of ruins, while its people were carried into captivity.

4. *The Period of Restoration* (B. C. 587–70 A. D.). After lying desolate for 50 years, the city was again occupied under Zerubbabel, by the decree of Cyrus, B. C. 536. For nearly a century it remained unwalled and was thinly inhabited, until its wall was rebuilt by Nehemiah, B. C. 445. Thenceforward it grew rapidly, and soon became again the metropolis as well as the capital of the Jewish state. Alexander the Great visited it, B. C. 332, and gave the Jews certain privileges in his empire. The city was taken by Ptolemy Soter, king of Egypt, B. C. 320, because the Jews would not fight on the Sabbath. In B. C. 203 it was taken by Antiochus, the king of Syria, and, after a revolt, again by his son, Antiochus Epiphanes, in B. C. 170 and B. C. 168. The latter capture was followed by a bitter persecution of the Jewish

religion, in which thousands of lives were sacrificed. But a deliverer arose, in the family of the priest Matta-thias, whose son, Judas Maccabeus, rescued the city and restored the worship in the Temple. Under the Macca-bean princes Jerusalem was generally prosperous, though with occasional reverses. The Romans first besieged and took the city under Pompey, B. C. 65. Herod the Great beautified the city, erected many buildings, and rebuilt the Temple throughout. But the most terrible of all scenes in Jerusalem's annals, were those which took place in the revolt of the Jews against the Roman em-pire, and the destruction of the city by Titus, A. D. 70. For years it was the arena of riot, of the bloody strife of factions, and of massacre, which scarcely ceased dur-ing the final siege. At last the city and Temple were taken by Titus, demolished and burned, and for a second time Jerusalem was left an utter desolation.

5. *The Roman Period* (A. D. 70–637). For fifty years after its destruction Jerusalem is not mentioned, and probably remained uninhabited. But, after the attempt of the false Messiah Bar-cocheba to rebuild the city and Temple, and restore the independence of the Jews, — an attempt which was only quelled by calling forth all the power of the empire,— the emperor Hadrian resolved to establish a heathen city upon its site. He named it Ælia Capitolina, built on Moriah a temple to Jupiter, and allowed no Jews to enter the walls, a prohibition which remained until the empire became Christian. Constantine, the first Christian emperor, restored the an-cient name; and his mother, Helena, made a pilgrimage to the city, A. D. 326, which now began to be regarded as a sacred place by Christians. At this time the first Church of the Holy Sepulchre was built, over the place where Helena discovered the tomb of Jesus. The empe-ror Julian, A. D. 362, out of hatred to the Christians, undertook to rebuild the Temple, and make it once more a Jewish centre; but was defeated in his plans by earth-quakes and the leaping forth of subterranean fires, as is related by Ammianus Marcellinus, himself a heathen, the friend and companion in arms of the emperor. He

states: "Horrible balls of fire, breaking out near the foundations, with frequent and reiterated attacks, ren-dered the place from time to time inaccessible to the scorched and blasted workmen; and, the victorious element continuing in this, obstinately and resolutely bent, as it were, to drive them to a distance, the under-taking was abandoned." In 529 A. D. the emperor Justinian founded a church upon the site where now is the Mosque el Aksa, and a tide of pilgrims, increasing with each generation, began to pour upon the holy places. In 614 A. D. the city was taken by the Persian king, Chosroes II., the churches were destroyed, and multi-tudes of priests and monks were slain; but 14 years after-ward it was retaken by the emperor Heraclius, and held, though but for a short time, by the Christians.

6. *The Mediæval Period* (A. D. 637–1517). In 637 Palestine and Jerusalem passed under the dominion of the Moslems, then ruled by the Caliph Omar; but the holy places were respected, and the Christians were allowed to retain their churches. Under the Fatimite caliphs of Cairo the Christians were persecuted, and the Church of the Holy Sepulchre was several times de-stroyed and rebuilt. The pilgrims from Europe brought trade and tribute, so that the city flourished, in spite of frequent pillagings and captures by various Arab and Turkish hordes. On July 15, 1099, it was taken by the Crusaders, after a terrible assault, and for 88 years was the seat of a Christian kingdom. Saladin reconquered it in 1187; and various changes in its government and several sieges followed, until 1517, when it finally passed under the rule of the Turks, who have since been its masters.

7. *The Modern Period*, from A. D. 1517 until the present, has witnessed comparatively few changes in the city's condition. The present wall was built by the sultan Suleiman in 1542. In 1832 it was seized by Mo-hammed Ali, Pasha of Egypt, but was again restored to the sultan, through the interference of the European powers. It is now a city of a population variously estimated at from twenty to fifty thousand.

OUTLINE FOR TEACHING AND REVIEW.

Have two blackboards (or a large one), and use one for the outline of the lesson, the other for the map.

I. Teach the *Names*. Salem, Jebus, Jerusalem, Ariel, Ælia Capitolina, El Khuds.

II. *Location*. 1. Latitude. 2. Longitude. 3. Distances. 4. Elevation.

III. *Geologic Formation*.

IV. *Valleys*. Draw a rough map showing the valleys, and name them, indicating them by initial letters on the map. 1. Kedron. 2. Tyropœon. 3. Hinnom.

V. *Mountains*. Describe each, and indicate by initial letter. 1. Zion. 2. Acra. 3. Moriah. 4. Bezetha 5. Olives. Peaks: (1.) Scopus. (2.)

"Viri Galilæi." (3.) Ascension. (4.) Prophets. (5.) Offense. (6.) Evil Counsel.

VI. *Walls*. Draw them on the board, describe and name. First. (David.) Second. Third. (Agrippa.)

VII. *History*. 1. Patriarchal. (Melchizedek.) 2. Jebusite. (Adoni-zedek.) 3. Royal. (David, Jehoshaphat, etc.) 4. Restoration. (Zerubbabel, Alex-ander, Ptolemy, Antiochus, Judas Maccabeus, Pompey, Herod, Titus.) 5. Roman. (Bar-cocheba, Hadrian, Constantine, Julian, Justinian, Chosroes.) 6. Mediæval. (Omar, Crusaders, Saladin.) 7. Modern. (Suleiman, Mo-hammed Ali, etc.)

JERUSALEM,

DESCRIPTION OF

1. The Mohammedan Quarter occupies the northeastern half
the city, and is the foreground of our view. Its principal objec
of interest are, the Church of St. Mary Magdalene, the Church of S
Anne, two convents, two mosques, a building known as Pilate
Hall, and the narrow and crooked street known as the Via Doloros
"The Sorrowful Way," through which Christ is (traditionally) said
have carried his cross; a street crowded with places commemorati
different events in the passion of our Lord.

2. The Temple Enclosure, called by Moslems *Haram esh Sher*
"The Noble Sanctuary," is in the southeastern part of the Moha
medan Quarter (on the left foreground of the picture). It occupi
the site of the Temple, and probably a part also of the Tower
Antonia. (See map and description of Ancient Jerusalem, page 7:
It is now a quadrangle of 1,042 feet on the north, 1,530 east (alo
the front wall in the picture), 922 south, and 1,601 west, embraci
about 35 acres. Its most prominent building is the *Kubbet es Sakhr*
"The Dome of the Rock," often called, but incorrectly, the Mosq
of Omar. This is an octagonal building, each of its sides being
feet long, 170 in height, and surmounted by a dome. Directly und
the dome rises a rough native rock, standing at present nearly 5 f
above the pavement. Some regard this as the place where the A

51 52 53 54 55 56 57 58 59 60 61 62

ROM THE MOU

DERN JERUSALEM.

of the Covenant rested in Solomon's Temple; but most authorities consider it the site of the Altar of Burnt Offering, and of Araunah's threshing-floor. (2 Sam. 24:18.) In the southeast corner of the Enclosure stands the Mosque el Aksa (left of the picture), adjoining the southern wall.

3. The Jewish Quarter is west of the Temple Enclosure. In the picture, beyond the trees in the Enclosure, may be seen the steep side of the Tyropœon Valley. The Jews' Wailing Place, adjoining the Temple Enclosure, is hidden in the picture by the Mosque el Aksa, but may be located upon the map. Here the wall contains large blocks of stone, which may have belonged to the foundations of the court of the ancient Temple; and at this place a Jewish service of lamentation is held every week, over the destruction of the Temple and the city. Two domed buildings may be noticed on the hill beyond the Tyropœon Valley, the two synagogues of the Ashkenasim Jews. This quarter, once filthy and mean, has been greatly improved by the liberality of Sir Moses Montefiore.

4. The Armenian Quarter is west of the Jewish, in the southwestern corner of the city. Its most prominent building is the Citadel of David (el Kabaa), an irregular, castellated edifice, containing a lofty tower. This may occupy the site of the castle built by David, where

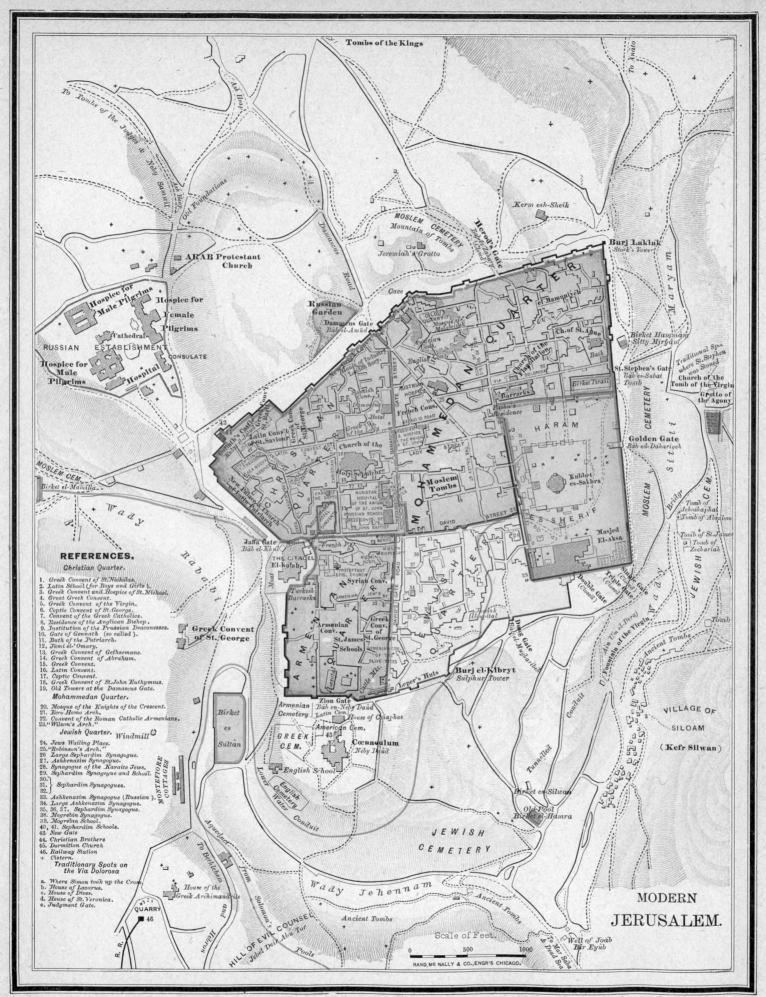

REFERENCES.
Christian Quarter.
1. Greek Convent of St. Nicholas.
2. Latin School (for Boys and Girls).
3. Greek Convent and Hospice of St. Michael.
4. Great Greek Convent.
5. Greek Convent of the Virgin.
6. Coptic Convent of St. George.
7. Convent of the Greek Catholics.
8. Residence of the Anglican Bishop.
9. Institution of the Prussian Deaconesses.
10. Gate of Gennath (so called).
11. Bath of the Patriarch.
12. Jami el-'Omary.
13. Greek Convent of Gethsemane.
14. Greek Convent of Abraham.
15. Greek Convent.
16. Latin Convent.
17. Coptic Convent.
18. Greek Convent of St. John Euthymius.
19. Old Towers at the Damascus Gate.
Mohammedan Quarter.
20. Mosque of the Knights of the Crescent.
21. Ecce Homo Arch.
22. Convent of the Roman Catholic Armenians.
23. "Wilson's Arch."
Jewish Quarter.
24. Jews Wailing Place.
25. "Robinson's Arch."
26. Large Sephardim Synagogue.
27. Ashkenazim Synagogue.
28. Synagogue of the Karaite Jews.
29. Sephardim Synagogue and School.
30.
31. } Sephardim Synagogues.
32.
33. Ashkenazim Synagogue (Russian).
34. Large Ashkenazim Synagogue.
35, 36, 37. Sephardim Synagogue.
38. Mogrebin Synagogue.
39. Mogrebin School.
40, 41. Sephardim Schools.
43. New Gate.
44. Christian Brothers
45. Dormition Church
46. Railway Station
+ Cistern.
Traditionary Spots on the Via Dolorosa.
a. Where Simon took up the Cross.
b. House of Lazarus.
c. House of Dives.
d. House of St. Veronica.
e. Judgment Gate.

MODERN
JERUSALEM.

Scale of Feet.

0   500   1000

RAND, MC NALLY & CO., ENGR'S CHICAGO.

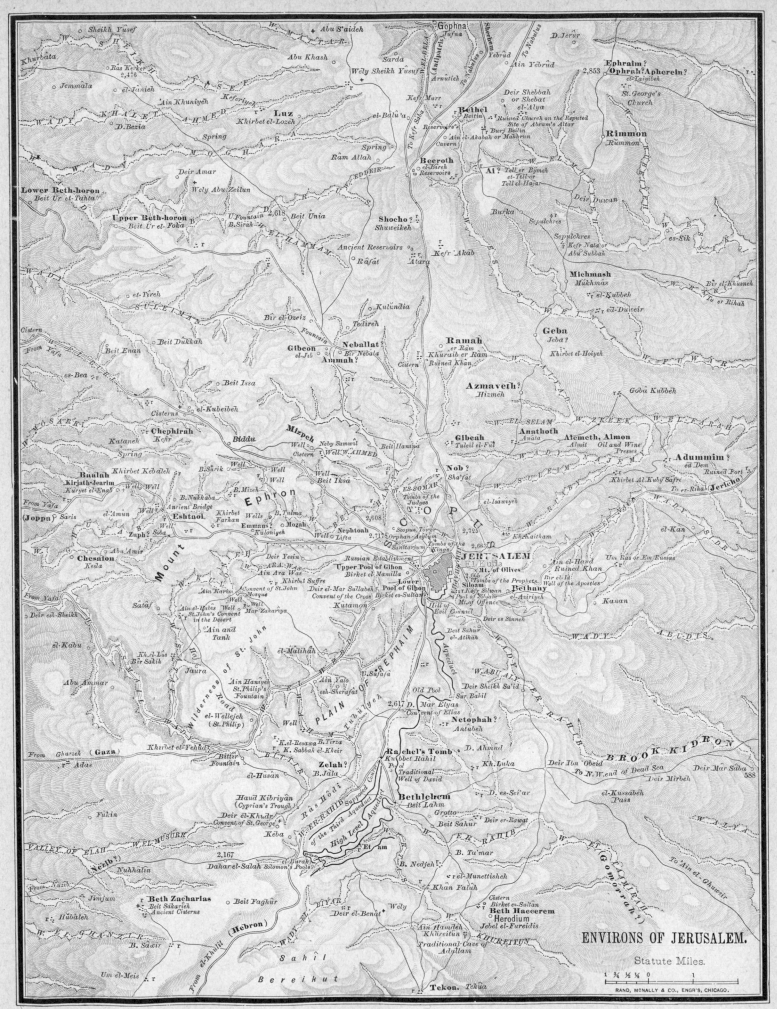

ENVIRONS OF JERUSALEM.

Statute Miles.

RAND, McNALLY & CO., ENGR'S, CHICAGO.

THE ENVIRONS OF JERUSALEM.

THE city of Jerusalem occupies a prominent place, not only in the history but also in the topography of the Holy Land. It is one of the most elevated sites in a land whose important places were among the mountains. There are many peaks higher than Mount Zion, on which the city stands; but few cities in Palestine are built upon a site so lofty. This fact explains many of the allusions in the Psalms. "Beautiful for situation," "I will look unto the hills," etc.

There are six roads leading to Jerusalem from different parts of the land. Starting from the city by each one of these roads, let us notice the important places upon either side of it.

I. **The Northern Road.** This starts from the Damascus Gate and leads almost due north through the centre of the mountain region, toward Shechem and Damascus, passing more of the historic localities than any other. Explorers, however, are not agreed upon the identification of all the places; and our space permits us only to give conclusions without naming reasons or authorities for the opinion in all cases.

1. About a mile north of Jerusalem, on the west of the path, we find *Scopus*, the eminence from which Titus, the Roman conqueror, obtained his first view of the doomed city. According to some authorities this was also the location of *Mizpeh*, the place of assembly for Israel during the time of the Judges. But later investigators place Mizpeh at *N~by Samwil*, on the northwestern road, and we have accepted their conclusions. (See next page.) Both the location of Mizpeh and that of Ramah are uncertain. One word means "watchtower," the other "height," so they may be identical, though the references seem to point to different localities.

2. A mile further, and on the west of the path, is *Nob* (*el Isawiyeh*), named as a city of the priests. At this place the Tabernacle was kept during the reign of Saul; David visited the high-priest and received the sword of Goliath; and the priest and 70 of his associates were slain by command of Saul. (1 Sam. 21:1-9; 22:9-19.)

3. *Gibeah* (*Tuleil el Ful*, "hill of beans," lies on the east of the road, 2½ miles from the city. The place is first mentioned in the painful story of the Levite (Judges 19); but its principal interest is in the fact that it was the home and court of King Saul. "It is now dreary and desolate, with scarce any ruins save a confused mass of stones, which form a sort of cairn on the top."—*Tristram.*

4. *Anathoth* (*Anata*), the birthplace of the prophet Jeremiah, and a priestly city, is 3 miles northeast of Jerusalem, upon a path branching out of the main road. It is now a village of about 20 houses.

5. Some locate *Ramah*, the home of Samuel, at *Er Ram*, on the east of the road; but others favor the place at *Neby Samwil*, to be noticed below.

6. *Michmash*, the scene of Jonathan's daring exploit, lies on a hill adjoining a ravine, 7 miles northeast of the city; and a mile away, in plain sight, lies *Geba*, the camping place of Saul's army at the time of the battle. (1 Sam. 13.) It is now called *Mukmas*.

DEFILE BETWEEN JERUSALEM AND JERICHO.

7. *Ai*—the place where Joshua's army was repulsed by the Canaanites, on account of the crime of Achan (Josh. 7), and which, after his punishment, was taken and destroyed by the Israelites—is 9 miles from the city; a desolate heap, known as *el Tell*.

8. *Beeroth* (wells), now *el Bireh*, 10 miles north, was one of the Gibeonite cities which made peace with Israel. (Josh. 9:17.) According to tradition, this is the place where Joseph and Mary, returning from Jerusalem, first missed the boy Jesus (Luke 2:44); and it is now the halting place of caravans going north.

9. *Bethel*, "the house of God" (now *Beitin*), 10 miles north, is a place of many Scriptural associations. Here Abraham pitched his tent and built his altar, on his entrance upon the Land of Promise (Gen 12:8); here Jacob lay down to rest and saw the glorious vision of

the heavenly ladder (Gen. 28:11–22), and on his return from Syria again consecrated the place to God's service. (Gen. 35:6–15.) During the period of the Ten Tribes it was a sanctuary of idols, but also the seat of a prophetic school. (1 Kings 12:29–33; 2 Kings 2:2, 3.) It is now an uninhabited ruin.

10. East of Bethel, and 11 miles north of Jerusalem, is the rock *Rimmon* (now *Rummon*), where the remnant of the tribe of Benjamin found a refuge after the civil war. (Judges 20, 21.)

11. Two miles north of Rimmon is the site of *Ophrah*, in the New Testament *Ephraim*, the retreat of Jesus after the raising of Lazarus. (John 11:54.) It is in a wilderness, on the edge of the Jordan Valley, and outside the line of travel; now called *et Taiyibeh*.

II. **The Eastern Road** from Jerusalem leads through a barren region of crags and ravines, almost without inhabitants, except the robbers who have haunted it since the days when "a certain man went down from Jerusalem to Jericho, and fell among thieves." (Luke 10:30.) The road is a continual descent from a height of 2,700 feet above the sea to 1,300 feet below it, in 20 miles.

The only place passed on the route is *Bethany* (now *el Azariyeh*), the home of Mary and Martha, the place where Lazarus was raised from death, and near which Jesus ascended. (Luke 24:50.) It is on the eastern slope of the Mount of Olives, and about a mile and a quarter from Jerusalem. Beyond this place the road grows more steep, descending toward the Jordan Valley.

III. **The Southern Road,** leading along the crest of the hill country toward Hebron, also passes few places of historical interest.

1. Just south of the city is the *Plain of the Rephaim*, where, after the capture of Jerusalem, David twice met and vanquished the Philistines. (2 Sam. 5:18–25.) The name may be a reminiscence of the most ancient people who inhabited the mountain region of Palestine, before the Amorites were in the land.

2. Four miles from the city the traveler passes *Rachel's Tomb*. This may represent the place where Jacob, while journeying southward, lost his beloved wife Rachel, the mother of Joseph and Benjamin. (Gen. 35:16–20.) The monument now standing is of comparatively recent date; but it may occupy the site of one more ancient.

3. Six miles southeast of the city we come to *Bethlehem*, a small town, yet having the deepest interest as the birthplace of David, and of David's greatest descend-

ant, the Saviour of the world. It lies upon the side and summit of a steep hill, and contains now about 2,000 inhabitants. Many places connected with the birth of Jesus are shown; but there is no authority for their precise location except tradition. In a cave near this village Jerome wrote most of his translation of the Bible, the Vulgate version, recognized as the standard Bible by the Roman Catholic Church.

4. A little beyond Bethlehem is the head of the *Valley of Elah*, in which, but at a distance to the west, David fought with Goliath, and gained his earliest honors before Israel. (1 Sam. 17.)

5. There are no more places of interest to the Bible reader until we reach *Hebron*, 18 miles from Jerusalem. This is one of the most ancient towns in the world, occupied before the time of Abraham; the burial place of the Patriarchs, the capital of David's kingdom of Judah, and the place where Absalom's rebellion was begun. It is still a large town, inhabited by intolerant Mohammedans, who closely guard the sanctity of the Mosque which covers the graves of Abraham, Isaac and Jacob. It is now called *el Khalil*, "the Friend," *i. e.*, Abraham, "the friend of God."

SOLOMON'S POOLS.

6. The region between Hebron and the Dead Sea is wild and desolate, with but few inhabitants. It was called *Jeshimon*, "the waste," and is the place generally recognized as "the wilderness of Judæa," where David wandered during his exile when he was persecuted by Saul, and in constant danger of his life, and where Christ was tempted after his long fast of forty days.

IV. **The Southwestern Road** is that "that goeth down from Jerusalem unto Gaza, which is desert." (Acts 8:26.) It passes through ravines and among mountains, descending through successive plateaus, from the mountain region to the Shefelah, or low hills, and thence to the plain by the Mediterranean. It is "desert," in the sense that no towns lie along the route. The fountain where Philip baptized the Ethiopian treasurer is shown at *Ain Haniyeh*, 4 miles southwest of Jerusalem; but it has only tradition in support of its claim.

V. **The Western Road** leads to Joppa, descending from the mountains to the sea.

1. Four miles from Jerusalem it passes *Emmaus* (*Kuloniyeh*), the place to which the two disciples were walking when they were joined by the risen Christ. (Luke 24:13.) The place, however, is disputed. Dr. Thomson locates it at *Kuriet el Enab*, further from Jerusalem; and others at *el Kubeibeh*, 7 miles northwest of the city.

2. *Kirjath-jearim*, or *Baalah*, is 7 miles from Jerusalem, at *Kuriet el Enab*, named above. Here the Ark of the Covenant was brought from Beth-shemesh, after its return from the Philistines, and remained until it was removed by David to Jerusalem. (1 Sam. 6:21; 2 Sam. 6:2.) It is now a small village, with ruins and a church.

VI. **The Northwestern Road** branches from the Northern Road just beyond Gibeah, and winds down the mountains to the sea-shore at Joppa. Among its places of interest are the following:

1. *Mizpeh*, "watch-tower," is probably the hill known as *Neby Samwil*, 4 miles northwest of Jerusalem. Here Samuel gathered the people for reformation, and won his great victory over the Philistines. This may also have been *Ramah*, the birthplace and burial-place of Samuel.

2. *Gibeon* is at *el Jib*, a hill 6 miles from Jerusalem. This was the head of the Hivite league of cities which made peace with Israel and were spared by Joshua at the time of the conquest (Josh. 9:17); which led to the battle of Beth-horon, the decisive event of the war.

Here a skirmish took place between the soldiers of David and of Abner (while David was reigning over Judah), and Asahel, the brother of Joab, was killed. (2 Sam. 2:12–24.) At this place the Tabernacle was standing during David's reign, while the ark was at Zion; here was "the great high place" where Solomon offered sacrifice at the opening of his reign; and here Solomon had a vision, and made his choice of wisdom. (1 Kings 3:4–14.)

3. Five miles beyond Gibeon is *Beth-horon*, celebrated as the place where was fought the great battle of the conquest, which, measured by its results, was the most important battle in the history of the world, since upon it was staked the world's religion. If ever the sun might stand still, it was then, when earth's destiny was in the balance. (Josh. 10:9–14.) The "upper Beth-horon" is at *Beit ur el Foka*, and the lower at *Beit ur et Tahta*, two miles beyond it.

In this brief view we have compassed the most important places upon the map within 15 miles around the city of Jerusalem.

OUTLINE FOR TEACHING AND REVIEW.

SUGGESTIONS FOR TEACHING.

1. Locate upon the blackboard Jerusalem as a centre, and in presence of the class draw the general direction of the roads leading from it. It is scarcely necessary to draw the valleys and mountains, as they are but rarely referred to by name. The teacher may mark the line of the road in French chalk or common slate-pencil upon the blackboard, in advance of the lesson, making a faint line, which can be followed with the crayon afterward.

2. Then take each road in order, going out from Jerusalem, and indicate the places near it, stating the events of Bible History in connection with each place.

3. It would be a good plan to write on slips of paper the references to texts, distribute them among the class, and have each text read by a student as its event is named.

REVIEW.

I. *Northern Road.* 1. Scopus. (Titus.) 2. Nob. (Slaughter of priests.) 3. Gibeah. (Saul's court.) 4. Anathoth. (Jeremiah.) 5. Ramah. (?) (Samuel.) 6. Michmash. (Jonathan's exploit.) 7. Ai. (Achan.) 8. Beeroth. (Gibeonites; Jesus lost in Temple.) 9. Bethel. (Jacob's ladder.) 10. Rimmon. (Benjamin.) 11. Ephraim. (Christ's retirement.)

II. *Eastern Road.* 1. Bethany. (Lazarus.) 2. Steep descent. 3. Jericho.

III. *Southern Road.* 1. Plain of Rephaim. (David's victory.) 2. Rachel's Tomb. 3. Bethlehem. (David, Jesus.) 4. Valley of Elah. (David and Goliath.) 5. Hebron. (Abraham's sepulchre.) 6. Jeshimon. (Wilderness).

IV. *Southwestern Road.* "Jerusalem to Gaza." (Philip.)

V. *Western Road.* 1. Emmaus. (Risen Christ.) 2. Kirjath-jearim. (Removal of ark.)

VI. *Northwestern Road.* 1. Mizpeh. (Samuel.) 2. Gibeon. (Solomon's choice.) 3. Beth-horon. (Joshua's victory.)

GETHSEMANE.

THE
DIVISION
OF
SOLOMON'S EMPIRE.

Statute Miles

RAND, Mc NALLY & CO., ENGR'S, CHICAGO.

THE DIVISION OF SOLOMON'S EMPIRE.

ON the death of Solomon, B. C. 935, the empire which had been won by the sword and consolidated by the statesmanship of David, fell asunder, and five kingdoms took the place of one.   These were:

1. The portion of Solomon's empire north of Mount Hermon and extending to the Euphrates revolted, and formed the **Kingdom of Syria,** having Damascus for its capital. This kingdom, at first small, soon rose to power, and at its height, under Hazael, was the leading nation in Asia, west of the Euphrates. It fell, about B. C. 750, under the power of Assyria.

2. South of Syria was the **Kingdom of Israel,** or the Ten Tribes, founded by Jeroboam, B. C. 935, soon after the death of Solomon. This included by far the larger portion of Palestine Proper, having 9,400 square miles, while the rival kingdom of Judah had but 3,400.

uncertain.   The Shefelah, or low hills, and the sea-coast, were probably controlled by the Philistines, though nominally belonging to Judah. This kingdom remained loyal to the house of David during all its history, and was ruled by twenty-one kings, all of one family. It was destroyed by Nebuchadnezzar, B. C. 587.

4. **Moab** lay east of the Dead Sea, between the brooks Arnon and Zered. It was nominally subject to Israel (the northern kingdom); but, from the indications of the history and of the Moabite Stone (a monument of Mesha, the king of Moab, erected in the time of Elisha the prophet), it may be inferred that it had its own government, and only occasionally paid tribute to the Ten Tribes. Strong kings, like Omri, Ahab and Jeroboam II., may have held power over it; but during most of the time it was practically independent.

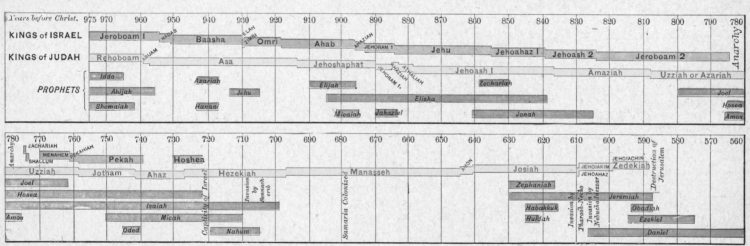

CHRONOLOGICAL CHART OF KINGS OF ISRAEL AND JUDAH.

It received the allegiance of all the tribes on the east of the Jordan. The boundary line between the two kingdoms ran south of Jericho, Bethel and Joppa. This line was, however, very variable, being moved northward or southward, according to the relative power of the kingdoms. Over this kingdom reigned nineteen kings, representing several dynasties, with intervals of anarchy and frequent change. Its capital was at first Shechem, then Tirzah, until Omri, the founder of the third dynasty, chose a permanent location at SAMARIA, which soon became to Israel all that Jerusalem was to Judah, and in time gave its name to the entire province. Its two religious sanctuaries were at Dan on the north, and at Bethel on the south, where the national worship to Jehovah, was maintained under the form of a calf or young ox.

3. **The Kingdom of Judah** included the tribe of that name, a portion of Benjamin, and perhaps of Simeon also, though the southern boundary was always

5. **Edom,** south of the Dead Sea, had been conquered by David, and remained subject during the reign of Solomon. After the disruption it held to Judah about the same relation that Moab held to Israel, dependent and tributary, but not annexed as a part of the realm. There was a king of Edom during the reign of Jehoshaphat (2 Kings 3:9), but evidently subject to Judah. The Edomites finally gained their independence during the reign of Jehoram, the son of Jehoshaphat (2 Kings 8:16-22), despite a defeat which they suffered at Zair (probably Seir, or Sela). Like all the kingdoms around it, this kingdom fell under the rule of Nebuchadnezzar.

These five provinces or kingdoms are represented upon the map according to their general boundaries during most of the time from the age of Solomon to that of Nebuchadnezzar, when all the East was united under one mighty sceptre. Historically, the epoch requires the consideration of several periods, as follows:

1. **The Period of Division** (B. C. 935-842), during

which three kingdoms—Syria, Israel and Judah—strove for supremacy. This extends from the reign of Jeroboam to that of Jehu in the north; and from Rehoboam to Joash in Judah. During the first half-century of this period, wars were constant between Israel and Judah. During the latter half-century the growing power of Syria compelled an alliance between the rival kingdoms, and nearly all the battles were between Israel

sion of Judah by the Ethiopians under Zerah, and the victory of Asa at Mareshah. (2 Chron. 14.) (5.) The introduction of the worship of Baal into Israel, by Ahab, and with it the appearance of the prophet Elijah. (1 Kings 16–19.) (6.) The wars with Syria, with the victory of Israel at Aphek, and the defeat at Ramoth-gilead. (1 Kings 20–22.) (7.) The invasion of Judah, in the reign of Jehoshaphat, by the allied forces of Ammon, Moab and Edom, and their slaughter at Berachah. (2 Chron. 20.) (8.) The allied war of Israel and Judah with Moab, and the battle of Kir-haraseth, commemorated by the Moabite Stone, recently discovered. (2 Kings 3.) (9.) The revolt of Edom from Judah, in the

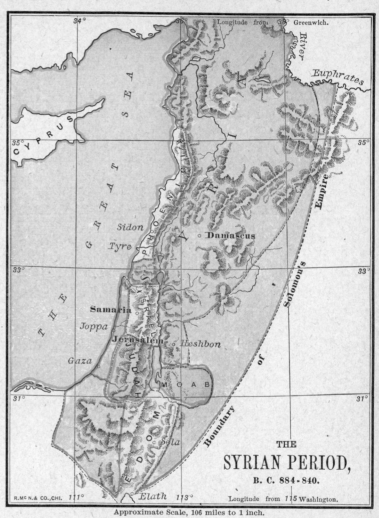

THE SYRIAN PERIOD, B. C. 884–840.

Approximate Scale, 106 miles to 1 inch.

MOABITE STONE.

and Syria. The leading events of this period were: (1.) The accession of Rehoboam, followed by the disruption of the kingdom, and the breaking up of Solomon's empire. (2.) The invasion of Judah by Shishak, king of Egypt, and the loss of all the treasures of David and Solomon (2 Chron. 12), which permanently crippled the kingdom. (3.) The wars of Jeroboam with Judah, culminating in the battle of Zemaraim, near Bethel, a signal defeat for Israel. (2 Chron. 13.) (4.) The inva-

reign of Jehoram. Jehoram gained a victory at Zair (probably Sela, or Petra), but could not retain supremacy over the Edomites.

2. **The Syrian Period,** B. C. 842–799, began with revolutions in the same year in Damascus, Samaria, and Jerusalem; by which Hazael mounted the throne of Syria, Jehu of Israel, and Athaliah, the queen-mother, usurped the throne of Judah. Hazael established a powerful kingdom. (2 Kings 8:7–15.) He conquered all of Israel east of the Jordan (2 Kings 10:32, 33), reduced Israel under Jehoahaz to a condition of vassalage (2 Kings 13:1–8), took Gath from Judah, and was only withheld from besieging Jerusalem by the payment of a heavy tribute. (2 Kings 12:17, 18; 2 Chron 24:23,

24.) We insert an outline map of his kingdom and conquests.

The principal events of this period were as follows: (1.) The accession of Hazael in Syria, Jehu in Israel, and Athaliah in Judah, B. C. 842. (2.) The destruction of Baal worship in Israel. (2 Kings 10.) (3.) The conquests of Hazael on the east of Jordan. (2 Kings 10:32, 33.) (4.) The slaughter of Athaliah, and accession of Jehoash in Judah. (2 Kings 11.) (5.) The repairs of the Temple by Jehoiada. (2 Kings 12.) (6.) The prophecies of Jonah and Joel. (7.) The subjection of Israel under Hazael. (8.) Hazael's campaign against Judah, and capture of Gath. (9.) The death of Hazael.

3. **The Restoration of Israel,** B. C. 779–742. The Syrian conqueror, Hazael, left as his successor a weak prince, Ben-hadad III., who was unable to hold his dominions against the ability of the third king of the house of Jehu in Israel, Jehoash, or Joash, and his greater son, Jeroboam II. Under these two able rulers the kingdom of the Ten Tribes arose to its culmination, the territory lost was regained, nearly all Syria was conquered, Judah was made tributary, and Samaria gave laws to a large part of Solomon's empire. This period was marked as the era of two great prophets, Jonah and Joel; and, from its brilliant but brief prosperity, has been called "the Indian Summer of Israel." At the opening of this epoch, Amaziah reigned in Judah. He won a victory in Edom, but, venturing to attack Israel, was routed at Beth-shemesh; and, for the only time in Judah's history, the army of the Ten Tribes entered Jerusalem as victors. (2 Kings 14.) Uzziah, his successor, was more successful, and held his kingdom in security both against Israel and the enemies on the south. The outline map represents the kingdoms during the reign of Jeroboam II., about B. C. 800.

4. **The Fall of Israel,** B. C. 742–721. The decline of Israel after the reign of Jeroboam II. was rapid. A succession of usurpers seized the throne, the foreign conquests melted away, and anarchy prevailed. The cause of these sudden changes was the growth of the Assyrian power under a succession of warlike kings, who made Nineveh the capital of the Eastern world. Syria fell before their arms, and Israel soon followed. In the reign of Menahem, Israel became tributary to Assyria; and in that of Pekah, B. C. 735, the portion of Israel on the north, including the tribe of Naphtali, was carried into captivity by Tiglath-pileser. (2 Kings 15:29.) In the reign of Hoshea, Samaria itself was taken (B. C. 721) by Sargon (having been besieged by Shalmaneser); and the Ten Tribes were finally carried into captivity to Halah and Habor. (2 Kings 17.) This period belongs to the map of the Assyrian Empire.

5. **The Fall of Judah,** B. C. 721–587. The kingdom of Judah lasted more than a hundred years after that of Israel, though most of the time as a subject-nation to the "great king" of Assyria, to whom Ahaz and most of the kings of Judah after him paid tribute. The most important events of this period were: (1.) The reforms

10

of King Hezekiah, and the deliverance of Jerusalem from the Assyrians under Sennacherib. (2 Chron. 30–32.) (2.) The captivity of King Manasseh among the Assyrians, and his return. (2 Chron. 33.) (3.) The attempt at reformation by King Josiah, and his death at the battle of Megiddo. (2 Chron. 34, 35.) (4.) The rise of the power of Babylon, and Nebuchadnezzar's first invasion of Judah, in the reign of Jehoiakim, B. C. 606. From this date Judah was subject to Babylon, and the "seventy years' captivity" began. (5.) The rebellion of Zedekiah, the last king, against Nebuchadnezzar, the siege of Jerusalem, the destruction of the kingdom, and the final carrying of Judah into captivity to Babylon, B. C. 587.

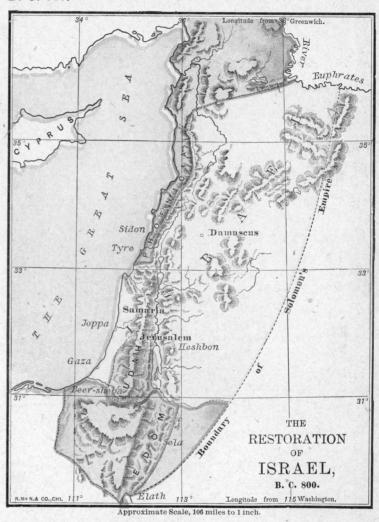

THE
RESTORATION
OF
ISRAEL,
B. C. 800.

Approximate Scale, 106 miles to 1 inch.

We notice the most important wars, sieges and battles of this period, indicated upon the map of the Division of Solomon's Empire, by flags.

1. The battle of **Zemaraim,** near Bethel, fought between Jeroboam and Abijah, the second king of Judah, B. C. 917, and resulting in the defeat of Israel, and the ruin of Jeroboam's plans of ambition. (2 Chron. 13.)

2. The battle of **Mareshah,** in Judah, on the border of the mountain region, in which King Asa defeated Zerah, the Ethiopian king of Egypt, and an immense host, B. C. 900. (2 Chron. 14.)

3. The siege of **Samaria,** by Ben-hadad, king of Syria, in the reign of Ahab, who was able to repel the

invaders. (1 Kings 20.) We notice, that from this time, for a century, the principal wars of Israel are with Syria.

4. The victory at **Aphek,** won by Ahab over Ben-hadad and the Syrians. Ahab, however, allowed the fruits of the victory to be lost, when he might have made it decisive in its results. (1 Kings 20:26–43.)

5. The battle of **Ramoth-gilead,** in which the Syrians, under Ben-hadad, were victorious over allied Israel and Judah, and Ahab was slain. (1 Kings 22.)

6. The slaughter of the allied Moabites, Ammonites and Edomites, at **Berachah,** "the valley of blessing," in the reign of Jehoshaphat, king of Judah. (2 Chron. 20.)

7. The war of Israel, Judah and Edom, against the Moabites, in which a great battle took place at **Kir-haraseth,** in the land of Moab, when the king of Moab offered his own son as a sacrifice in presence of the contending armies. (2 Kings 3.) This was during the reign of Jehoshaphat in Judah, and of Jehoram in Israel.

8. A second siege of **Samaria,** by the Syrians, under Ben-hadad, in the reign of Jehoram; and a miraculous deliverance. (2 Kings, 6, 7.)

9. A battle at **Zair** (probably Sela, or Petra), in Edom, in which Jehoram was surrounded by the revolting Edomites, and won a victory, yet could not prevent the Edomites from gaining their liberty. (2 Kings 8: 21, 22.)

10. The capture of **Gath,** by the Syrians, under Hazael, in the reign of Jehoash, king of Judah. (2 Kings 12:17.)

11. The victory of King Jehoash, of Israel, over the Syrians, at **Aphek,** foretold by Elisha. (2 Kings 13: 17–25.)

12. The battle of **Beth-shemesh,** a victory of Israel over Judah, resulting in an Israelite army entering Jerusalem, in the reign of Amaziah. (2 Kings 14.)

13. The final capture of **Samaria** by the Assyrians, and the extinction of the kingdom of the Ten Tribes. (2 Kings 17:1–6.)

14. The battle of **Megiddo,** in which King Josiah, of Judah, lost his life while resisting the invasion of Pharaoh-necho, the king of Egypt. (2 Kings 23:29.)

15. Two battles at **Carchemish,** near the Euphrates, in the first of which, Pharaoh-necho, of Egypt, was victorious (B. C. 608) over the Assyrians, and in the second (B. C. 606) was thoroughly defeated by Nebuchadnezzar, and compelled to relinquish all his conquests in Asia. (2 Chron. 35:20.)

16. The destruction of **Jerusalem** by Nebuchadnezzar, and the extinction of the kingdom of Judah. (2 Kings 25.)

OUTLINE FOR TEACHING.

1. Draw on the blackboard the map of *Solomon's Empire*, as already given, showing its boundaries, and placing on it the city of Jerusalem, the river Jordan, etc.

2. Divide the map into the *five kingdoms* of *Syria, Israel, Judah, Moab* and *Edom*, and show their capitals and political relations.

3. Drill the class upon the leading events of the *five historical periods*

named in the above description, placing upon the map the localities named in the history.

4. Name the *battles* of the periods, and state the circumstances of each battle, placing them upon the map in their historical order.

5. Through all the work let the class draw their own maps, following that upon the board, and at the close carefully review all the work. This subject might require several lessons in a normal class.

MOSQUE EL AKSA.

THE GREAT ORIENTAL EMPIRES.

THE history of the Bible is so interwoven with that of the East, that a view of its great empires is necessary. All the lands between the Persian Gulf and the Mediterranean were united at different periods under one government, and formed an empire which was constantly changing according to the power or weakness of its dominant state; for in the Oriental world there never has existed anything like a confederation of states on an equality. At different periods Ur, Babylon or Nineveh conquered all the surrounding lands; or at other periods a single race, as the Medes and Persians, obtained supremacy. The empire thus arose and fell, to be succeeded by a similar empire with another centre. During the Old Testament history, between the days of Abraham and of Ezra, more than 1,500 years, four successive empires appeared in the East. These were:

I. The Early Babylonian Empire. B. C. 2280–1120.

II. The Assyrian Empire. B. C. 1120–626.

III. The Babylonian Empire. B. C. 606–538.

IV. The Persian Empire. B. C. 538–330.

I. **The Early Babylonian Empire** began about 3000 B. C., with several states, each having a city as its capital. Among these were Ur (*Mugheir*), Lagesh (Shirpurta), and Isin. These separate kingdoms were united in an empire, of which Babylon was the capital, in the reign of Hammurabi (the Amraphel of Gen. 14:1), about 2280 B. C. It lasted, with varying fortunes, for 1,000 years. A map of this empire, in the time of Abraham, is given on page 34.

II. **The Assyrian Empire** arose from the small country Asshur, about 25 square miles in extent, lying east of the Tigris and north of the lower Zab. Its capital was the city Asshur, now called *Kileh Sherghat*, 60 miles south of Nineveh. The city rose to power in the 14th century B. C., when, under Tukulti-ninib, Babylon was captured and the Babylonian empire became the Assyrian. Afterward *Nimrud*, 20 miles south of Nineveh, became the capital. Not until 702 was NINEVEH made by Sennacherib the royal residence. It soon surpassed the earlier capitals in size and magnificence, and became one of the largest cities of the East. It then included four cities, surrounded by one wall, and forming a parallelogram, as shown on the plan on page 96. The

greatest kings of this empire were: Shalmaneser, who made war on Samaria, and erected the "Black Obelisk," which now stands in the British Museum, and by its inscriptions furnishes the best record of the kingdom down to its own age; Sargon, who completed the conquest of Samaria, and otherwise added to the empire; Sennacherib, who enlarged and beautified Nineveh, warred from Babylon to Egypt, and extorted tribute from Hezekiah, king of Judah; and Esar-haddon, son of the preceding, who saw the empire at its height, embracing, besides Assyria, Armenia, Media, Babylonia, Elam, Mesopotamia, Syria, Israel, Judah, and the northern

AN ASSYRIAN PALACE.

portion of Egypt. These lands, however, for the most part retained their own rulers, customs and government, but recognized themselves as vassals to the "Great King," as he is styled in the inscriptions. Esar-haddon took Manasseh, king of Judah, captive to Babylon, and repopulated Samaria with colonists from other lands. His son, Asshur-bani-pal, witnessed his kingdom declining, and was the last of the great kings, though he built a vast palace at Nineveh. There was no coherence or unity in the empire, whose provinces were held together only by the strong arm of the king; and, on the death of Asshur-bani-pal, a general revolt took place among the subject nations, his son perished, and Nineveh was utterly destroyed, never again to appear in history.

The boundaries of the Assyrian empire are given upon the map according to the best authorities. On the north they were the Armenian Mountains, the river Cyrus (now called the *Kur*), north of the Araxes, and the

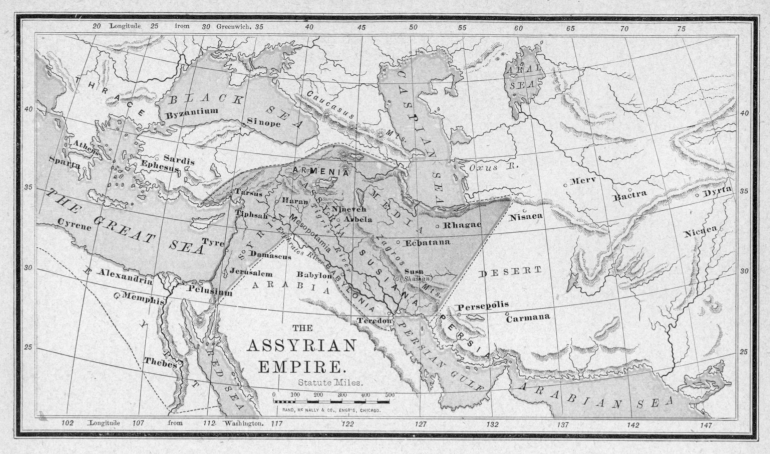

northern range of Mount Taurus; on the east, the Caspian Sea and the great salt desert; on the south, the Persian Gulf, the Arabian desert and Upper Egypt; on the west, the Mediterranean and the river Halys.

III. **The Babylonian Empire,** B. C. 606–538. This period has been more correctly termed that of the "four kingdoms," since the East was not then, as during the Assyrian period, under one government. The destruction of Nineveh had been wrought by the union of the Medes and Babylonians, under their kings, Cyaxares and Nabopolassar, and these peoples succeeded to most, but not all, of the conquests of Assyria.

1. Media won its own independence, and obtained possession of Armenia, Assyria Proper (north of the Tigris), and Elam. Persia had already been conquered, so that the largest, though less important, portion of the Assyrian empire now belonged to Media.

2. Babylonia obtained Chaldea, Mesopotamia, Syria and Palestine. Most of these countries had claimed their independence on the fall of Assyria; and their conquest occupied the reign of Nabopolassar, and his greater son, Nebuchadnezzar. Thus the important parts of the Bible world were nearly all under the rule of Babylon.

3. A new kingdom arose in Asia Minor, that of Lydia,

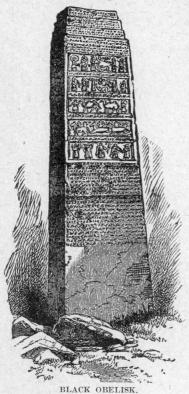

BLACK OBELISK.

embracing all the lands between the Ægean Sea and the river Halys; destined, however, to a short history, for it formed one of the earliest conquests of Cyrus the Great.

4. Cilicia also appears for the first time upon the map, being situated between the Euphrates and Lydia, north of Syria, and south of the Halys river, and retained its independence until the close of the Babylonian period, when it was annexed to Persia, though even then it retained its own kings.

5. To these might be added Egypt, though outside of the Asiatic world. It soon shook off the yoke of Assyria, and resumed its independence; but, endeavoring to contest with Babylon the empire of the East, was defeated at Carchemish by Nebuchadnezzar, and compelled to retire from Asia. Some suppose that it was conquered by Babylon; and it is possible that for a few years Egypt may have recognized the supremacy of Nebuchadnezzar by paying tribute, but it was never a part of his empire.

The map of the Oriental world, as thus reconstructed, lasted about a century, though with varying boundary lines; as, for instance, Elam, or Susiana, sometimes formed a part of Babylonia, and at other times of Media. During this period BABYLON was the metropolis of the East. It was raised to greatness by Nebuchadnezzar, who finished the Tower of Belus, raised the Hanging Gardens, and built great palaces. Two-thirds of the bricks unearthed in the ruins of Babylon bear his name. The city formed a square, on both sides of the Euphrates, covering an area of 130 miles, about that of the city and

county of Philadelphia. It was surrounded with double walls, one of which is said to have been 300 feet high, and so wide that six chariots could be driven abreast along its summit. The greatness of the city was short-lived. It was taken by the Medes and Persians, B. C.

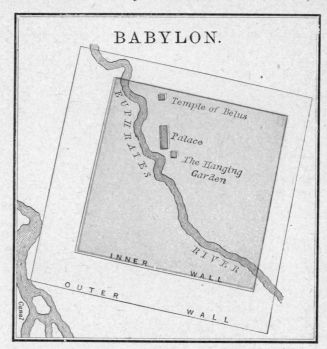

536, and soon began to decline, though it remained, in a decaying condition, for nearly 1,000 years afterward.

IV. **The Persian Empire,** B. C. 538–330. As the Babylonian power arose with Nebuchadnezzar, the Persian began with Cyrus the Great. He was the hereditary king of the Persians, and headed a revolt against the Medes, which resulted in reversing the relations of the two races, so that the Persians became dominant. He

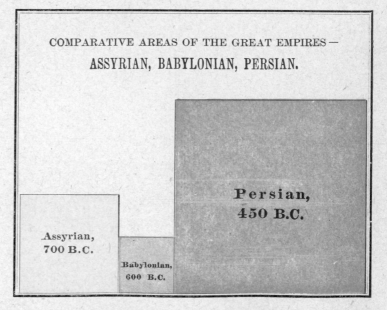

then led his united people westward, and conquered Crœsus, the king of Lydia, thus extending his dominion from the Persian Gulf to the Ægean Sea. The power of Babylon began to fall on the death of Nebuchadnezzar, whose successors were weaklings, and in B. C. 538

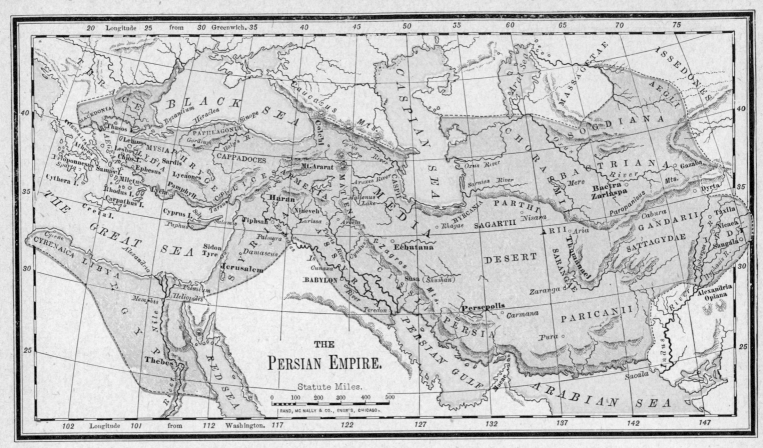

THE
PERSIAN EMPIRE.

Statute Miles.

Cyrus took the city of Babylon. His dominions were now larger than those of the old Assyrian empire; and under his successors the conquests of Persia were pushed both eastward and westward, until, under Darius the Great, they embraced all the lands from the Indus to the Nile. The map represents the empire of Persia at this period, with the twenty satrapies, or provinces, into which it was divided by Darius. This empire lasted for

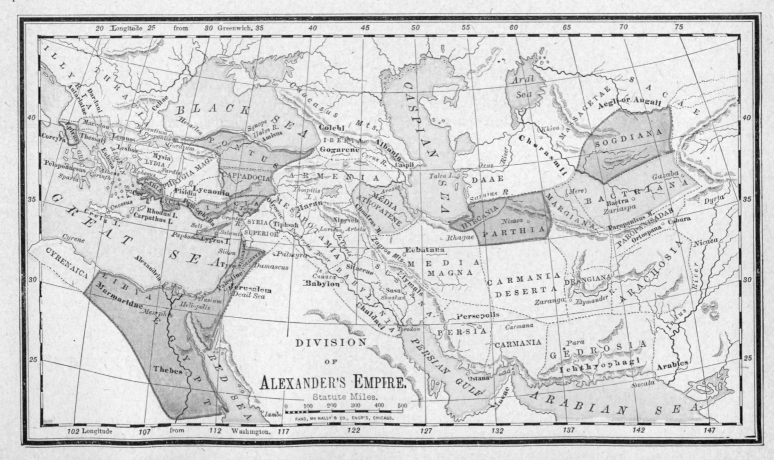

DIVISION
OF
ALEXANDER'S EMPIRE.

Statute Miles.

200 years, until its conquest by Alexander the Great, B. C. 330, when the sceptre of the East passed into European hands, and Greece gave law to Asia. In the extent of its territory, in the strength of its dominion, and in the consolidation of its conquests, Persia was far greater than either Assyria or Babylon. It will be observed that the scale of all the maps of the Assyrian, Babylonian and Persian Empires, is the same, so that their relative proportions may be seen.

The map of the Persian Empire represents the political state of the Oriental world at the conclusion of the Old Testament period. When Ezra and Nehemiah were at Jerusalem, and Haggai and Malachi were the prophets of Judah, all the lands were under the dominion of Persia, and were governed from "Shushan the palace," or Susa.

PERIOD OF RESTORATION 536 B. C.–70 A. D.

The closing portion of Old Testament history, from the edict of Cyrus the Great, B. C. 536, permitting the captive Jews to return to Palestine, is known as the Period of Restoration. From that time until the end of the Jewish history, the land was under foreign rule. The Period of Restoration, from the return from captivity to the birth of Christ, may be divided as follows:

1. **The Persian Supremacy,** B. C. 538–330. During the 200 years of the Persian empire, the Jews were kindly treated by their sovereigns, and permitted to regulate their own affairs. Under Darius the Great, who reigned B. C. 521–486, the second Temple was completed. Under Xerxes, the next monarch, called in the Bible, Ahasuerus, occurred the romantic events of Esther's deliverance, and the downfall of Haman. Under his successor, Artaxerxes Longimanus, B. C. 465–425, the Jewish state was reformed by Ezra, and the walls of Jerusalem were built by Nehemiah. Soon after this occurred the separation of the Samaritans, and a rival temple was built on Mount Gerizim.

2. **The Macedonian Supremacy,** B. C. 330–321, though brief, brought to pass vast results. Alexander the Great, in a brilliant series of battles, subjugated the entire Persian empire, and became the master of the Oriental world. He dealt kindly with the Jews, not-

BABYLON.

withstanding their loyalty to the Persian throne, and permitted them to enjoy freedom of worship and of government. We do not give a map of Alexander's empire, as its boundaries in Asia varied but little from those of Persia, and it has no direct relation to Bible history. Soon after Alexander's death, his generals formed a compact for the government of his empire; but it was soon broken, and out of his conquests four kingdoms arose, of which the most important were those of Seleucus in Asia, and of Ptolemy in Africa. In the first division, B. C. 323, Palestine became a part of Syria.

3. **The Egyptian Supremacy,** B. C. 321–198. Palestine was taken from Syria by Ptolemy Soter, the ruler of Egypt; and his successors, the Greek kings of Egypt, all named Ptolemy, held the Holy Land for 120 years. During this time the Jews were governed, under the king of Egypt, by their high-priests. The most important event of this epoch was the Septuagint translation of the Old Testament, made at Alexandria about 285 B. C. The map of the Division of Alexander's Empire represents the Oriental world at this period, after the lands had settled down into something like order under stable governments.

Omitting the minor states and free cities, the kingdoms of that epoch were as follows:

1. *The kingdom of the Seleucidæ,* sometimes known as Syria, was founded by Seleucus, B. C. 312. It included the largest portion of Alexander's conquests, embracing most of Asia Minor, and those provinces of the Bible world known as Syria, Mesopotamia, Babylonia, Persia Proper, Southern Media, and far beyond them eastward to the Indus. Throughout its history of 250 years, it remained a Greek government, though in Asia, and introduced the Greek language and literature to all the lands of the Orient.

2. *The kingdom of the Ptolemies* included Egypt, Libya, Palestine, Phœnicia, and the southern provinces of Asia Minor. It was ruled by a succession of Greek monarchs, descended from Ptolemy Soter, and, with changing boundaries, endured until the death of its last queen, the famous Cleopatra, when it became a part of the Roman empire.

3. There were other kingdoms in Asia at this time,

appearing upon the map. *Pontus* and *Cappadocia* intervened between the two sections of the empire of the Seleucidæ. Southwest of the Caspian, and near the sea, *Media Atropatene* had gained its independence, and on the southeast *Parthia* was rising to power; while beyond, on the east, was *Bactriana*. Other lands of less importance might also be named; but these are all that are necessary to the reader of the history.

During this epoch of 125 years, Palestine remained under the control of Egypt.

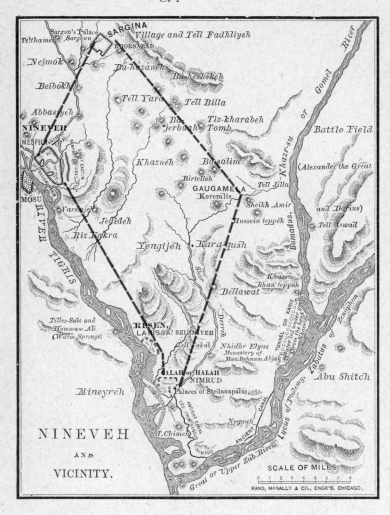

4. The Syrian Supremacy, B. C. 198–166. By the battle of Mount Panium, Antiochus of the Seleucid line wrested Palestine from Egypt. The Syrian domination, though short, brought to the Jews greater trials than any previous period in their history. Jerusalem was twice taken and sacked, the Temple was desecrated and closed, the Jewish religion was forbidden, and those who remained steadfast to it were subjected to a cruel persecution. The trials named in Heb. 11: 35–37, belonged to this period, when every attempt was made by Antiochus Epiphanes to destroy the worship of Jehovah, and introduce Greek customs and religion among the Jewish

people. But the very violence of the tyranny reacted, and led to a complete deliverance and a more thorough devotion.

5. The Maccabean Independence, B. C. 166–40. A priest named Mattathias raised the banner of revolt; and, after his death, his five sons in succession led the efforts of the Jews for freedom. The greatest of them, though all were heroes, was Judas, called Maccabeus, "the hammer." In B. C. 165 he took possession of Jerusalem; and, after his death, his brother Simon won the recognition of the freedom of Palestine. Other Maccabean princes extended the boundaries of the land over Edom, Samaria and Galilee. Under a succession of

these rulers, also called Asmonean kings, Palestine was virtually independent, though nominally subordinate to either Syria or Egypt.

6. The Roman Supremacy, B. C. 40 – A. D. 70. Perhaps this period should begin with B. C. 63, when the Roman general Pompey entered Jerusalem, and the Romans began to exercise a controlling influence. But the representatives of the Maccabean line were allowed to reign until B. C. 40, when they were set aside, and Herod the Great, an Idumean (Edomite), was made king by the Romans. It was in the closing portion of his reign that JESUS CHRIST was born. The last 70 years of the Roman period belong to New Testament history, and will be considered in connection with the maps of that period.

THE ROMAN EMPIRE.

THE last of the Old World empires was that having its capital on the seven hills of ROME. Like most of the others, it was the dominion of a single city; but, unlike others, it represented the conquests, not of a single conquering king, as Nebuchadnezzar or Cyrus, but of a self-governing and conquering people; and, unlike its predecessors, it was not a loose aggregation of states, ready to fall apart as soon as the hand that fettered them was removed, but an empire, carefully welded together, building up in every land its own civilization, and developing a national unity which held its possessions together for a thousand years.

At the close of the Old Testament period, the Persian empire stood in all its power. Four hundred years later, at the opening of the New Testament epoch, the Persian empire had given place to that of Alexander; that had broken up into many fragments; and most of these in turn had been united under the eagles of Rome. The world's capital had moved westward, and the Mediterranean was now a Roman lake. The principal provinces of this empire, omitting minor subdivisions, were:

I. **European Provinces.** 1. Italy. 2. Hispania, now known as Spain, subdivided into three provinces. 3. Gallia, now France, including also parts of Germany and the Netherlands, embracing five provinces. 4. The Danubian provinces of Rhætia, Noricum Pannonia, and Mœsia, to which Dacia was

afterward added by the emperor Trajan. 5. The Grecian provinces of Thracia, Macedonia, Achaia, and Illyricum.

II. **The Insular Provinces** were: 1. Britannia. 2. Sicilia. 3. Sardinia and Corsica, united. 4. Cyprus. The other islands were attached, either to these, or to governments upon the mainland.

III. **The Asiatic Provinces** were: 1. Asia, a term referring only to the western end of Asia Minor. 2. Pontus and Bithynia, united. 3. Galatia. 4. Pamphylia and Lycia. 5. Cilicia. 6. Syria, of which Palestine was a part. To these were added, after the New Testament period, Armenia, Mesopotamia, and Arabia Petræa; but they were soon lost to the empire.

IV. **The African Provinces** were: 1. Ægyptus, or Egypt. 2. Cyrenaica, called, in Acts 2:10, "parts of

THE COLOSSEUM AT ROME.

Libya about Cyrene." 3. Africa, the district around Carthage. 4. Mauritania, now Morocco.

This empire was the most thoroughly organized and the longest in duration of any in ancient history. It lasted until Rome fell under the attacks of barbarians from the North, A. D. 476. Even after this, the eastern division of the empire remained with almost unbroken power for centuries, and was not finally extinguished until 1453, the close of the Middle Ages.

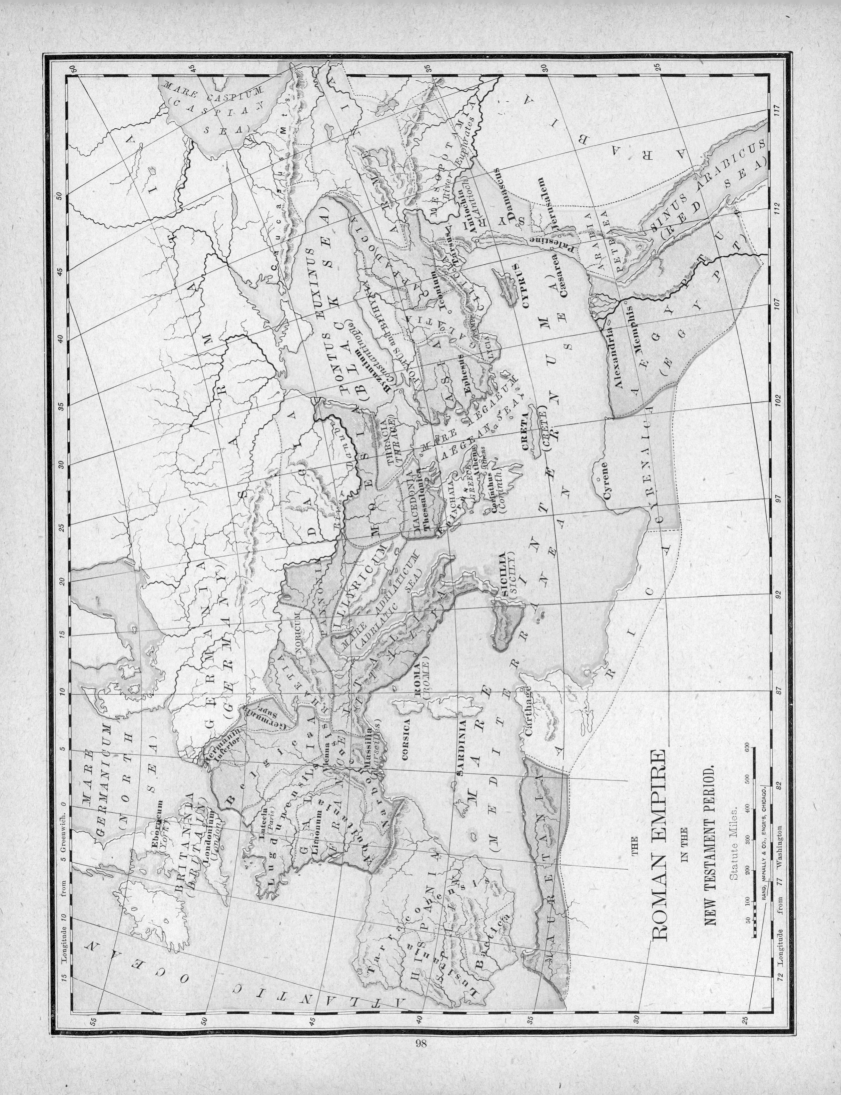

THE

ROMAN EMPIRE

IN THE

NEW TESTAMENT PERIOD.

Statute Miles.

RAND, McNALLY & CO., ENGR'S, CHICAGO.

OUTLINE FOR TEACHING AND REVIEW.

THE ANCIENT EMPIRES.

It is desirable to let the class see the comparative area and location of the Four Oriental Empires; hence they should be presented upon the same map. Each of these may form a separate lesson.

I. *The Early Chaldean Empire.* 1. Draw in the centre of the blackboard the outlines of the map of Chedorlaomer's Empire, on page 34, reserving space enough around it to embrace all the lands of the maps on page 92. 2. Draw the four important rivers: the *Tigris, Euphrates, Jordan* and *Nile.* 3. Show the *boundaries* of Chedorlaomer's empire, and its principal places: *Babylon, Ur, Nineveh, Haran, Damascus, Hebron.* 4. State briefly the *history* of the empire. 5. Review the lesson, and let the class state all the information given.

N. B. The outlines may be drawn in advance with slate pencil or soapstone, and then traced with chalk in the presence of the class. Also, the initial letters only of places or rivers should be written, as a hint to the memory; afterward the initial letters should be erased, and the class be called upon to name the places as located by the pointer.

II. *The Assyrian Empire.* 1. After erasing the boundaries of the first empire, leaving the general outline of sea-coast and lands the same, show the location of the conquering province, *Assyria,* and its capital, Nineveh. 2 Draw the *boundaries* of the Assyrian empire, explain them to the class,

and have them repeated in concert. 3. Locate and name the subject provinces: *Armenia, Media, Mesopotamia, Susiana, Babylonia, Syria, Palestine.* 4. Name its most important kings: *Tiglath-adar, Shalmaneser, Sargon, Sennacherib, Esar-haddon, Asshur-bani-pal.* With each king should be named the events associated with his reign. 5. Review the outline as before.

III. *The Babylonian Empire.* This may be given upon the same map as the two preceding. 1. Show the location and relations of the four kingdoms: *Babylonia, Media, Lydia, Cilicia.* 2. Give an account of Babylon, and its fall.

IV. *The Persian Empire.* Leaving the coast-line of the former maps on the board, add to it the lines in all points of the compass requisite to show the boundaries of Persia. The provinces, or satrapies, need not be specified (unless detailed knowledge is desired), for they do not relate to Bible history. Name the leading monarchs, Cyrus, Darius, Xerxes, Artaxerxes Longimanus, and give an account of the fall of the empire.

V. *The Empire of Alexander.* 1. This may be shown in outline; and its history be given. 2. The division of the empire and its leading kingdoms should be mentioned.

VI. *The Roman Empire.* This will require a new map. Draw in outline the lands around the Mediterranean Sea, and enumerate the provinces: European, Asiatic, African.

GROTTO OF JEREMIAH (UNDER MOUNT CALVARY).

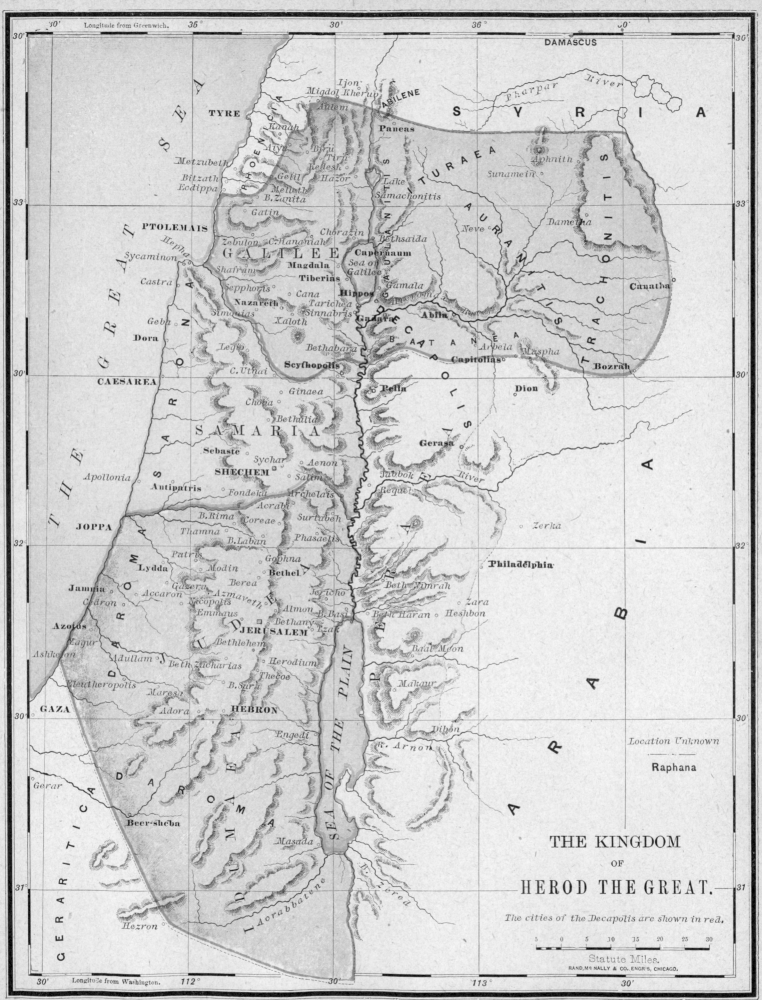

THE KINGDOM
OF
HEROD THE GREAT.

The cities of the Decapolis are shown in red.

Location Unknown

Raphana

Statute Miles.
RAND, McNALLY & CO. ENGR'S, CHICAGO.

NEW TESTAMENT PALESTINE.

THE political geography of Palestine, during the seventy years of New Testament history, is somewhat complicated, from the two facts, that new provinces are named in the annals, and also that the government was changed from regal to provincial, and from provincial to regal, oftener than once in a generation.

I. THE PROVINCES OF PALESTINE.

These were, on the west of the Jordan, Judæa, Samaria and Galilee; and on the east, Peræa, and a group of minor principalities, popularly, but not accurately, called Decapolis. They are indicated upon the map of the Kingdom of Herod the Great.

1. **Judæa** was the largest province in Palestine. It embraced the territory anciently belonging to the four tribes, Judah, Benjamin, Dan, and Simeon. On the east its boundary was the Dead Sea; on the south, the desert; on the west, the Mediterranean. The northern line, separating it from Samaria, is less definitely known; but we have adopted the

TIBERIAS.

boundary as given by Conder in "A Handbook to the Bible," where the evidences in its favor are shown. The southern portion was properly Idumaea, or western Edom. The Philistine plain, and the Negeb, or "South Country," were both known as Daroma.

2. **Samaria** was the central province, between Judæa and the Carmel range of mountains. Its share of the plain by the sea was known as Sarona (Sharon), and was occupied almost entirely by Gentiles; while its mountain region was held by the Samaritans, a people of mingled origin, partly descended from the remnant of the Ten Tribes after the captivity, and partly from heathen peoples deported to the territory, of which an account is contained in 2 Kings 17. They separated from (or rather, were disfellowshiped by) the Jews in the times of Nehemiah, and built a temple on Mount Gerizim, B. C. 400. A small remnant still remain in the ancient city of Shechem, and maintain their ancient worship.

3. **Galilee** was the northern province, extending from Mount Carmel to Lebanon, and from the Sea of Tiberias to the Mediterranean and Phœnicia. Its people were Jews, and profoundly attached to the law, but less superstitious than those of Jerusalem. In this province most of the ministry of Jesus Christ was accomplished.

4. **Peræa** extended from the Jordan and the Dead Sea on the west to the Syrian desert on the east, and from the river Arnon on the south to the town of Pella on the north; nearly corresponding to the location of the tribes of Reuben and Gad. The word means "beyond"; and the country was sometimes called (Mark 10:1) "Judæa by the farther side of Jordan." It was inhabited during the New Testament period by Jews, among whom were established many villages of Gentiles.

5. The remaining province has no correct geographical name. It is sometimes called **Decapolis;** but the term is not precise, and strictly refers to ten cities, not all of which were in the province. It embraced no less than five sections, as may be seen upon the map. (1.) Gaulanitis, the ancient Golan, now *Jaulan*, east of the Jordan, Tiberias, and Lake Merom, which was then called Samachonitis. (2.) Auranitis, now *Hauran*, the flat country of Bashan. (3.) Trachonitis, "rugged," the mountainous district of Bashan, now known as *el Ledja*. (4.) Iturea, now called *Jedur*, between Mount Hermon and the *Ledja*, on the north. (5.) Batanea, an Aramaic form of the Hebrew word Bashan, south of the Hieromax.

Decapolis was "the land of the ten cities." These were ten confederated Gentile cities standing in Palestine; and, though surrounded by a Jewish population, preserving their heathen character, and protected by the Roman government. Their names, as given by different historians, do not entirely agree; but the best list is: (1.) Scythopolis (Beth-shean). (2.) Gadara. (3.) Gerasa. (4.) Canatha. (5.) Abila. (6.) Raphana. (7.) Hippos. (8.) Dion. (9.) Pella. (10.) Capitolias. To these may

PALESTINE DURING THE MINISTRY of JESUS. A. D. 26.

be added: (11.) Philadelphia (Rabbath Ammon). (12.) Damascus. As far as identified, they are named upon the map in red letters. Many of these cities were destroyed, and their inhabitants massacred, by the Jews, in the beginning of the final war before the destruction of Jerusalem by Titus.

II. THE POLITICAL HISTORY OF PALESTINE, B. C. 4–A. D. 70.

1. **The Kingdom of Herod the Great** included all the provinces indicated upon the map, and described above. This organization came to an end B. C. 4, when Herod died.

2. **The Tetrarchy,** B. C. 4–A. D. 41. The word means "a government of four," and points to the division of the kingdom after Herod's death, when Archelaus was made tetrarch of Judæa and Samaria; Antipas (called in the New Testament "Herod the tetrarch"), of Galilee and Peræa; and Philip, of the fifth province, east of the Sea of Tiberias. The fourth tetrarch was Lysanias, who ruled over the small district of Abilene, between Mount Hermon and Damascus, a separate dominion from that of Herod. In A. D. 6 Archelaus was deposed,

and Judæa and Samaria were annexed directly to the empire, and governed by a series of procurators, of whom Pontius Pilate was the sixth. This was the political arrangement of Palestine during the ministry of Jesus, of which a map is given.

3. **The Kingdom of Herod Agrippa,** A. D. 41–44. Herod Agrippa was a grandson of Herod the Great, and an intimate friend of the emperor Caligula, from whom he received the title of king, and all the dominions of Herod the Great, with Abilene added; so that he reigned over more territory than any Jewish king after Solomon. He was the "Herod the king" who slew the apostle James, imprisoned Peter, and died by the judgment of God at Cæsarea. (Acts 12.)

4. **The Two Provinces,** A. D. 44–70. On the death of Herod Agrippa, his son, Herod Agrippa II., was a youth of 17. The emperor Claudius gave him only the tetrarchies formerly held by Philip and Lysanias, "the fifth province" of Palestine, and Abilene. Over these he reigned until the final extinction of the Jewish state by Titus, A. D. 70, when he retired to a private station at Rome. This was the "King Agrippa" before whom the apostle Paul bore testimony. (Acts 25, 26.) During

THE TWO PROVINCES. A. D. 44–70.

his reign, Judæa, Samaria, Galilee and Peræa formed the province of Judæa, under Roman procurators, having their headquarters at Cæsarea. When the last rebellion of the Jews had been quelled by the destruction of Jerusalem, the entire country was annexed to the province of Syria, and the history of Judæa ended.

THE LIFE OF CHRIST.

As THE life of Jesus Christ on earth is the most important not only in all Bible history, but in all human history as well, it is desirable that the Bible student, and especially the Bible teacher, should obtain a clear understanding of its leading events, associate them with the places where they occurred, and arrange them in chronological order. Of the 150 principal events, about 100 are fixed as to their chronological order by the common consent of the leading harmonists; about 25 are agreed upon by the majority; while the remaining 25 are altogether uncertain. In the outline here given, the authorities most relied upon are Andrews, Robinson, Geikie, and Strong, yet no one of them is exclusively followed. We divide the earthly life of Jesus into nine periods, to each of which is given a separate map, so that the student may not be confused among the various lines of the Saviour's journeying.

The periods are as follows:

I. Period of Preparation, 30 years, from the Birth to the Baptism of Jesus.

II. Period of Inauguration, 15 months, from the Baptism to the Rejection at Nazareth.

III. Period of Early Galilean Ministry, 4 months, from the Rejection at Nazareth to the Sermon on the Mount.

IV. Period of Later Galilean Ministry, 10 months, from the Sermon on the Mount to the Feeding of the Five Thousand.

V. Period of Retirement, 6 months, from the Feeding of the Five Thousand to the Feast of Tabernacles.

VI. Period of Judæan Ministry, 3 months, from the Feast of Tabernacles to the Feast of Dedication.

VII. Period of Peræan Ministry, 4 months, from the Feast of Dedication to the Anointing at Bethany.

THE POOL OF SILOAM.

VIII. Period of the Passion, 8 days, from the Anointing at Bethany to the Resurrection.

IX. Period of the Resurrection, 40 days, from the Resurrection to the Ascension.

I. PERIOD OF PREPARATION.

This includes the events of 30 years, from the Birth of Jesus to his Baptism, and though the longest, contains the fewest recorded incidents of any. Upon the map are indicated by red lines four journeys of Jesus.

1. **The Presentation in the Temple.** (From Bethlehem to Jerusalem and return.) From Bethlehem, his birthplace, the infant Jesus, at the age of 40 days, was taken to Jerusalem, to be presented before the Lord in the Temple. Here he was recognized as the Messiah of Israel, by Simeon and Anna, and then was taken back to Bethlehem. (Luke 2:22–38.)

2. **The Flight into Egypt.** (From Bethlehem to Egypt.) After the visit of the Wise Men, the Saviour, still an infant, was taken down to Egypt, in order to escape the jealousy of Herod the Great. (Matt. 2:1–18.)

3. **The Settlement at Nazareth.** (From Egypt to Nazareth.) After the death of Herod, Jesus was taken from Egypt to Galilee, to the village of Nazareth, the early home of Joseph and Mary. Here he spent his youth. (Matt. 2:19–23.)

4. **The Visit to the Temple.** (From Nazareth to Jerusalem and return.) The only recorded event of the Saviour's youth, is his journey to Jerusalem, at the age of 12 years, to attend the Passover. On the return journey, he was lost by his parents, and after three days, found in the Temple (probably in the Court of the Women), conversing with the doctors of the law. He returned with Joseph and Mary to Nazareth (Luke 2:40 –52), and thenceforth no events in his life for 18 years are related.

The places in this period are : (1.) Bethlehem, a village six miles southwest of Jerusalem, now *Beit-lahm.* (2.) The Temple in Jerusalem. (See plan on page 138.) (3.) Nazareth, a village on the border of the Plain of Esdraelon, in Galilee. now *en Nasireh,* a place of 6,000 population.

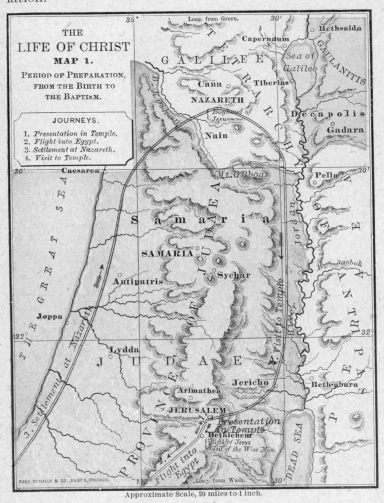

OUTLINE REVIEW OF JOURNEYS—FIRST PERIOD.

PERIOD OF PREPARATION.

1. *Presentation in the Temple.* (Bethlehem to Jerusalem and return.) Recognized by Simeon and Anna.

2. *Flight into Egypt.* (Bethlehem to Egypt.) Escape from Herod.

3. *Settlement at Nazareth.* (Egypt to Nazareth.) Childhood and youth.

4. *Visit to the Temple.* (Nazareth to Jerusalem and return.) Found among the doctors.

II. PERIOD OF INAUGURATION.

This embraces 15 months, from the Baptism of Jesus to the Rejection at Nazareth, and contains the record of five journeys. Its places are as follows: 1. Nazareth, already located. 2. Bethabara was formerly supposed to be the ancient Beth-Nimrah, now *Nimrin,* on a small stream east of the Jordan, not far from the Dead Sea. But Conder locates it at *Abarah,* a ford of the Jordan above Beth-shean, and near the Sea of Galilee. 3. "The Wilderness" is probably the uninhabited region of Judæa near the Dead Sea, though it may have been the desert far to the south. 4. Cana is located at *Kefr Kenna,* northeast of Nazareth, though Dr. Robinson places it

at *Kana el Jelil,* 9 miles north of Nazareth. 5. Capernaum was probably at *Khan Minyeh,* on the west of the Sea of Galilee, though long located at *Tell Hum,* on the north. 6. Jerusalem. 7. Sychar, the ancient Shechem, now *Nablus,* beside Mount Gerizim. The journeys of this period are named, each from its leading event.

1. **The Baptism.** (From Nazareth to Bethabara.) Near the close of John the Baptist's ministry, Jesus left his carpenter shop at Nazareth, and journeyed down the Jordan Valley to Bethabara. There he was baptized by John, and received from heaven the testimony of his sonship. (Matt. 3:13–17.)

2. **The Temptation.** (From Bethabara to the Wilderness and return.) (1.) Immediately after his baptism, Jesus was led by the Spirit into the Wilderness, where he fasted 40 days, and overcame the temptations of Satan. (Matt. 4:1–11.) (2.) Returning to Bethabara, he received the testimony of John the Baptist, and met his earliest followers, Andrew and Peter, John, Philip, and Nathanael. (John 1:37–50.)

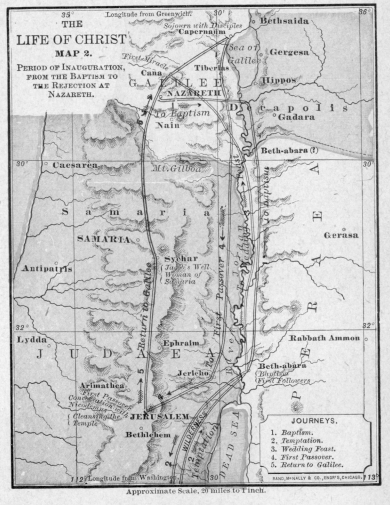

3. **The Marriage at Cana.** (Bethabara to Cana and Capernaum.) (1.) Jesus left Bethabara, journeyed up the Jordan Valley to Galilee, and over the mountains to Cana, near Nazareth. Here he was present at a wedding, and wrought his first miracle, turning the water into wine. (2.) Thence, with his mother and brothers,

he went down to Capernaum, by the Sea of Galilee, and remained a few days. (John 2:1–12.)

4. The First Passover. (Capernaum to Jerusalem.) (1.) Soon after the wedding feast Jesus went up to Jerusalem, probably by way of the Jordan Valley, to attend the first Passover of his ministry. (John 2:13.) (2.) At Jerusalem he asserted his authority by cleansing the Temple from the traders. (John 2:14–22.) (3.) He held the conversation with Nicodemus concerning the new birth, and remained for a time in Judæa, gathering a few disciples, yet not making his ministry prominent, while his forerunner was still preaching. (John 3:1–36.)

5. The Return to Galilee. (Jerusalem to Sychar and Cana.) (1.) As soon as the teaching of John the Baptist was ended by his imprisonment, Jesus left Judæa to open his own public ministry. (2.) He went through Samaria, and paused at Jacob's well for the conversation with the Samaritan woman, and then remained at Sychar, the ancient Shechem, two days. (3.) At Cana, the place of his earlier miracle, he spoke the word of healing for a nobleman's son, who was sick at Capernaum. (John 4:1–54.)

OUTLINE REVIEW OF JOURNEYS— SECOND PERIOD.

Period of Inauguration.

1. *Baptism.* (Nazareth to Bethabara.)
2. *Temptation.* (Bethabara to Wilderness and return.) (1.) The temptation. (2.) The first followers.
3. *Marriage at Cana.* (Bethabara to Cana and Capernaum.) (1.) The first miracle. (2.) The visit to Capernaum.
4. *First Passover.* (Capernaum to Jerusalem.) (1.) The Passover. (2.) Cleansing the Temple. (3.) Discourse with Nicodemus.
5. *Return to Galilee.* (Jerusalem to Sychar and Cana.) (1.) The departure. (2.) The woman of Samaria. (3.) The nobleman's son.

III. PERIOD OF EARLY GALILEAN MINISTRY.

This is a period of about four months, from the Rejection at Nazareth to the Sermon on the Mount. It brings to notice six places, most of which have been already noticed. 1. Cana. 2. Nazareth. 3. Capernaum. 4. Eastern Galilee, the region on the shore of the Sea of Galilee. 5. Jerusalem. 6. The mountain of the sermon. This was probably *Kurûn Hattin,* "the horns of Hattin," a mountain with a double peak, a few miles from the Sea of Galilee. The journeys of this period are four in number.

1. The Opening of the Ministry. (From Cana to Nazareth and Capernaum.) (1.) He came (perhaps from Cana) to Nazareth, with the intention of commencing his ministry in his own home. But his towns-people

rejected his message, and would have slain him if he had not escaped from their hands. (Luke 4:16–31.) (2.) Rejected in his own city, he removed to Capernaum, which thenceforward was the centre of his ministry for more than a year. (Luke 4:31.) (3.) Here he called from their work at the seaside his four earliest disciples, Simon and Andrew, James and John. They had known him before, but now left all to follow him. (Luke 5:1–11.) (4.) In the synagogue, on the sabbath, he cast out an evil spirit (Luke 4:33–36), and healed the mother of Peter's wife. (Luke 4:38–40.)

2. The Tour in Eastern Galilee. (From Capernaum through Eastern Galilee and return.) (1.) This journey was probably near the Sea of Galilee, and may

BETHLEHEM.

not have occupied more than a few weeks. (2.) During its progress he healed a leper, whose testimony led such multitudes to come seeking miracles that Jesus was compelled to go into retirement. (3.) On his return to Capernaum he healed a paralytic let down through the roof, and (4.) called the publican Matthew to be one of his disciples. (Luke 5:17–28.)

3. The Second Passover. (From Capernaum to Jerusalem and return.) (1.) In the spring of the second year of his ministry he went up to the feast at the capital, and while there healed a cripple at the Pool of Bethesda. (John 5:1–47.) (2.) On his return, while walking through the wheat fields, he asserted his authority as "Lord of the sabbath." (Luke 6:1–5.) (3.) On a sabbath soon after, he healed in the synagogue a man with a withered hand. (Luke 6:6–11.)

4. The Sermon on the Mount. (From Capernaum to the mountain.) (1.) The opposition of the Pharisees caused Jesus to leave Capernaum and instruct the people by the sea-shore. (Mark 3:7–12.) (2.) He ascended a mountain, probably *Kurûn Hattin,* and, after a night in prayer, appointed the Twelve Apostles. (Luke 6:12–16.) (3.) To the disciples and the multitude he preached the Sermon on the Mount. (Matt. 5–7.)

OUTLINE REVIEW OF JOURNEYS—THIRD PERIOD.

Period of Early Galilean Ministry.

1. *Opening of the Ministry.* (Cana to Nazareth and Capernaum.) (1.) Rejection at Nazareth. (2.) Settlement at Capernaum. (3.) Calling of Simon and Andrew, James and John. (4.) Demoniac healed, and Peter's wife's mother healed.

2. *Tour in Eastern Galilee.* (Capernaum to Eastern Galilee and return.) (1.) Preaching in Galilee. (2.) Leper healed. (3.) Paralytic healed. (4.) Matthew called.

3. *Second Passover.* (Capernaum to Jerusalem and return.) (1.) The cripple at Bethesda. (2.) Through the wheat fields. (3.) Withered hand healed.

4. *Sermon on the Mount.* (Capernaum to the mountain.) (1.) By the sea. (2.) Calling the Twelve. (3.) The sermon.

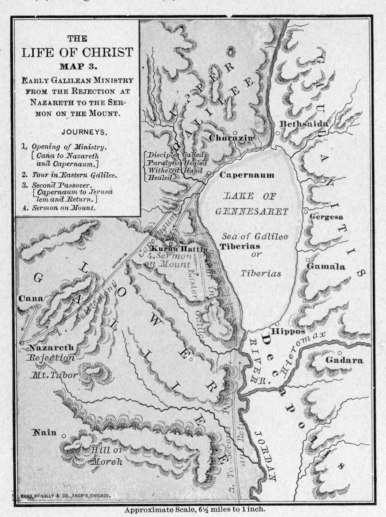

Approximate Scale, 6½ miles to 1 inch.

IV. THE LATER GALILEAN MINISTRY.

This period of ten months, from the Sermon on the Mount to the Feeding of the Five Thousand, was a time of opposition on the part of the ruling classes, but continued popularity among the people. The places which Jesus visited at this time were: 1. Capernaum, already noticed, and still the headquarters of his ministry. 2. Nain, now called *Nein*, on the northwestern edge of Little Hermon, six miles southeast of Nazareth, in full view of Mount Tabor. 3. "The country of the Gadarenes" (Mark 5:1); called by Matthew (8:28) "the country of the Gergesenes." Gadara was the largest city of the region, situated south of the Sea of Galilee, and giving its name to the district; Gergesa, the little village east of

the Sea of Galilee, now called *Khersa*. 4. Nazareth, already noticed under Period I. 5. Bethsaida, a city at the head of the Sea of Galilee, supposed by some to have been on both sides of the Jordan, by others on the east side. 6. The plain of Gennesaret, near to Capernaum. We arrange the events of this period under four journeys.

1. **The Tour in Southern Galilee.** (From Capernaum to Nain and return.) The following events belong to this tour: (1.) At Capernaum, before starting, Jesus healed the slave of a believing centurion. (Luke 7:1–10.) (2.) On the next day he led his disciples southward to Nain, where he raised to life the widow's son, about to be buried. (Luke 7:11–17.) (3.) Perhaps at the same time and place he received the messengers and answered the questions of John the Baptist. (Luke 7:18–35.) (4.) During the journey he was entertained by a Pharisee, at whose house "a woman who was a sinner" washed his feet. (Luke 7:36–50.) (5.) On his return the healing of a dumb demoniac occasioned the Pharisees to assume an open opposition, and to declare that his miracles were wrought by the power of the evil spirit. (Luke 11:14–26.) (6.) At the same time occurred the interference of his mother and brethren, desiring to restrain him. (Luke 8:19–21.)

2. **The Gadarene Voyage.** (Capernaum to Gergesa and return.) With this journey are associated four events. (1.) The opposition of the enemies caused Jesus to leave the city, and to teach in parables by the sea. (Matt. 13:1–53.) (2.) From the shore, near Capernaum, he set sail for the country of the Gadarenes, east of the Sea of Galilee, and on the voyage stilled a sudden tempest. (Mark 4:35–41.) (3.) At the eastern shore, near the village of Gergesa, he restored two demoniacs, permitted the demons to enter a herd of swine, and as a result was besought by the people to leave their coasts. (4.) Returning across the sea to Capernaum, he raised to life the daughter of Jairus the ruler. (Luke 8:41–56.)

3. **The Tour in Central Galilee.** (From Capernaum to Nazareth and return.) (1.) Starting from Capernaum with his disciples, he visited Nazareth a second time, but was again rejected by its people. (Mark 6:1–6.) (2.) He then gave the Twelve a charge, and sent them out to preach. (Matt. 10:5–42.) (3.) While they were absent upon their mission, Jesus himself also journeyed preaching through Central Galilee. (Mark 6:6.) This was his third tour in Galilee. (4.) On his return to Capernaum, he received the report of the Twelve, and the news of John the Baptist's murder by Herod Antipas. (Mark 6:14–30.)

4. **The Retirement to Bethsaida.** (1.) The multitudes following him led Jesus to leave Capernaum by sea for a retired place near Bethsaida. (Mark 6:31, 32.) (2.) The people hastened after Jesus, and met him as he landed, so that he was compelled to teach them all day, and wrought in the afternoon the miracle of the Five Loaves. (Mark 6:32–44.) (3.) After the miracle he sent the disciples out upon the sea, and at midnight walked to them upon the water. (Mark 6:45–51.) (4.) In the

morning they landed at the plain of Gennesaret, near Capernaum, where Jesus wrought many miracles (Mark 6:52–56), and then returned to Capernaum. (5.) Here he completed his Galilean ministry by a discourse in the synagogue on the "Bread of Life." (John 6:25–59.)

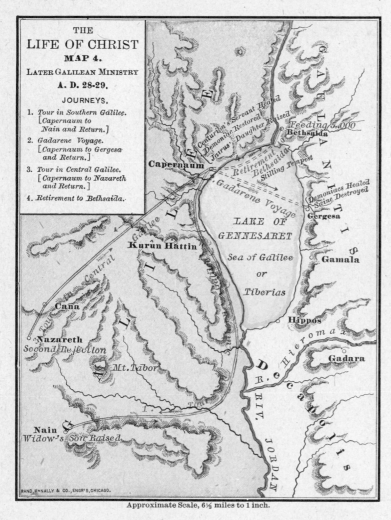

Approximate Scale, 6½ miles to 1 inch.

OUTLINE REVIEW OF JOURNEYS—FOURTH PERIOD.

PERIOD OF LATER GALILEAN MINISTRY.

1. *Tour in Southern Galilee.* (Capernaum to Nain and return.) (1.) Centurion's servant healed. (2.) Widow's son at Nain raised. (3.) Messengers from John. (4.) Washing the Saviour's feet. (5.) Dumb demoniac, and opposition of Pharisees. (6.) Interference of relatives.

2. *Gadarene Voyage.* (Capernaum to Gergesa and return.) (1.) Parables by the sea. (2.) Stilling the tempest. (3.) Gadarene demoniacs. (4.) Jairus' daughter raised.

3. *Tour in Central Galilee.* (Capernaum to Nazareth and return.) (1.) Second rejection at Nazareth. (2.) Mission of the Twelve. (3.) Third tour in Galilee. (4.) Report of the Twelve, and death of John the Baptist.

4. *Retirement to Bethsaida.* (Capernaum to Bethsaida and return.) (1.) Seeking retirement. (2.) Feeding the five thousand. (3.) Walking on the sea. (4.) Miracles at Gennesaret. (5.) Discourse on the "Bread of Life."

V. PERIOD OF RETIREMENT.

During most of the six months, from the Feeding of the Five Thousand to the Feast of Tabernacles, in the fall before Christ's crucifixion, he remained in retirement, engaged in instructing his disciples in the deeper truths of the gospel. The places visited at this time were: 1. Phœnicia, "the coasts of Tyre and Sidon," probably

only the borders near Galilee, not the cities themselves. 2. Decapolis, the region of the "ten cities," southeast of the Sea of Galilee; a country mainly inhabited by a heathen population. 3. Dalmanutha, a village on the western shore of the Sea of Galilee, not certainly identified, but perhaps at *Ain el Barideh,* two miles from Tiberias. 4. Bethsaida, already noticed under Period IV. 5. Cæsarea Philippi, at the foot of Mount Hermon, now *Banias.* 6. Capernaum, already noticed under Period II.

1. **The Journey to Phœnicia.** (From Capernaum to the borders of Tyre and Sidon.) (1.) The discourse in the synagogue, showing the spiritual nature of Christ's kingdom, led to the defection of the multitude, and the retirement of Jesus and the Twelve. (John 6:60–71.) (2.) At the "coasts," or frontiers, of Tyre and Sidon, he restored the demoniac daughter of a Syrophœnician woman. (Mark 7:24–30.)

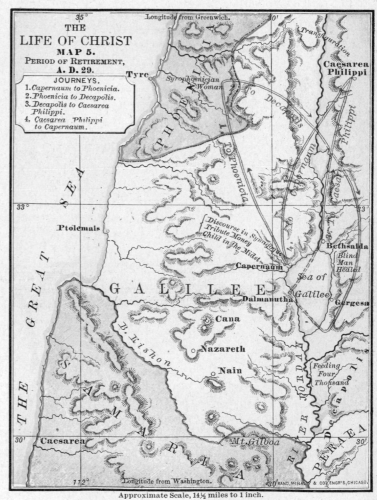

Approximate Scale, 14½ miles to 1 inch.

2. **The Journey to Decapolis.** (From the borders of Tyre and Sidon to Decapolis.) (1.) The crowds gathering around Jesus in Phœnicia, he crossed Galilee, and sought seclusion in Decapolis, southeast of the Sea of Galilee. (Mark 7:31.) (2.) Here he wrought two miracles, healing a deaf stammerer, and feeding the four thousand. (Mark 7:31–37; 8:1–9.)

3. **The Journey to Cæsarea Philippi.** (From Decapolis to Dalmanutha, Bethsaida and Cæsarea Phi-

lippi.) (1.) He sailed across the lake to Dalmanutha, but was met by the Pharisees with unbelieving demands for a sign, so took ship again. (Mark 8:10–13.) (2.) He sailed northward to Bethsaida, where he healed a blind man, who saw "men as trees walking." (Mark 8:22–26.) (3.) Pursuing his way up the Jordan, he came to Cæsarea Philippi, at the foot of Mount Hermon, where he remained several days. (4.) Here occurred Peter's confession, "Thou art the Christ," the transfiguration, and the restoration of the demoniac boy. (Luke 9:18–45.)

4. The Last Return to Capernaum. (From Cæsarea Philippi to Capernaum.) He probably went down the Jordan to Bethsaida, and thence by the shore of the sea to Capernaum. Here he kept in seclusion, and gave his disciples a lesson in humility, from "the child in the midst." (Mark 9:30–50.)

OUTLINE REVIEW OF JOURNEYS — FIFTH PERIOD.

PERIOD OF RETIREMENT.

1. *To Phœnicia.* (Capernaum to coasts of Tyre and Sidon.) (1.) Defection of the multitude. (2.) Syrophœnician woman.

2. *To Decapolis.* (Phœnicia to Decapolis.) (1.) Journey to Decapolis. (2.) Healing the stammerer, and feeding the four thousand.

3. *To Cæsarea Philippi.* (Decapolis to Dalmanutha, Bethsaida and Cæsarea Philippi.) (1.) Dalmanutha: a sign demanded. (2.) Bethsaida: blind man healed. (3.) Cæsarea Philippi. (4.) Transfiguration.

4. *To Capernaum.* (Cæsarea Philippi to Capernaum.) The child in the midst.

VI. PERIOD OF JUDÆAN MINISTRY.

This includes the events of about three months, from the Feast of Tabernacles to the Feast of Dedication. The following places are referred to during this period: 1. Capernaum, noticed under Period II. 2. The "village of the Samaritans" where Jesus was inhospitably treated, has been traditionally located at En-gannim, on the border of Galilee and Samaria. 3. Bethany, a small village on the Mount of Olives, east of Jerusalem, the home of Mary and Martha, now *el Nasiriyeh.* 4. Jerusalem. (See description on page 73.) 5. Bethabara, on the east of Jordan, referred to as the place of the baptism, in Period II.

This period embraces but two journeys, at its beginning and ending; the one before the Feast of Tabernacles, the other after the Feast of Dedication.

1. From Galilee to Jerusalem. (1.) Bidding farewell to Galilee, Jesus left Capernaum for the last time, and journeyed through Galilee toward Jerusalem. While starting he conversed with "the three aspirants" (Luke 9:57–62), and showed the duty of full devotion to his work. (2.) On the border of Samaria, perhaps at the village of En-gannim, he was rejected by the Samaritans, but refused to allow his disciples to call down fire from heaven, "as Elias did." (Luke 9:52–56.) (3.) While in Samaria he healed the ten lepers, of whom but one turned back to give him thanks. (Luke 17:11–19). (4.) He found a home at Bethany, with Lazarus and his two sisters, and reminded Martha of her needless care, while Mary was seeking "the good part." (Luke 10:38–42.) (5.) He came to Jerusalem during the Feast of Tabernacles, and gave the teachings embodied in John 7–10. (6.) While here he healed the blind man at the Pool of Siloam. (John 9:1–41.)

2. From Jerusalem to Bethabara. (1.) At the Feast of Dedication the teachings of Christ created such an opposition that he left the city. (2.) He went to Bethabara beyond Jordan, the place of the baptism, and there prepared for his tour in Peræa.

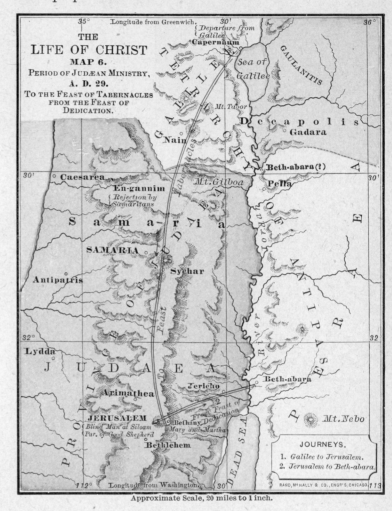

Approximate Scale, 20 miles to 1 inch.

OUTLINE REVIEW OF JOURNEYS — SIXTH PERIOD.

PERIOD OF JUDÆAN MINISTRY.

1. *From Galilee to Jerusalem.* (1.) Three aspirants. (2.) Rejected by Samaritans. (3.) Ten lepers. (4.) Mary and Martha. (5.) Feast of Tabernacles. (6.) Blind man at Pool of Siloam.

2. *From Jerusalem to Bethabara.* (1.) Departure from Jerusalem. (2.) At Bethabara.

VII. PERIOD OF PERÆAN MINISTRY.

This extends through four months, from the events immediately succeeding the Feast of Dedication, to the Anointing at Bethany, six days before the crucifixion. Its places are as follows: 1. Bethabara, already noticed in Period II. 2. Bethany. (See Period VI.) 3. Ephraim. This was probably the village in a wild region northeast of Bethel, in the Old Testament called Ophrah, now *et Taiyibeh.* 4. Peræa was the province on the east of Jordan, and south of the Hieromax river. It was governed by Herod Antipas, the slayer of John the Baptist, and was inhabited by a mixed population.

No towns are named as visited by the Saviour; but we have conjectured a route through most of the province, as shown on the map. 5. Jericho, at that time the largest city in the Jordan Valley, and recently beautified by Herod. It is now a miserable village, called *er Riha*. This period includes four journeys.

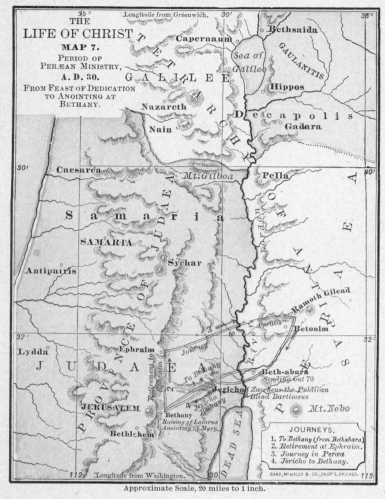

Approximate Scale, 20 miles to 1 inch.

1. From Bethabara to Bethany. (1.) While at Bethabara Jesus sent out the Seventy, to proclaim his coming in the Peræan villages. (Luke 10:1–16.) (2.) Hearing of the sickness of Lazarus, after some delay, he went to Bethany, and raised him from the dead, a miracle which caused the Jewish leaders to formally resolve upon putting Jesus to death. (John 11.)

2. The Retirement to Ephraim. The hour had not yet come for Jesus to die, and he therefore secluded himself from the rulers, in the village of Ephraim, in a wilderness north of Jerusalem, on the mountains overlooking the Jordan Valley. Here he remained several weeks, probably instructing the Twelve.

3. The Journey in Peræa. Descending the mountains, Jesus crossed the Jordan Valley, and entered the province of Peræa. His ministry, during this journey, was of teaching rather than miracle, and is mainly related by Luke. Its events were: (1.) The miracles of healing the woman bent together by an infirmity, and the man with the dropsy. (Luke 13:10–17, and 14:1–6.) (2.) The seven great parables, among them that of the

Prodigal Son. (Luke 14–16.) (3.) Blessing the little children. (Luke 18:15–17.) (4.) The rich young ruler's question, and Jesus' answer, "Sell all that thou hast," etc. (Luke 18:18–30.) (5.) The ambitious request of James and John, for the first places in the kingdom of Christ. (Matt. 20:20–28.)

4. From Jericho to Bethany. Jesus had now reached Jericho, on his last journey to Jerusalem, and from this point we notice the following events: (1.) The healing of Bartimeus at the gate of Jericho. (Luke 18:35–43.) (2.) The visit of Jesus at the house of Zaccheus the publican. (Luke 19:1–10.) (3.) At the end of his journey, the anointing by Mary at Bethany, on the Saturday evening before the Passover. (John 12:1–8.)

OUTLINE REVIEW OF JOURNEYS—SEVENTH PERIOD.

PERIOD OF PERÆAN MINISTRY.

1. *Bethabara to Bethany.* (1.) Sending the Seventy. (2.) Raising of Lazarus.
2. *Retirement to Ephraim.*
3. *Journey in Peræa.* (1.) Two miracles (infirm woman, and dropsy). (2.) Seven parables. (3.) Blessing little children. (4.) Rich young ruler. (5.) Request of James and John.
4. *Jericho to Bethany.* (1.) Bartimeus. (2.) Zaccheus. (3.) Anointing by Mary.

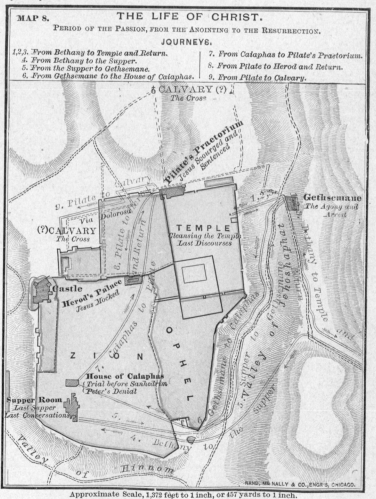

Approximate Scale, 1,372 feet to 1 inch, or 457 yards to 1 inch.

VIII. PERIOD OF THE PASSION.

Although this period embraces only the week from the Anointing by Mary to the Death of Jesus on the cross, its events are so minutely related by the Evangelists as to occupy one-third of the Gospels. If the entire life of Jesus were as fully written out, it would fill nearly 80 volumes as large as the Bible. The events of the Passion-Week took place in and near Jerusalem. The locations on the map are those of tradition only, and are largely conjectural, while the lines of the journeyings are entirely unknown. The map is intended merely as a guide to the student in presenting the order of events, and must not be regarded as fixing the places with any authority. We arrange the events under nine short journeys.

1, 2, 3. **From Bethany to the Temple and Return.** These three journeys took place on successive days, and were marked by distinctive events. (1.) The First Journey, on Sunday, was the triumphal entry into

NAZARETH.

the city and the Temple, after which Jesus returned for the night to Bethany. (Matt. 21:1–11.) (2.) The Second Journey, on Monday, was marked by the cleansing of the Temple, when for the second time the Saviour drove out of the Court of the Gentiles those who made it a place of trade. (3.) The Third Journey, on Tuesday, was made memorable by the last teachings of Jesus, to the people and rulers in the Temple, and to the Twelve on the Mount of Olives, looking down upon the city. (Matt. 21–25.) At the close of each of these three days Jesus returned to Bethany, where he remained in seclusion on Wednesday, no event of that day being left on record.

4. **From Bethany to the Supper.** The traditional place of the *Cœnaculum*, or supper-room, is on Mount Zion, where Jesus came with his disciples on Thursday evening. Here took place the Last Supper, and the farewell conversation of Jesus with his disciples. (John 13–17.)

5. **From the Supper to Gethsemane.** Near midnight of Thursday, Jesus and his disciples (Judas being absent) left the supper-room, and walked up the Valley of Jehoshaphat to the Garden of Gethsemane. Here Jesus endured the agony, and here he was arrested by the officers of the Jews, led by Judas. (Matt. 26:36–56.)

6. **From Gethsemane to the House of Caiaphas.** The fettered Jesus was dragged by the crowd, first to the house of Annas (John 18:13–15), for a brief examination, thence to the house of Caiaphas for the formal trial before the Sanhedrim. This place is traditionally located on Mount Zion, near the house of the Last Supper. Here he was condemned by the rulers, and mocked by their servants. (John 18:16–28.)

7. **From Caiaphas to Pilate.** Jesus was brought before the Roman procurator at his *prætorium*, or place of judgment. We are inclined to think that this was the castle built by Herod the Great on Mount Zion; but we give on the map the traditional location at the Tower Antonia, north of the Temple. Here Jesus was examined by Pilate, who vainly sought to deliver him, being convinced of his innocence. (John 18:28–38.)

8. **From Pilate to Herod and Return.** Wishing to avoid the responsibility of condemning Jesus, Pilate sent him to Herod Antipas, who was then in the city, probably in the palace of the Asmonean (Maccabean) kings. But Herod only mocked Jesus, and returned him to Pilate. (Luke 23:8–12.)

9. **From Pilate to Calvary.** At last Pilate gave orders for the crucifixion of Jesus. He was now led forth, bearing his cross, perhaps by the street called Via Dolorosa, "the Sorrowful Way," to the place Golgotha, or CALVARY, outside the wall, where three crosses were erected, and the Saviour of the world was crucified. As two locations of Calvary are now given, both are indicated, and a journey from Pilate's castle to each. The route to the northern locality is indicated by dotted lines.

OUTLINE REVIEW OF JOURNEYS—EIGHTH PERIOD.

PERIOD OF THE PASSION.

1. *Bethany to Temple and Return.* Triumphal entry.
2. *Bethany to Temple and Return.* Cleansing the Temple.
3. *Bethany to Temple and Return.* Last discourses.
4. *Bethany to Supper.* Last Supper.
5. *Supper to Gethsemane.* (1.) Agony. (2.) Arrest.
6. *Gethsemane to Caiaphas.* (1.) To Annas. (2.) To Caiaphas.
7. *Caiaphas to Pilate.*
8. *Pilate to Herod and Return.*
9. *Pilate to Calvary.* (1.) Crucifixion. (2.) Death. (3.) Burial.

IX. PERIOD OF THE RESURRECTION.

The events of the forty days between the Resurrection and the Ascension of Jesus cannot be arranged as journeys, since his resurrection body moved from place to place by the will of his spirit. The student may therefore consult the Map of Palestine during the ministry of Jesus for the places referred to in the account of this period. Of the ten recorded appearances, five were on the day of the resurrection, the first Easter Sunday.

1. **At Jerusalem,** on Easter morning, to Mary Magdalene, after the other women had received from the angels the news that he was alive. (John 20:1–18.)

2. **At Jerusalem,** soon afterward, to the other women, when Jesus greeted them with the words "All hail!" (Matt. 28 : 1–10.)

3. **Near Emmaus,** on Easter afternoon, to two disciples, not apostles, to whom he unfolded the Scriptures concerning himself. (Luke 24 : 13–33.) Various locations have been proposed for Emmaus, of which we prefer *Kulonieyeh,* four miles west of Jerusalem.

4. **At Jerusalem,** on the afternoon of the same day, to Simon Peter. (Luke 24 : 34.) No account of this appearance, more than the mention of the fact, has been preserved.

5. **At Jerusalem,** on Easter evening, to the ten disciples, Thomas being absent. (John 20 : 19–25.)

6. **At Jerusalem,** a week after the resurrection, to the eleven apostles, when Thomas received a tender rebuke for the slowness of his faith. (John 20: 26–29.) Perhaps these last two appearances were at the place of the Supper, on Mount Zion.

7. **Near the Sea of Galilee,** to seven apostles, when Peter received a new commission. (John 21: 1–23.)

8. **On a Mountain in Galilee,** perhaps *Kurûn Hattin,* the place of the Sermon on the Mount. Here were gathered 500 disciples, and the final commands of Christ were given. (Matt. 28 : 16–20; 1 Cor. 15 : 6.)

9. **At Jerusalem** (?). To James, the Lord's brother. Only a mention of this appearance is left on record. (1 Cor. 15 : 7.)

10. **Near Bethany.** Forty days after the resurrection, Jesus appeared to the eleven apostles, gave them his last charges, and ascended to heaven, from whence he has promised to come once more to earth. (Acts 1:9–12.)

THE VIA DOLOROSA.

OUTLINE REVIEW OF NINTH PERIOD.

PERIOD OF THE RESURRECTION.

The Ten Appearances of the Risen Christ :

1.	*Jerusalem.*	Mary Magdalene.	7.	*Sea of Galilee.* Seven apostles.
2.	*Jerusalem.*	Other women.	8.	*Mountain in Galilee.* Five hundred disciples.
3.	*Emmaus.*	Two disciples.		
4.	*Jerusalem.*	Peter.	9.	*Jerusalem* (?). James.
5.	*Jerusalem.*	Ten apostles.	10.	*Bethany.* Apostles. [Ascension.]
6.	*Jerusalem.*	Eleven apostles.		

OUTLINE FOR TEACHING AND REVIEW.

1. Let each period be given as a separate lesson.

2. Draw the map for the period on the blackboard, and show each place named in the period.

3. Let each scholar also draw the map, and locate the places upon it.

4. Draw the lines of the journeys in the period in colored chalk, naming the places and events of the journeys, and writing only initials or catch-syllables.

5. Review carefully and thoroughly each period, each journey under it, and each event of the journey.

6. Erase the map, and call upon the scholars to draw its different parts in turn; one the outlines, another the places, a third the journeys, a fourth the events, etc.

7. Review with each lesson the leading points in all the previous lessons, until the whole series is thoroughly understood and remembered.

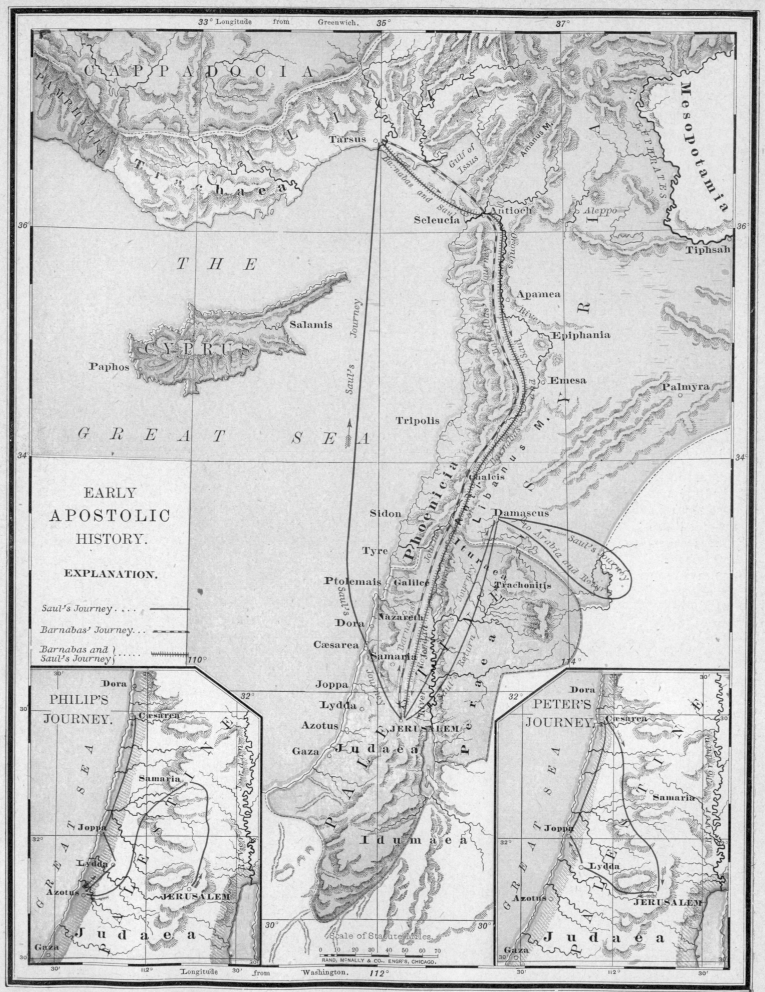

EARLY
APOSTOLIC
HISTORY.

EXPLANATION.

Saul's Journey . . . .

Barnabas' Journey . . .

Barnabas and
Saul's Journey } . . . . .

PHILIP'S
JOURNEY.

PETER'S
JOURNEY.

Scale of Statute Miles.
0 10 20 30 40 50 60 70

RAND, McNALLY & CO., ENGR'S, CHICAGO.

EARLY APOSTOLIC HISTORY.

During the seven years following the ascension of the Saviour, the Christian church was entirely Jewish in its membership, and, so far as we can learn, limited to the city of Jerusalem and the surrounding villages. There was at that time no thought of the gospel for the Gentiles, and the conception of the apostles was that the only door into the church lay through the profession of Judaism and the rite of circumcision. Probably the first to attain to wider views of the gospel was Stephen, and the persecution in which he became the first martyr arose from the tendency of his teachings toward extending among the Gentiles the privileges of the new kingdom. This state of affairs was suddenly ended by the death of Stephen, and the scattering of the church at Jerusalem. The more liberally inclined of its members, when driven abroad, were led to preach the gospel, first to Samaritans; then to believers in the Jewish faith who had not yet submitted to circumcision, and hence were called "Proselytes of the Gate"; and at last to the general Gentile world. The period from the death of Stephen, A. D. 37, to the first missionary journey of the Apostle Paul, A. D. 45, may, therefore, be regarded as an age of transition from Jewish to Gentile Christianity.

This period requires us to notice two provinces, Palestine and Syria. Palestine appears at this time under several forms of government in frequent succession. During the public life of Christ, Judæa and Samaria were under the direct rule of Rome, governed by a procurator, while Galilee and Peræa belonged to Herod Antipas, and the region north and east of the Sea of Galilee, anciently called Bashan, was held by Herod Philip, both of these having the title of *tetrarch*, "ruler of a fourth part." In A. D. 37 Herod Agrippa received Philip's tetrarchy, and in 41 he was made king of all Palestine. ("Herod the king," Acts 12.) In A. D. 44 he died, and his dominions were divided. Judæa, Samaria, Galilee and Peræa again became a procuratorship, under a succession of Roman rulers, until the final destruction of the Jewish state, A. D. 70. The principality of Bashan was given to Herod Agrippa II. in A. D. 53, and held by him until A. D. 70. Syria, the great region north of Palestine, extending from Damascus to Antioch, was, during this time, a province of the Roman empire, governed by a prefect.

The events of this period gather around seven cities.

1. **Jerusalem.** This place has been already described. (See page 73.) 2. **Samaria** (Acts 8:5–25), the field of Philip's early ministry, was the ancient capital of the Ten Tribes (see page 87), located 30 miles north of Jerusalem, and 6 miles northwest of Shechem. It had been rebuilt by Herod the Great, and named Sebaste, in honor of Augustus. It is now a village called *Sebastiyeh.* 3. **Cæsarea** (Acts 10:1), the place where the Gentile Cornelius became a disciple, was the Roman capital of Palestine, and the residence of the procurators. It was called Cæsarea Stratonis, to distinguish it from Cæsarea

DAMASCUS.

Philippi, under Mount Hermon; and was located on the sea-coast, 47 miles northwest of Jerusalem; and is now a desolate, uninhabited ruin, called *Kaisarieyeh.* 4. **Joppa,** where Dorcas was raised to life, and Peter received a vision (Acts 9:36–43; 10:11), is one of the most ancient towns in the world, in all ages the principal seaport of Palestine. It lies 30 miles south of Cæsarea, and 35 miles northwest of Jerusalem; and is now a flourishing city called *Yafa,* or *Jaffa.* 5. **Damascus,** the place where Saul was converted (Acts 9:1–25), is an ancient and famous city of Syria, 133 miles northeast of Jerusalem, beautifully situated in a plain at the foot of the Anti-Lebanon mountains. Recently it had a population of 150,000, but is rapidly decaying from the diversion of the Eastern trade through the Suez Canal. Its modern name is *el Shams.* 6. **Antioch,** seat of the first missionary church (Acts 11:19–30), was the metropolis of northern Syria, situated on the

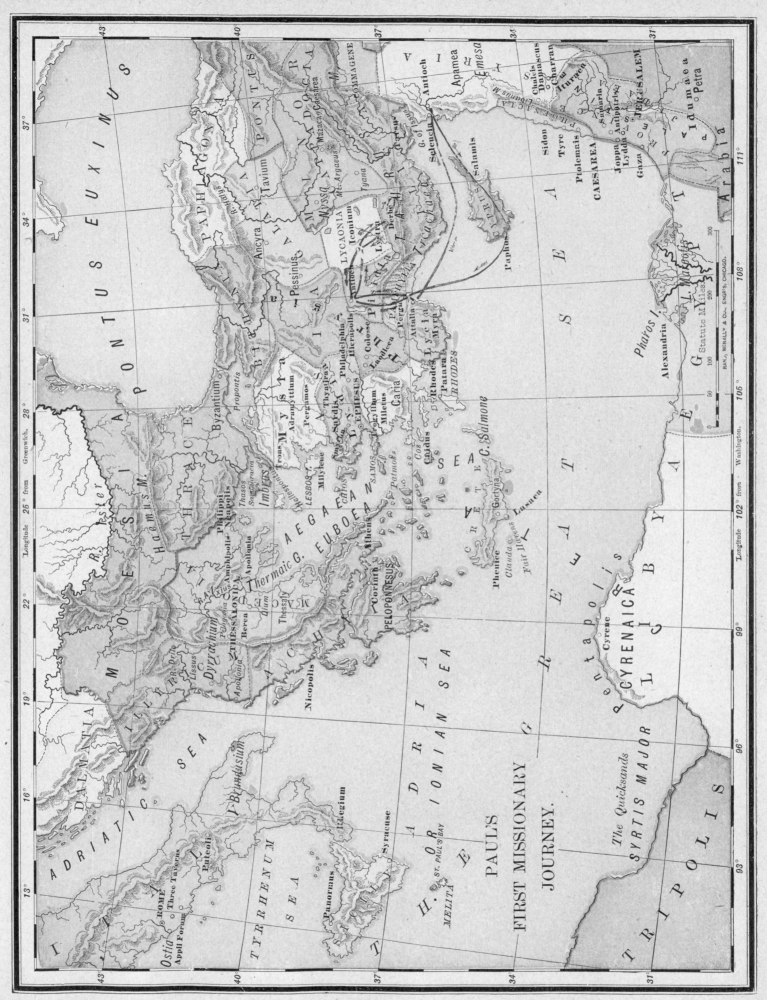

PAUL'S

FIRST MISSIONARY

JOURNEY.

JOURNEYS OF THE APOSTLE PAUL.

During the twenty years between A. D. 45 and 65, of which the events of church history are recorded in Acts 13–28, the most important personage is the apostle Paul. While the work of the original Twelve is scarcely referred to, the journeys of the last apostle are related with considerable detail. The probable reason for this is, that Paul was the leader in the great movement by which the church of Christ was broadened from an inconsiderable Jewish sect, scarcely known out of Jerusalem, to a religion for all the world. This distinction from the other apostles is considered of so much importance that he is called, almost universally, by the descriptive title he gave himself — the Apostle of the Gentiles. The localities and events of this period are represented upon four maps, three of Paul's Missionary Journeys, and the last of his Voyage to Rome.

THE PROVINCES OF ASIA MINOR.

As the first missionary journey was mainly in Asia Minor, a brief description of that peninsula is necessary. It embraces about 156,000 square miles, or about two-thirds the size of Texas, and was located between the Black, Ægean, and Mediterranean Seas on the north, west and south, and bounded on the east by the provinces of Armenia, Mesopotamia and Syria. The provinces which it contained at the New Testament epoch may be variously stated, since in their political, racial and geographical relations they were different. The map of the Roman Empire, on page 98, gives them according to their political arrangement, which united two or more under one government, and gave to some new names. Thus there were four districts united under the name ASIA, which in the New Testament never denotes the whole continent, nor yet the whole peninsula, but the seaboard provinces of Caria, Lydia, Mysia, and the interior land of Phrygia. So, too, Bithynia and Pontus formed one government, Lycaonia was included in Galatia, and Lycia and Pisidia in Pamphylia. We can best arrange these provinces of Asia Minor, according to territorial relations, in four groups. 1. The three northern provinces, on the Black Sea: Pontus, Paphlagonia, Bithynia.

2. The three western provinces, on the Ægean Sea: Mysia, Lydia, Caria. 3. The three southern provinces, on the Mediterranean Sea: Lycia, Pamphylia, Cilicia. 4. The five interior provinces: on the north, Galatia; on the east, Cappadocia; on the south, Lycaonia and Pisidia; and on the west, Phrygia. All of these fourteen provinces, except four, are named in the New Testament.

1. **The Provinces on the Black Sea.** (1.) *Pontus* (Acts 2:9; 18:2; 1 Pet. 1:1) was the northeastern province, between Paphlagonia and Armenia, and having Cappadocia on the south; now represented by *Trebizond*

ANTIOCH IN SYRIA.

in the Turkish empire. Some of its Jewish inhabitants were present in Jerusalem on the Day of Pentecost; Aquila, a helper of Paul, was a native of this region; and its Christian Jews were among those addressed in Peter's first Epistle. (2.) *Paphlagonia*, not mentioned in the New Testament, lay between Pontus and Bithynia, and north of Galatia. (3.) *Bithynia* (Acts 16:7; 1 Pet. 1:1) was the northwestern province, having the Propontis (now called the *Sea of Marmora*) on the west, and Mysia and Phrygia on the south, from which it was separated by Mount Olympus. Though the region is only incidentally named in the New Testament, two of its cities, Nicæa and Nicomedia, were prominent in the history of the Greek church.

2. **The Provinces on the Ægean Sea.** These are all included under the name Asia, by which the western portion of the peninsula was known to the Romans.

(1.) *Mysia* (Acts 16:7, 8) was separated from Europe by the Hellespont and the Propontis, and had Bithynia on the north, Phrygia on the east, and Mysia on the west. It contained Troas, on the ruins of ancient Troy, whence Paul could dimly see the hills of Europe on the west, and where the vision of "the man of Macedonia" led to the voyage for the evangelization of Europe. (2.) *Lydia*, once the centre of the great empire of Crœsus, extended along the Ægean Sea from Mysia to Caria, and eastward to Phrygia. Its principal city was Ephesus, the metropolis of Asia Minor, and one of Paul's most important fields of labor; and Sardis, Thyatira and Philadelphia were also large places and seats of churches addressed in the Apocalypse. (3.) *Caria* was the southwestern province, not named in the New Testament, though its cities, Cnidus and Miletus, are referred to;

MAP

GIVING COMPARATIVE SIZE

OF

ASIA MINOR AND TEXAS, U.S.

the latter as the place where Paul parted from the Ephesian elders. (Acts 20:15.)

3. **The Provinces on the Mediterranean.** (1.) *Lycia* (Acts 27:5) lay south of Mount Taurus, and opposite to the island of Rhodes. Two of its cities, Patara and Myra, were visited by the apostle Paul. (Acts 21:1; 27:5.) (2.) *Pamphylia* (Acts 13:13) was a small province between Lycia and Cilicia, and also between Mount Taurus and the sea. Its capital, Perga, was the first city in Asia Minor visited by Paul on his first missionary journey. On his return, he preached in its seaport, Attalia. (Acts 13:13; 14:24, 25.) (3.) *Cilicia* (Acts 6:9) is a long and narrow province, also lying between Mount Taurus and the sea, and separated from Syria by the Syrian Gates, a pass in the mountains. Its capital, Tarsus, was one of the leading cities of the Roman empire, and the birthplace of Paul.

4. **The Provinces in the Interior.** (1.) On the

north was *Galatia*, a land of uncertain and varying boundaries, but located between Bithynia, Cappadocia, Lycaonia and Phrygia. It received its name from a race of Gauls, who conquered it about 300 B. C., was twice visited by Paul, and its Christian population was addressed in the Epistle to the Galatians. (Acts 16:6; 18:23; Gal. 1:2.) (2.) *Cappadocia* lay on the southeast of Galatia, and south of Pontus. It was the largest province in Asia Minor. Some of its people were in Jerusalem at the Feast of Pentecost (Acts 2:9); and its churches were among those addressed in 1 Peter. (3.) *Lycaonia* (Acts 14:1–23) was not a political division, but a district in southern Galatia. It was west of Cappadocia and east of Phrygia, and separated by the Taurus range from Cilicia. Its principal places were Iconium, Derbe and Lystra, in all of which Paul preached the gospel and suffered persecution. (4.) *Pisidia* was politically connected with Pamphylia, but lay north of the Taurus, between Lycaonia and Phrygia. Its principal city was Antioch (to be distinguished from Antioch in Syria), twice, at least, visited by the apostle Paul. (Acts 13:14; 14:21.) (5.) *Phrygia* varied greatly at different periods, and in Paul's time had no separate existence as a province. In the earlier days, when Galatia was a part of it, it was said to touch in some way every other land in Asia Minor. In its southern section lay the three cities of Laodicea, Hierapolis and Colosse, all named in Paul's letters.

THE FIRST MISSIONARY JOURNEY.

1. Paul and Barnabas, with John Mark as their assistant, set forth upon the first missionary journey from *Antioch*, the metropolis of Syria (Acts 13:1), already described on page 107.

2. They descended the mountains to *Seleucia* (Acts 13:4), the seaport of Antioch, 16 miles from the city, named from its founder, Seleucus Nicator, B. C. 280. It is now a small village known as *el Kalusi*, having among its ruins an ancient gateway, still standing, through which Paul and Barnabas may have passed.

3. Setting sail, they crossed over the arm of the Mediterranean to the island of *Cyprus* (Acts 13:4–13), the early home of Barnabas, 60 miles west of Syria, and 40 miles south of Asia Minor; of irregular shape, 140 miles long and 50 wide; then thickly inhabited, and governed by a Roman proconsul, now under the rule of Great Britain.

4. Their first stopping place was at *Salamis* (Acts 13:5), on its eastern shore, on the river Pediæus, where they found a Jewish synagogue. The city is now desolate, and its unoccupied site is known as *Old Famagousta.*

5. They crossed the island from east to west, preaching on their way, and came to *Paphos* (Acts 13:6), the capital, and residence of the proconsul. This city contained a famous shrine of Venus, to whose worship, with all its immoralities, its people were devoted. There was an old and a new city, of which the former was

the one visited by Paul and Barnabas. It is now called *Baffa*.

6. Sailing in a northwesterly direction a distance of 170 miles, they reached Asia Minor, in the province of Pamphylia. Passing by Attalia for the present, they ascended the river Cestrus, and landed at *Perga* (Acts 13:13), 7½ miles from the sea. This was a Greek city, devoted to the worship of Diana: now in ruins, and called *Eski Kalessi*. Here their young assistant, Mark, left the two missionaries to prosecute the hardest part of the journey without his help.

7. Their next field of labor was *Antioch in Pisidia*, a city east of Ephesus, and northwest of Tarsus, now known as *Yalobatch*. Here Paul preached in the synagogue a discourse reported more at length than any other in his ministry, and here a church was founded. (Acts 13:14–52.)

8. Driven out of Antioch by the persecution of the Jews, they went on 60 miles eastward to *Iconium*, a large city, still in existence as *Konieh*, and in the Middle Ages the capital of a powerful Mohammedan kingdom. This region, in the apostle's time, was independent of the Roman empire. (Acts 14:1–5.)

9. Again compelled to endure persecution, they traveled to *Lystra*, a heathen city in the district of Lycaonia, where a miracle wrought by Paul led the superstitious people to offer worship to the two apostles as the gods Jupiter and Mercury (in Greek, Zeus and Hermes).

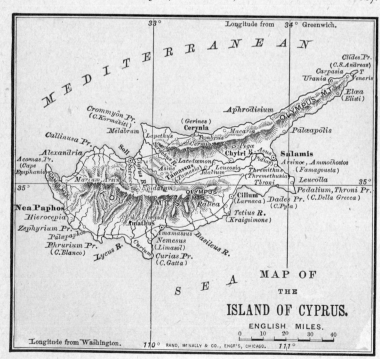

MAP OF THE ISLAND OF CYPRUS.

There is reason to suppose that Lystra was at the place now known as *Bin bir Kilisseh*, "the thousand and one churches," a mass of ruins in the *Kara Dagh*, or Black Mountain.

10. Paul having been stoned at Lystra, the apostles went on to *Derbe*, 20 miles distant, but in the same province, where they were suffered to labor in peace. It is supposed to be represented by the modern village of

Divle. This marked the furthest place reached by the evangelists. They were now quite near the pass in Mount Taurus, known as the Cilician Gates, and could easily have reached Tarsus, and thence taken a short voyage home.

11. But they preferred to return by the same route, perilous as the journey was from the enmities excited by their preaching; and revisited Lystra, Iconium and

REVIEW CHART OF PAUL'S FIRST JOURNEY.

Antioch, confirming the churches which they had planted, and establishing new ones in other neighboring places in Pisidia and Pamphylia, as in *Attalia*, a seaport on the river Katarrhaktes, 16 miles from Perga, now known as *Adalia*, where they took ship once more, and thence sailed over the Cilician section of the Mediterranean, north of Cyprus, to Antioch in Syria, where they were gladly received by the church which had sent them forth

OUTLINE FOR TEACHING AND REVIEW.

1. Draw on the blackboard the subjoined Review Chart of Asia Minor, and let the class also draw the same on slates or paper, in a rough sketch. Then insert the provinces, and drill the class upon their names, reviewing from the beginning after each group is given.

Black Sea. Pontus, Paphlagonia, Bithynia.

Ægean Sea. Mysia, Lydia, Caria.

Mediterranean Sea. Lycia, Pamphylia, Cilicia.

Interior. Galatia, Cappadocia, Lycaonia, Pisidia, Phrygia.

2. Draw in colored chalk the line representing *Paul's travel*, calling attention to the places and events; and frequently review the list, as a new name is presented. (1.) Antioch in Syria. (2.) Seleucia. (3.) Island of Cyprus. (4.) Salamis. (5.) Paphos. (6.) Perga. (7.) Antioch in Pisidia. (8.) Iconium. (9.) Lystra. (10.) Derbe. (11.) Return, and Attalia.

THE SECOND MISSIONARY JOURNEY.

The map presents the field of the apostle Paul's labor during four of the most active years of his life, according to Alford's chronology, from A. D. 50 to 54. To this period belong two journeys: a journey from Antioch to Jerusalem and return, and the second missionary journey, through Asia Minor, Macedonia and Greece.

The journey to Jerusalem, not indicated upon the

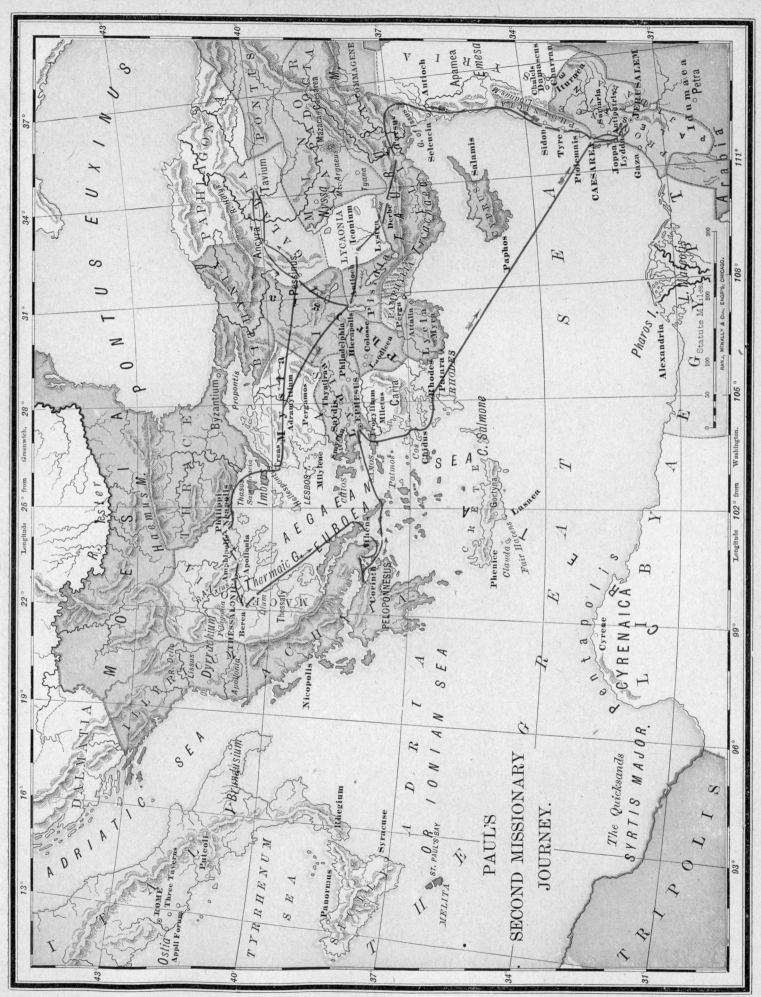

PAUL'S
SECOND MISSIONARY
JOURNEY.

map, was Paul's third visit to that city after his conversion. His first visit was in A. D. 40, when Barnabas introduced him to Peter and James (Acts 9:26–30); his second was in A. D. 45, when with Barnabas he brought the gifts of the church at Antioch (Acts 11:30); his third was in A. D. 50, when, again accompanied by Barnabas, he attended the council in Jerusalem, called to establish the principle upon which Gentiles were to be received into the Christian church. (Acts 15:1–30.)

The second missionary journey began with an unfortunate disagreement between Paul and Barnabas, which resulted in their separation, Barnabas going to the island of Cyprus, and Paul to the mainland. (Acts 15:36–40.) The apostle chose as his companion Silas, or Silvanus, and was afterward joined by Timothy, and Luke, the author of the third Gospel and the Acts. We may subdivide this journey into three sections, as follows:

I. The Stations in Asia, seven in number.

II. The Stations in Europe, eight in number.

III. The Stations of the Return, four in number.

I. **The Asiatic Stations.** These are mostly the names of provinces in Asia Minor already described in connection with a previous map.

THE ACROPOLIS AT ATHENS. (AREOPAGUS ON THE LEFT.)

1. Starting from Antioch, Paul first traveled through *Syria*, visiting the churches. (Acts 15:41.) This tour was probably through northern Syria only, in the region around Antioch; and the general direction was toward Asia Minor, which he probably entered through the Syrian Gates, now the Beilan Pass in Mount Amanus. No cities are named in this region as visited by the apostle; but the principal places were Issus and Alexandria, both of which lay along the route of his journey.

2. The next province visited was *Cilicia* (Acts 15:41), the land of Paul's birth. As everywhere he made the chief cities his stations of labor, we may suppose that he passed through Mopsuestia and Adana, on his way to Tarsus, the metropolis of the province. From Tarsus he journeyed westward toward Mount Taurus, the northern boundary of the province, and crossed the range through the Cilician Gates, from which he emerged upon the great Lycaonian plain.

3. We read of a station at *Derbe*, where he had

14

planted a church on the first journey, and which was now strengthened by his second visit. (Acts 16:1.)

4. Next, at *Lystra*, where in other days he had been first worshiped and then stoned. Here he found a church, the result of his early labors, and was joined by his life-long companion, Timothy. (Acts 16:1–4.)

5. We read of Paul and Silas as having next "gone throughout *Phrygia*." Probably this refers to a tour among the churches at Iconium and Antioch in Pisidia, the fields of former labors. There is no indication in the Acts or Epistles that he preached in any new places in this district.

6. From Antioch he turned northward and entered for the first time the province of *Galatia*. (Acts 16:6.) But W. M. Ramsay has shown that Lycaonia itself was only a district in the political province of Galatia, and that the Galatian journey (and also the Galatian epistle) may refer to the region of Derbe, Lystra, and Iconium, not to the entire province. In that case the dotted red line on the map may indicate Paul's journey, and the line through Pessinus, Ancyra, and Tavium should be omitted.

These conclusions are not, as yet, generally accepted.

7. Paul's desire was to preach the word throughout the Roman proconsular province of Asia, which comprised Phrygia, and the maritime districts of Mysia, Lydia and Caria. But divine influences closed up his path, both in this direction and northward toward Bithynia; so he journeyed westward across Phrygia and Mysia, and at last reached the shore of the Ægean Sea at *Troas*. (Acts 16:6–8.) This was the site of ancient Troy, the scene of Homer's Iliad, and has been the place of great discoveries in modern times. There was a city near the ancient site in Paul's time; and it is probable that in it he founded a church, for there he was joined by Luke, the historian of the Acts and author of the third Gospel, and in a later journey met "the disciples" of the place. (Acts 20:7.) Here the vision of the "man of Macedonia" summoned Paul from Asia to Europe (Acts 16:9, 10), and opened a new chapter in the history of Christianity.

II. **The European Stations.** All the places named as visited by the apostle in this journey were included in the two provinces of Macedonia and Greece, of which the Roman name was Achaia.

Macedonia was the province north of Greece, and famous in history from its conquering kings, Philip, and his greater son, Alexander. Its boundaries were: on the north, the Hæmus or Balkan Mountains; on the east, Thrace and the Ægean Sea; on the south, Achaia (Greece); on the west, the Pindus Mountains, separating it from Epirus and Illyricum. It consists of two great plains, watered respectively by the Axius, near Thessalonica, and the Strymon, near Apollonia. Between these two rivers projects a peninsula, having three points, like a hand of three fingers, across the palm of which, in Paul's time, ran the great Roman road known as the Ignatian Way. It was divided by the Romans into four districts, of which the capitals were Amphipolis, Thessalonica (the residence of the provincial proconsul), Pella (the birthplace of Alexander the Great), and Pelagonia. Of these, Amphipolis had become less important than the rival city of Philippi, in the same district.

Achaia was the Roman name of the little land of Greece, whose fame has filled all history. In the later period of its independence, its ruling state had been Achaia, which gave its name to the entire province when annexed to the Roman empire. In the apostolic age, Corinth was its metropolis and political capital, though Athens still retained its fame as a centre of art and literature.

The apostle Paul and his companions sailed across the Ægean Sea from Troas, in a northwesterly direction, passing the storied isles of Tenedos and Imbros; anchored for the first night off Samothracia, "the Thracian Samos," a rocky island near the coast of Thrace; and the next day passed northward of Thasos, and anchored in the harbor of Neapolis, on the border of Thrace. They did not remain at the seaport, but pressed inland to the larger city, which was to be memorable as the first foothold of the gospel in Europe. In the European part of the second missionary journey we notice eight places visited by the apostle.

1. *Philippi* (Acts 16:12–40). This was an ancient town, enlarged and renamed by Philip, the father of Alexander the Great. Near it was fought the great battle between Augustus and Antony on one side, and Brutus and Cassius on the other, in which the hope of a Roman republic perished, and the empire was ushered in. It had been made a *colony;* that is, a branch of Rome itself, and enjoyed certain privileges of self-government, so that its magistrates bore Roman titles, as noticed by Luke. Here Lydia, the first convert in Europe, was baptized, and a church was planted; Paul and Silas were scourged and imprisoned, and set free by divine power; the jailer was brought to Christ; and the officials of the city were made to tremble at having inflicted violence upon citizens of Rome.

2. *Amphipolis* was 33 miles southwest of Philippi, and 3 miles from the Ægean Sea. It was a town of

ancient fame; but, in Paul's time, decayed in population; and, having no synagogue or Jewish population, was not yet made a field of his labors. After a delay of only a day, he journeyed on still further westward. (Acts 17:1.)

3. *Apollonia* was 30 miles from Amphipolis, and an important city; but for some reason Paul did not choose to labor in its vicinity, and remained there but a day. (Acts 17:1.)

4. *Thessalonica* (Acts 17:1–9) was the capital of the entire province, and 40 miles from the preceding station. It was named after a sister of Alexander the Great, and had many historic associations. An arch is still standing, and was doubtless seen by the apostle, which commemorated the victory at Philippi. There was a large Jewish population, and a synagogue, in which Paul preached for three sabbaths. He succeeded in founding a church, mostly of Gentiles, to which he soon after wrote his two earliest epistles, First and Second Thessalonians. But the Jews excited a riot, and the apostles were compelled to leave the city by night. Thessalonica, now called *Saloniki*, is still the second city of European Turkey, and contains 80,000 inhabitants.

5. *Berea* (Acts 17:10–13) was a small city, chosen by the apostle on account of its retired situation. It lay on the eastern side of Mount Olympus. Its people were generous in hearing the truth, and candid in examination of its claims; so that many of them believed, and "the Bereans" have furnished a name for earnest students of the Bible in all lands. The place is now called *Verria*, and has a population of about 6,000.

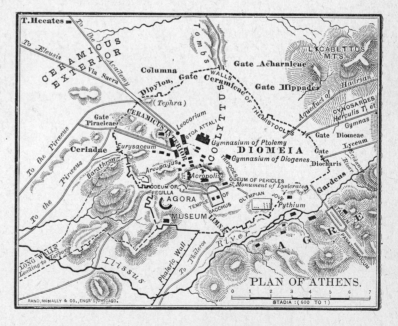

PLAN OF ATHENS.

6. *Athens* (Acts 17:15–34) was one of the most famous cities of the world. It was situated 5 miles northeast of the Saronic Gulf, between the two little streams Cephissus and Ilissus, and connected by long walls with its two seaports, the Piræus and the Phaleric Gulf, where probably Paul landed. Around it stand mountains noted in history, and within its walls rise four important hills:

the Acropolis, surmounted by the Parthenon, the most perfect specimen of Greek architecture; the Areopagus, northwest of the Acropolis, where Paul delivered his memorable discourse; the Pnyx, still further west; and, on the south, the Museum. In Paul's time Athens was no longer the political capital, but was still the literary centre, not only of Greece, but of the civilized world. Paul's discourse before its philosophers was not attended with immediate results, as no church appears to have been founded; but, four centuries afterward, the Parthenon became a Christian church, and the Athenians were among the most bitter foes of image worship. After many changes of fortune — at times being without inhabitants — Athens is now the growing capital of the kingdom of modern Greece, and the seat of a university.

7. *Corinth* (Acts 18:1–18), the next station of the apostle, was 40 miles west of Athens, on the isthmus between Hellas and Peloponnesus, which is here 10 miles

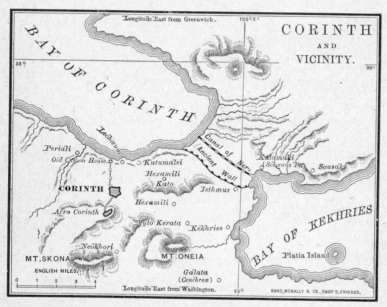

wide. In Paul's time it was the commercial and political metropolis of Greece, being the residence of the Roman proconsul. It was, however, a most wicked city, and a by-word for corruption and licentiousness. Paul preached in Corinth for a year and a half, working meanwhile at his trade as a tent-maker, and during his stay wrote the two Epistles to the Thessalonians. After leaving, he wrote to the Corinthian Christians two of his longest Epistles, First and Second Corinthians. The site of the city is now desolate, except for a small and wretched village, named *Gortho*.

8. *Cenchrea* (Acts 18:18), more accurately Cenchreæ, is named merely as the place from which Paul set forth on his return journey, and where he performed the Levitical service of cutting off his hair in token of a vow. We know, however, that he had, directly or indirectly, planted a church here, as its deaconess, Phebe, is named. (Rom. 16:1, 2.) This was the eastern harbor of Corinth, on the Saronic Gulf, 9 miles from the city. It is now called *Kekhries*.

III. **The Return Stations** of the apostle, in his journey from Corinth to Antioch, are given as four in number, though the journey was more than a thousand miles in length.

1. Sailing eastward across the Ægean Sea, and passing many celebrated islands, after a voyage of 250 miles, he reached *Ephesus*. (Acts 18:19–21.) He had been hindered from preaching in this region before, and now remained but a few weeks, though urged by the Jews to remain longer. He left behind him his friends Aquila and Priscilla, by whose labors the brilliant young Apollos of Alexandria was led into the church, and the way was prepared for Paul's labor on his second visit, in connection with which Ephesus will be noticed again.

2. A voyage around the southwestern border of Asia Minor, thence past the isle of Rhodes in a southeasterly direction, leaving Cyprus on the northeast, brought the apostle to *Cæsarea*. (Acts 18:22.) This was the Roman capital of Palestine, and a harbor. Here Paul debarked from the vessel on which he had sailed 600 miles, and entered once more the Holy Land. (For an account of Cæsarea, see page 113.)

3. *Jerusalem.* (Acts 18:22.) The apostle climbed the mountains, and for the fourth time since his conversion entered the Holy City. He stayed only to salute the church, and perhaps leave the gifts of the Gentile Christians to the poorer saints of Judæa, and then left once more.

4. He traveled, overland most probably, to *Antioch*, his home, if any place might be so named; for here were his nearest friends, here he had begun his missionary journey, and here he doubtless received a glad welcome from the church. He brought with him, on his return, not only Silas, who had set out as his companion, but Timothy, and perhaps also Aristarchus, Gaius and Erastus, whose names we find associated with Paul's soon after.

OUTLINE FOR REVIEW.

I. Draw the map of Asia Minor, and review the names of its provinces as already given.

II. Notice the *Stations in Asia*, and the events of the journey associated with them. 1. Syria. 2. Cilicia. 3. Derbe. 4. Lystra. 5. Phrygia. 6. Galatia. 7 Troas.

III. Notice the *Stations in Europe*. 1. Philippi. 2. Amphipolis. 3. Apollonia. 4. Thessalonica. 5. Berea. 6. Athens. 7. Corinth. 8. Cenchrea.

IV. Notice the *Stations of the Return Journey*. 1. Ephesus. 2. Cæsarea. 3. Jerusalem. 4. Antioch.

THE THIRD MISSIONARY JOURNEY.

This journey of the apostle, beginning at Antioch, led him as far west as Corinth, and then as far east as Jerusalem. It probably occupied about four years, from A. D. 54 to 58, and may be subdivided into two stages. I. The Outward Journey, from Antioch to Corinth, including seven stations. II. The Return Journey, from Corinth to Jerusalem, with fifteen stations. More than half of this period was spent at Ephesus, where Paul preached for nearly three years.

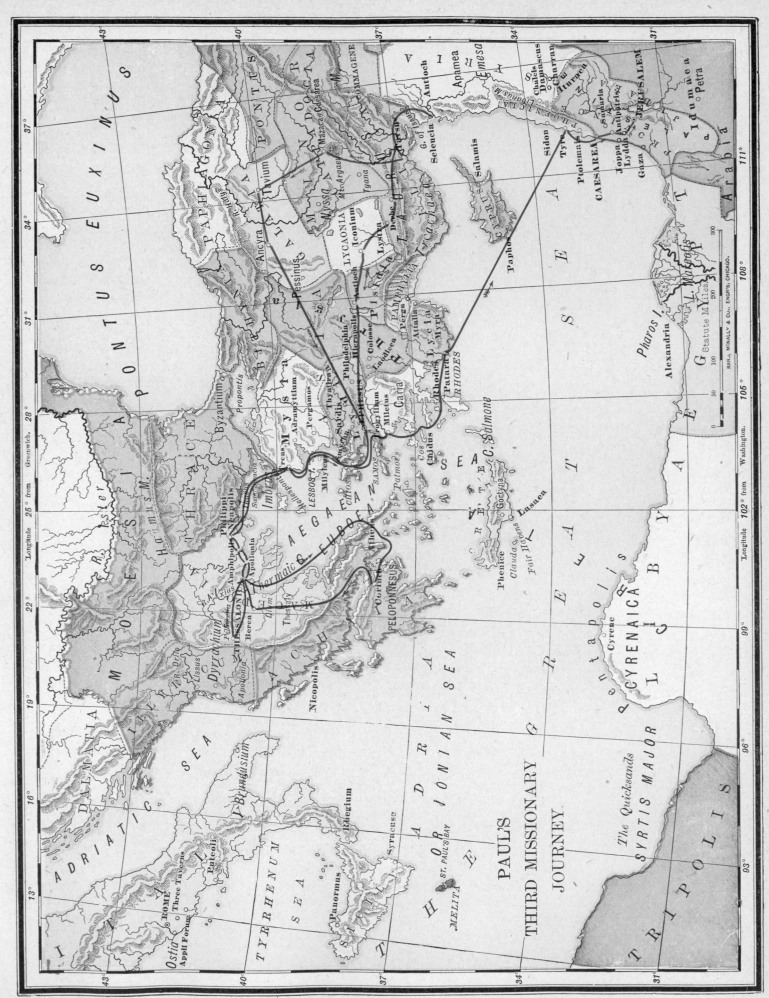

PAUL'S
THIRD MISSIONARY
JOURNEY

I. **The Outward Journey.** (Acts 18:23–20:3.)

1. We note *Antioch*, the starting point for each of Paul's three missionary journeys. This place has been already described, on page 113, in connection with the map of the Early Apostolic History.

2. His westward course lay through *Galatia* (Acts 18:23), where he visited the churches planted upon his former tour. But as before, this may refer to the part of Galatia embraced in Lycaonia; and we have thus indicated upon the map by a dotted line. (See page 121.)

3. Still journeying westward toward the coast, Paul passed through *Phrygia* (Acts 18:23), already described on page 118. No events of this part of the journey are related.

4. He came from the highlands of the interior to *Ephesus*, where he had touched on his previous journey,

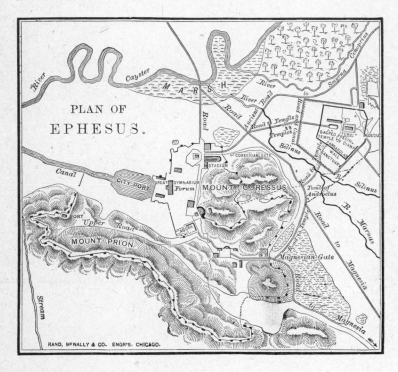

PLAN OF EPHESUS.

RAND, McNALLY & CO. ENGR'S. CHICAGO.

and was now to remain longer than at any other place during his active ministry. (Acts 19:1–20:1.) Ephesus was the metropolis of Proconsular Asia, and may be regarded as the third capital of Christianity, as Jerusalem had been its birthplace, and Antioch the centre of its foreign missions. It stood a mile from the Ægean Sea, fronting an artificial harbor, in which met the ships of all lands, and above which rose the Temple of Artemis (Diana), celebrated as the most magnificent building in Asia Minor, though the image which it enshrined was only a shapeless block. Its population was principally Greek, though with a large Oriental mixture. Here a preparation for Paul's labor had been made by Apollos, who had instructed a small company of Jews up to the twilight of John the Baptist's teachings concerning the Messiah. From Paul's friends, Aquila and Priscilla, he had learned the gospel of Christ; and, just before the apostle's arrival, had gone to Corinth. For three

months Paul labored in the synagogue with the Jews and inquiring Gentiles; but, when the Jewish opposition endangered the work, he took the step (at this time first in the history of Christianity) of calling the believers in Christ out of the synagogue. Paul remained at Ephesus in all more than two years, working at his trade through the week, while preaching on the Jewish Sabbath. Through his endeavors most of "the Seven Churches," addressed long afterward by John, were founded at this time. Just before Paul's departure a riot arose, and a tumultuous mob occupied the theatre, whose ruins may still be seen. Ephesus is now an utter desolation, haunted by wild beasts. Near its ruins is a small Turkish village, called *Ayasalouk*. Near the close of his stay at Ephesus, Paul wrote the First Epistle to the Corinthians.

5. The next stopping place of the apostle was at *Troas*. (2 Cor. 2:12, 13.) This is mentioned, not in the Acts, but in the Epistle written soon afterward. Here he had expected to meet his companion Titus, with news from the church at Corinth. While waiting, he found an opportunity for preaching, and success in winning souls. But, as the expected tidings did not come, Paul again took ship, and sailed once more (see the previous journey) from Asia to Europe.

6. His next station is named as *Macedonia* (Acts 20:2); but it may be inferred that he visited Philippi, Thessalonica and Berea, the places of former labors, already described in the account of the second journey. Perhaps it was at this time that he journeyed "round about unto Illyricum," which was a province on the Adriatic Sea, west of Macedonia. (Rom. 15:19.) While in Macedonia, perhaps at Philippi, Paul wrote the Second Epistle to the Corinthians.

7. The last place in Paul's outward journey is mentioned as *Greece*, the province elsewhere called Achaia. (Acts 20:2, 3; 18:27.) His principal errand was to Corinth (already described on page 123), where troubles in the church required his attention. While here he wrote the Epistle to the Galatians, and his great statement of Christian doctrine, the Epistle to the Romans.

II. **The Return Journey.** (Acts 20:6–21:6.) This was undertaken with the desire of reaching Jerusalem in time for the Feast of Pentecost, A. D. 58. For some reason, probably on account of a Jewish plot to murder him, Paul did not take the direct route, but went around the Ægean Sea by way of Philippi and Troas, and was accompanied by a number of friends.

1. From Corinth, Paul and his friends journeyed overland, through Greece and Macedonia, to *Philippi* (Acts 20:3–6), a place now visited for the third time. Here Paul was rejoined by Luke the Evangelist, who henceforth shared his dangers to the end of his life.

2. Most of Paul's company sailed from Philippi across the Ægean Sea to *Troas*, in advance of the apostle, but were soon followed by Paul and Luke. (Acts 20:5–13.) At Troas they remained for a week with the church; and here Eutychus was restored to life by the apostle.

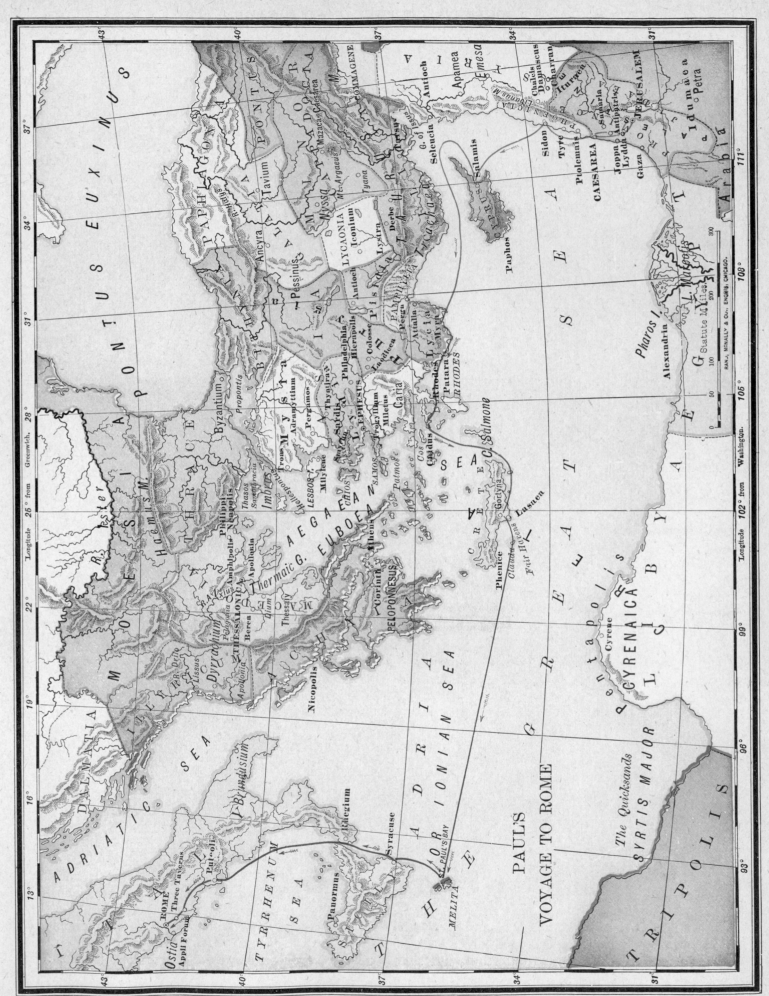

PAUL'S
VOYAGE TO ROME

3. From Philippi, most of the company set sail for Palestine, but Paul went on foot as far as *Assos*, where he was taken on board. (Acts 20:13, 14.) This place was situated 19 miles from Troas, and is now marked by extensive ruins.

4. *Mitylene.* This was on the island of Lesbos, famed as the home of Sappho, the Greek poetess. Here they anchored for the night, as the channel was not easy to follow among the islands. (Acts 20:14.) This and the succeeding stations in the Ægean Sea may be noticed on the map of the islands and coasts of Asia Minor, on page 132.

5. *Chios.* (Acts 20:15.) This is an island 32 miles long, and 5 miles from Asia; said to have been the birthplace of Homer; and now called *Scio.* Here Paul's ship anchored only for a night.

6. *Samos.* (Acts 20:15.) This is an island near the mainland, 42 miles southwest of Smyrna; and 27 miles long. It was the birthplace of the philosopher Pythagoras. They barely touched at the island, and then sailed across to the shore of Asia Minor.

7. *Trogyllium* (Acts 20:15) is a town and cape on the coast of Asia Minor, at the foot of Mount Mycale. The place at which they anchored for the night is still called *St. Paul's Port.* On the next day they sailed past the harbor of Ephesus without stopping, for Paul's stations were controlled by the movements of the ship and its masters.

8. *Miletus.* (Acts 20:16–38.) This was at the mouth of the river Mæander, 36 miles south of Ephesus; and at that time on the shore, though now ten miles inland, by the changes in the coast. Here, while the ship was delayed, Paul sent for the elders of the church at Ephesus, and gave to them a farewell address of deep tenderness. This place is now a small village, called *Melas.*

9. *Coos*, or Cos (Acts 21:1), where they next anchored, is a small island, northwest of Rhodes; now called *Stanchio.*

10. *Rhodes* (Acts 21:1) is an island of note in both ancient and modern history, 13 miles from Asia Minor, 46 miles long, and 18 wide. Upon it had stood the Colossus, a figure over 100 feet high, but overthrown by an earthquake, B. C. 224, and prostrate at the time of Paul's visit.

11. *Patara* (Acts 21:1) was a seaport in the province of Lycia, in Asia Minor, opposite Rhodes. Here the vessel ended its voyage, and the apostolic company found another, which was bound for Phœnicia. The place is now a ruin, and buried in the encroaching sand.

12. The disciples took another ship at Patara, and sailed in a southeasterly direction for Phœnicia, passing by Cyprus without stopping. The vessel paused for a week at *Tyre* to unlade its burden, and here Paul found a church, perhaps planted by Philip the evangelist. Tyre had once been the great commercial metropolis of the Mediterranean, known as "the strong city" as early as the time of Joshua. It was the capital of Phœnicia, and in Old Testament times held friendly relations with

Israel, but was idolatrous and abominably wicked. It was besieged by Nebuchadnezzar for 13 years, was destroyed by Alexander the Great, rebuilt by the Seleucidæ, and, in Paul's time, was still a large city. It is now a miserable village, called *Sur*, and, in the fulfillment of prophecy, "a place for the spreading of nets." (Ezek. 26:14.)

13. Taking ship once more, for the last time, they sailed southward along the coast of Palestine to *Ptolemais.* (Acts 21:7.) This was the Old Testament Accho, in the tribe of Asher, but never possessed. It was 8 miles north of Mount Carmel. In mediæval history it sustained a siege by the Crusaders, and was known as *St. Jean d'Acre.* Here Paul spent a day with the church, and then journeyed with his friends southward over the Plain of Esdraelon and Mount Carmel.

14. At *Cæsarea*, the next station, they were entertained by Philip, who, years before, had been driven out of Jerusalem by Saul of Tarsus. (See Philip's Journey, page 112.) Cæsarea was the Roman capital of Palestine, and was in all respects a heathen city, though containing many Jews. Here Paul received a message from the aged prophet Agabus, warning him not to go to Jerusalem; but he persisted in his purpose.

15. For the fifth time in his life as a Christian, and for the last time, Paul entered the city of JERUSALEM, from which he was soon to go forth "the prisoner of the Lord."

OUTLINE FOR REVIEW.

I. *Outward Journey.* 1. Antioch. 2. Galatia. 3. Phrygia. 4. Ephesus. 5. Troas. 6. Macedonia. (Philippi.) 7. Greece. (Corinth.)

II. *Return Journey.* 1. Philippi. 2. Troas. 3. Assos. 4. Mitylene. 5. Chios. 6. Samos. 7. Trogyllium. 8. Miletus. 9. Coos. 10. Rhodes. 11. Patara. 12. Tyre. 13. Ptolemais. 14. Cæsarea. 15. Jerusalem.

THE VOYAGE TO ROME.

The last of Paul's recorded journeys was that which he took as a prisoner under Roman power. He was seized by a Jewish mob in the Court of the Women in the Temple (see plan of the Temple on page 141), in or near the room set apart for the ceremonies of a Nazarite's vow. Dragged by the crowd into the Court of the Gentiles, he would have been slain but for the arrival of a company of Roman soldiers from the Tower of Antonia. He made an address to the throng from the stairs leading from the Court of the Gentiles to the Tower, and was then taken to the prison in the tower.

1. From *Jerusalem* he began his journey, as a prisoner. The immediate cause of his departure from the city was the information received by the Roman officer in charge of the Tower of Antonia, that a band of Jews had formed a plan to slay Paul. That night he was sent, under a strong escort, out of the reach of his enemies.

2. The guard paused at *Antipatris* (Acts 23:31, 32), beyond which the soldiers were not needed, so they were sent back, and Paul journeyed the rest of the way under an escort of cavalry. Antipatris was built by Herod the

Great, and named for his father, Antipater. It was 26 miles southeast of Cæsarea, on the direct road from Jerusalem, and 16 miles northeast of Joppa. Its location is not identified with certainty, but is probably to be found at a ruin known as *Ras el 'Ain*.

3. The apostle was taken to *Cæsarea* (Acts 23:33), where he was remanded to prison. Here he remained for more than two years, was tried by Felix, and made his memorable defense before the younger Herod Agrippa. (Acts 24–26.) Having appealed, as a Roman citizen, to the supreme court of the emperor at Rome, he was sent on shipboard for the voyage with a company of prisoners, and a guard commanded by the centurion Julius. Luke and Aristarchus were with Paul on the vessel. (Acts 27:1, 2.)

4. The day after starting from Cæsarea, the vessel touched at *Zidon*, and Paul was permitted to go on shore with the soldier to whom he was chained. (Acts 27:3.) Zidon was one of the most ancient towns in history, and the mother city of Tyre, which was 20 miles south of it. It lay in the limits of the tribe of Asher, but was never possessed by Israel. Its commerce was extensive, but early superseded by that of Tyre. It was a battle ground more than once during the Crusades, and changed masters frequently. Its site is now occupied by a small fishing village, called *Saida*.

5. The wind being unfavorable, the vessel was carried to the north of Cyprus, and sailed over waters traversed by Paul more than once, in the northeastern corner of the Mediterranean, past his church home at Antioch, and his birthplace, Tarsus, to the harbor of *Myra*, a city in the province of Lycia, in Asia Minor. (Acts 27:4–6.) This city stood at the entrance to a gorge in Mount Taurus, two miles from the sea. Its port, where Paul landed to be transferred to another vessel, was called Andriadice. It is now in ruins.

6. The next station was to have been Cnidus, 100 miles from Myra, on the coast of Caria; but the vessel only reached it with difficulty, and was unable to enter, on account of contrary winds: so the prow was turned southward toward the island of *Crete*. This lies at the entrance to the Ægean Sea, and is 140 miles long by 35 wide. They rounded Cape Salmone, at the eastern point of the island, and anchored for a time at a place then known, and still known, as *Fair Havens*, on the southern coast, about midway between the two extremes of the island. Here they were delayed for some time, and Paul urged the centurion to remain during the winter, and escape impending dangers. But it was resolved to follow along the shore still further westward, to the more commodious harbor of Phenice. But in this they were disappointed; for they were driven out to sea, and to the final result predicted by the apostle. (Acts 27:7–13.)

7. Soon after leaving Fair Havens, the storm set in. It was of the kind then called Euroclydon (Revised Version, Euro-aquilo, "east-northeaster"), now known as "a Levanter." They were able to run under the lee of

the little island of Clauda, 23 miles from Fair Havens, where they strengthened the vessel for the gale by "frapping," or winding ropes around the hull. Thence for fourteen days and nights they were driven before the wind in a westward direction, until hope perished in every heart save Paul's. They were driven 476 miles, upon the island of *Melita*, which is 62 miles south of Sicily, and is 17 miles long by 8 or 9 wide. It is of irregular oval shape, and its coast is indented by many bays. The one in which the apostle was shipwrecked is on the northeastern side of the island, and is known as St. Paul's Bay. A close investigation of the locality, its surroundings, and the soundings of the sea approaching it, show the remarkable accuracy of Luke's statements. The island is now known as *Malta*, and is under British

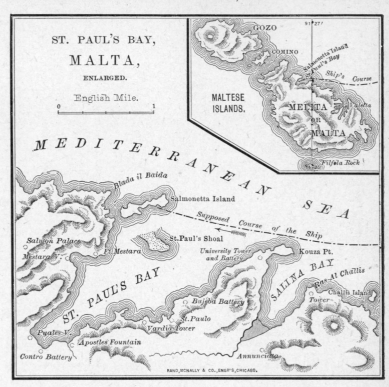

rule. Some years ago an ancient inscription was found on the island, giving to its ruler the same title, *protos*, "first or chief man" (Acts 28:7), given by Luke.

8. After wintering in the island of Melita, Paul and the other prisoners were placed on board an Alexandrian ship which was bound toward Rome. The first stopping place in this part of the voyage was at the historic city of *Syracuse*, on the eastern shore of Sicily. (Acts 28:12.) Here they paused for three days, and then continued their voyage.

9. The next station was at *Rhegium*, where they lay, awaiting a favorable wind, for one day. (Acts 28:13.) This is at the "toe" of the Italian boot, opposite Sicily, from which it is separated by a strait, only 6 miles wide. It is now a flourishing town, called *Rheggio*.

10. The vessel ended its voyage, and Paul and his fellow-prisoners disembarked, at *Puteoli*, near Naples. This was one of the leading ports of Italy, being to Rome what Liverpool is to London. Here Paul found a Christian church, and was permitted to remain for a

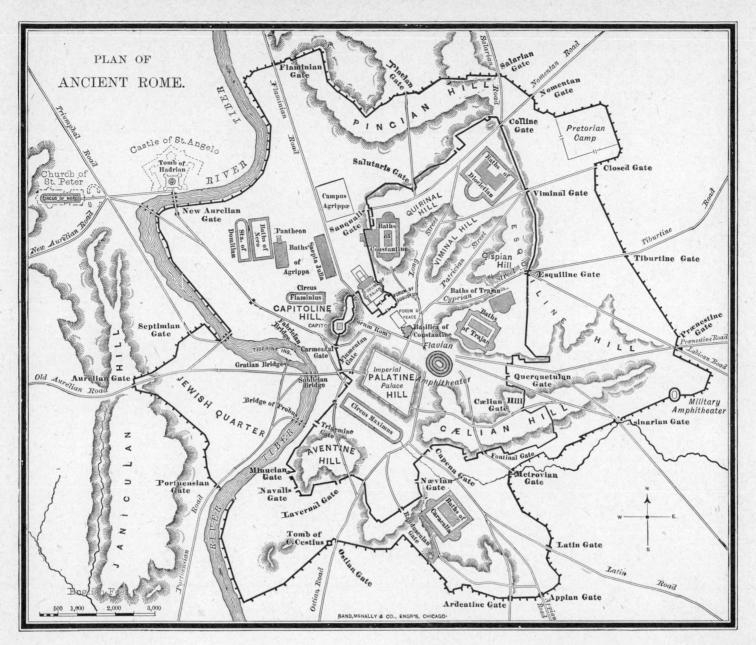

week before going onward to the capital, 141 miles distant. The city is now called *Pozzuoli*.

11. At a place called *Appii Forum*, "the forum of Appius," a village on the Appian Way, 43 miles from Rome, and again at the "Three Taverns," 10 miles nearer, Paul was met by some Christians, who had heard of his coming, and came to give him a welcome, which rejoiced his heart.

12. At last great ROME was reached, and the apostle was at the end of his long journey. For two years he dwelt as a prisoner at large, chained to a Roman soldier, but in "his own hired house." At this point ends all that is positively known of the journeys of the apostle.

The city of Rome stands on the river Tiber. In the period of its greatness it occupied ten hills, with the valleys between them, and a plain near the river. The apostle lived near the Pretorian Camp, on the northeastern border of the city, and at the opposite end of the city from the Jewish quarter, which was on the west of the Tiber. At the time of Paul's imprisonment, Rome contained about 1,200,000 inhabitants. One-half of the population were slaves, and two-thirds of the rest were paupers, supported in idleness by the free distribution of food. During the two years of Paul's imprisonment he wrote at least four Epistles — Ephesians, Philippians, Colossians, and Philemon. After about two years of imprisonment, Paul was released and spent two or more years at liberty.

OUTLINE FOR REVIEW.

1. Jerusalem. 2. Antipatris. 3. Cæsarea. 4. Zidon. 5. Myra. 6. Crete. (Fair Havens.) 7. Melita. 8. Syracuse. 9. Rhegium. 10. Puteoli. 11. Appii Forum and Three Taverns. 12. Rome.

THE LAST JOURNEYS OF PAUL.

The definite history of the apostle Paul ends with the last verse of the Acts of the Apostles; but, from the later Epistles and the dim light of early tradition, we may gather a few facts, and perhaps can indicate a few more journeys. From Philippians and Philemon,

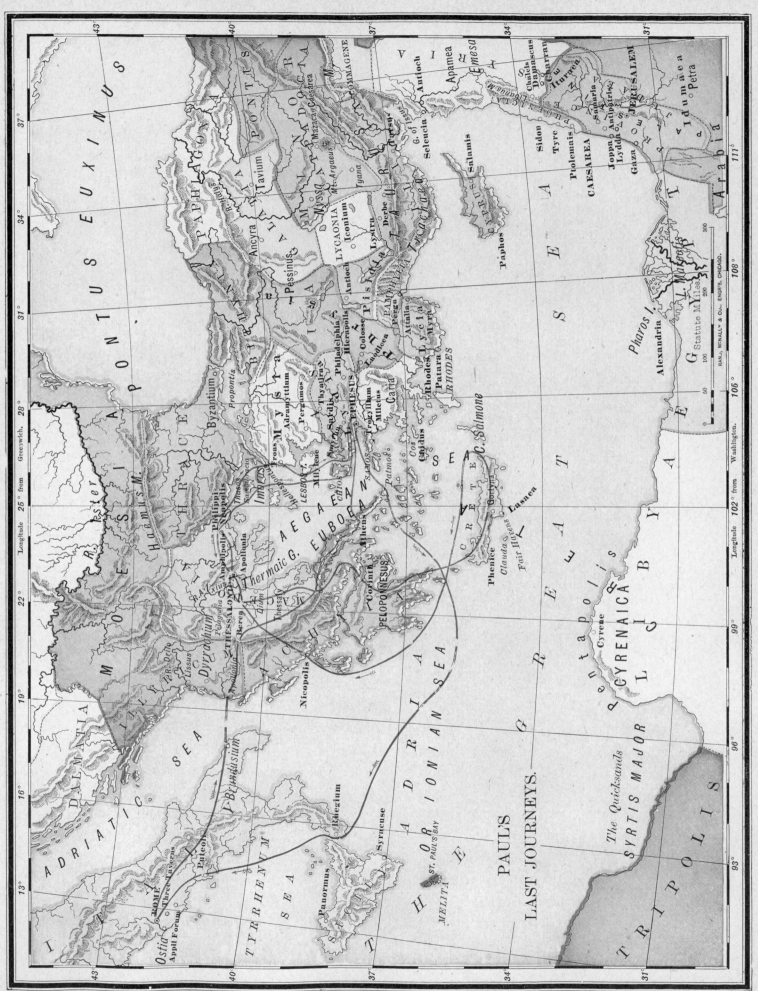

PAUL'S LAST JOURNEYS.

it is clear that Paul expected an acquittal and release; from 1 Timothy and Titus, it is evident, that after his imprisonment there were two years, perhaps more, of liberty. Combining the allusions in the Epistles, we offer a conjectural outline of the apostle's journeys during that year, following mainly the order of Canon Farrar.

1. Near the close of his imprisonment he expressed an expectation of speedily visiting the churches of Proconsular Asia, especially that at *Colosse* (Philem. 1:22), and desired a lodging to be prepared for him at the house of Philemon. We may take for granted that this purpose was accomplished, and that *Ephesus*, as well as Colosse, was visited at this time. Ephesus has been already described. (See page 125.) Colosse, called also Colassæ, was a city on the Lycus, near Hierapolis and Laodicea, and on the great caravan road from Ephesus to the Euphrates. At one time it was a large and flourishing place, but declined as other cities gained its Eastern trade. Paul had never before visited this city, and its church had been founded by Epaphras. Yet Paul was well acquainted with several of its members, and addressed to it, during his imprisonment, the Epistle to the Colossians; and to one of its members the Epistle to Philemon. The site of the ancient city is near the modern village of *Chonas*.

2. Just before his release, Paul dispatched Timothy to Philippi, expecting soon to follow him. (Phil. 2:19–24.) Timothy fulfilled his mission, and came to Ephesus, where Paul left him in charge of the church, and himself went to *Macedonia*. (1 Tim. 1:3.) Here he doubtless visited the churches which he had planted in Philippi, Thessalonica and Berea, and probably journeyed as far south as Corinth.

3. We judge that to this time belongs his visit to *Crete*. (Titus 1:5.) He had touched at this island during his voyage to Rome, and may have gone on shore at Fair Havens; but now he organized the church, and left it under the care of Titus, who had accompanied him to the island.

4. We find that after this Paul was at *Nicopolis*, a place not previously mentioned in his history. (Titus 3:12.) There were no less than ten cities of this name in the ancient world; but it must have been one of three among them: Nicopolis of Thrace, of Cilicia, or of Epirus. The latter has been generally accepted as the one where Paul "determined to winter." It was in the Roman province of Achaia, near the Adriatic Sea and the Ionian Isles; and was built by Augustus to commemorate his victory at Actium. The place is now called *Paleo-prevesa*, "old Prevesa," and contains extensive ruins, among which is a building said to have been Paul's place of prayer. Some think that Paul was arrested here before his final imprisonment; but there is no certainty concerning it.

5. *Troas.* (2 Tim. 4:13.) It is evident that Paul passed through this place, and stopped with a certain person named Carpus, where he left his mantle for winter wear, and some manuscripts. Farrar is of the opinion that he was here arrested, and in such haste that he could not obtain these articles. He may have come from Nicopolis by way of Macedonia, passing through Philippi, and sailing across the Ægean Sea.

6. An allusion in 2 Tim. 4:20 hints at another place visited by the apostle, perhaps as a prisoner. If arrested at Troas, he would probably be sent to *Ephesus*, the residence of the proconsul, for trial. And at Miletus, near that city, we find that he left his companion, Trophimus, who had been with him at the time of his former arrest in Jerusalem. It is a slight confirmation of this view, that there is among the ruins of Ephesus a place pointed out as the prison of Paul.

7. From Ephesus he may have set sail once more as a prisoner for *Rome*. He was accompanied by several friends, as Titus, who had left Crete once more to follow him; Luke the physician, his companion to the last; and Tychicus. We know nothing concerning the voyage, and therefore represent it on the map by the most direct route from Ephesus. At Rome we know only that his imprisonment was short; that his friends were few, for the church had been scattered by the terrible persecution of Nero; that Paul was left alone at his first hearing, his friends having gone in various directions, some on errands of duty, and others in fear of the world; that he wrote earnestly to Timothy to come, bringing Mark with him (2 Tim. 4:9, 11); and we infer from his own expectations and the tradition of the church, that his martyrdom was not long delayed.

The traditional place of his execution is shown at Aquæ Salvæ, now *Tre Fontane*, three miles from Rome, near the road to Ostia.

OUTLINE FOR REVIEW.

1. Colosse and Ephesus. 2. Macedonia. (Philippi, Thessalonica, Berea, Corinth.) 3. Crete. 4. Nicopolis. 5. Troas. (Arrest?) 6. Ephesus. 7. Rome. (Martyrdom.)

THE

ISLES OF GREECE

AND THE

SEVEN CHURCHES.

Scale of Statute Miles.

EXPLANATIONS.

Seven Churches in
Asia . . . . . **PERGAMOS**
Other New Testament
Places . . . . . . APOLLONIA

THE ISLES OF GREECE AND THE SEVEN CHURCHES.

I. As THE islands of the Ægean Sea are often referred to in the Acts, especially in the account of Paul's voyage to Phœnicia, in his third missionary journey, we present a map representing them upon a larger scale, with those portions of Asia and Europe adjoining them. Such of the islands as are mentioned in the history have been already described. One of the smallest is brought to our notice in the book of Revelation, **Patmos,** to which the apostle John was banished. This lies 20 miles south of the island of Samos, 24 miles west of Asia Minor, and about 70 miles southwest of Ephesus. It is about 20 miles in circumference, and is rocky and barren. Its loneliness and seclusion made it a suitable place for the banishment of criminals; and to it the apostle John was banished by the emperor Domitian, near the close of the first Christian century: though some scholars give an earlier date, under the emperor Nero. A narrow isthmus divides the island into two parts, north and south. On a hill in the southern part is a monastery named after the apostle John, and near it is the cave where it is said by tradition that he received the vision of the Apocalypse. In the Middle Ages the island was called Patmosa, and it is now known as *Patmo.*

II. The term **Asia** was used by the ancients in varied extent of meaning. 1. Its earliest use in Homer refers only to a meadow near Troy (Troas), which was called the "Asian meadow." 2. The lands of Mysia, Lydia, Caria, and a part of Phrygia, were known as Proconsular Asia, as they formed the province of Asia under the Roman government. This was originally the dominion of the last king of Pergamos, whose title was "king of Asia"; and was by him bequeathed to the Romans. 3. Asia Minor, as a whole, was sometimes called by the name Asia, though not often. 4. The entire Asiatic continent was known by this name in ancient times; but this use of the word is not found in Scripture.

III. **The Seven Churches of Asia** were all located in Proconsular Asia, in the immediate neighborhood of Ephesus. There were other churches besides these, as

Hierapolis and Colosse, both near Laodicea, and referred to in the Pauline Epistles; but these are named as the most important, and a group of seven is the arrangement most frequently found in the Bible, especially in its symbolical writings. To these Seven Churches were sent the messages in the opening chapters of the Revelation.

1. *Ephesus* (Rev. 2:1) was the most important city of the district, its church was the largest, and it was the first addressed. (A description and plan of this city may be found on page 125.)

LAODICEA FROM HIERAPOLIS.

2. *Smyrna* (Rev. 2:8) is north of Ephesus, about 40 miles in a direct line, though longer by the route of travel. It is on the Ægean Sea, at the head of the Hermæan Gulf, at the foot of Mount Pagus. The earliest city was built B. C. 1500, by the Greeks, and destroyed and rebuilt several times. From the time of Alexander the Great, who was one of its builders, it became an important city. Its earliest mention in Christian history is in the Revelation. Polycarp, a pupil of John, was martyred here A. D. 155. His grave is still shown on a hill near the city. Despite fires, earthquakes and wars, it has retained its importance, and is now the largest city on the Asiatic side of the Ægean Sea, having a population of nearly 200,000 people. The modern city is about two miles from the ancient site.

3. *Pergamos* (Rev. 2:12), more properly Pergamum,

was 60 miles northeast of Smyrna, in the district of Mysia, 3 miles north of the little river Caicus, and 20 miles from the Ægean Sea. It was the capital of a small but wealthy kingdom, which arose in the breaking up of Alexander's empire. It was celebrated for its large library, which at one time contained 200,000 manuscripts, but was by Mark Antony presented to Cleopatra, and removed to Alexandria. The city was devoted to the worship of Æsculapius, the patron divin-

ISLE
OF
PATMOS.

ity of medicine; and was, like most idolatrous places, corrupt in its morals. It is now a city of 25,000 inhabitants, called *Pergama*.

4. *Thyatira* (Rev. 2:18) was a city in the province of Lydia, on the road from Pergamos to Sardis. It was founded by Alexander the Great, who planted it with people from Macedonia, which may account for the fact that "Lydia of Thyatira" was found by Paul at Philippi, in Macedonia. It was a prosperous manufact-

uring town, but never a great city, and its scarlet cloth still has a reputation throughout the Orient. It is now a place with a population of from 17,000 to 20,000, and is called *ak Hissar*, "white castle."

5. *Sardis* (Rev. 3:1) lay 30 miles south of Thyatira, between the river Hermus and Mount Tmolus. It was the capital of Crœsus, the wealthy king of Lydia, whose empire was overthrown by Cyrus the Great. After the time of Alexander it belonged to the kingdom of Pergamos, until its absorption into the Roman empire. It was a place of extensive commerce, which led to prosperity, and the worldliness of the Christian church, rebuked in the message of the Revelation. It is now a miasmatic region, with scarcely an inhabitant, and bears the name *Sert Kalessi*.

6. *Philadelphia* (Rev. 3:7) was about 25 miles southeast of Sardis, on the river Cogamus, a branch of the Hermus. It was built and named by Attalus Philadelphus, king of Pergamos, and was the centre of a rich farming region, which has kept it inhabited through all the vicissitudes of the centuries. It was destroyed by an earthquake A. D. 17, but rebuilt. Its population is now about 10,000, and its modern name is *Allah Shehr*, "city of God."

7. *Laodicea* (Rev. 3:14) was the capital of Phrygia, and was 50 or 60 miles from Philadelphia, according to route. It was on the bank of the Lycus, near Hierapolis and Colosse. Its ancient name was Diospolis, but was changed by the Syrian king, Seleucus II., in honor of his wife, Laodice. In A. D. 62 it was destroyed by an earthquake; but its people were sufficiently rich to decline the aid of the Romans in rebuilding their city. Its worldly prosperity was reflected in its church, which received the sharpest rebukes of the Revelator. The Mohammedans destroyed the city, which is now a mass of ruins, surrounding a village called *Eski-hissar*.

It will be noticed, that, in the order of the Revelation, the Seven Churches are arranged in a circuit, as one would find them, starting from Ephesus, and traveling north to Smyrna and Pergamus, then southeast to Thyatira, Sardis and Philadelphia, until the southern and eastern limit is reached at Laodicea.

OUTLINE FOR REVIEW.

I. Let the teacher draw the outlines of the coast of both Europe and Asia, and call attention to the lands as already noticed under other maps. Then locate and name the principal *Islands*, especially those referred to in Paul's voyage to Palestine (map on page 122), and *Patmos*.

II. Explain the four meanings of the name Asia, as used by the ancients.

III. Locate and name the *Seven Churches*, as given in Revelation. *Ephesus, Smyrna, Pergamos, Thyatira, Sardis, Philadelphia, Laodicea.*

THE TABERNACLE.

I. **Its Origin.** The Tabernacle was the tent in which the emblems for divine worship were kept from the time of Moses to that of Solomon, 400 years. It represented the idea of God dwelling among his people, in the centre of the camp of Israel. The earliest institution for worship was the Altar, built wherever the patriarchs pitched their tents. Next we find a place consecrated and kept for the house of God, as Jacob's pillar at Bethel, to which the patriarch returned as to a sanctuary in after years. The Tabernacle arose when Israel was no longer a family, but a nation, needing a centralizing power and a system of worship as the uniting element among the tribes. It was erected under the direction of Moses, by divine command, while the Israelites were encamped at Mount Sinai.

II. **Its History.** During all the journeys of the Israelites through the wilderness, the Tabernacle stood in the centre of their camp, or, while on the march, was taken apart and carried by the Levites. At the time of the conquest, it remained at Gilgal, the fortified camp of Israel, near Jericho. After the war it was established at Shiloh, in the tribe of Ephraim, where it continued until the great defeat of Israel at Ebenezer (1

THE TABERNACLE, ACCORDING TO FERGUSSON.

Sam. 4 : 1–11), when the ark was taken, and probably Shiloh was ravaged. The Tabernacle was removed to Nob, in the tribe of Benjamin, where it remained until Saul's slaughter of the priests. (1 Sam. 21:1–6; 22: 18, 19.) It seems to have been at Gibeon, while the ark was in seclusion at Kirjath-jearim. (2 Chron. 1:4.) There is no mention of the Tabernacle after the building of the Temple; but a Jewish tradition is that its curtains were rolled up and laid away in one of the rooms connected with the Temple.

III. **The Departments of the Tabernacle.** This will require us to notice : 1. The Court. 2. The Altar. 3. The Laver. 4. The Tent. 5. The Holy Place. 6. The Holy of Holies. The dimensions of these are given in cubits ; and, as the authorities differ as to the length of the cubit, we will consider it here as being about a foot and a half, or 18 inches, the length generally given.

1. *The Court* was 150 feet long by 75 wide. It was separated from the camp by a curtain of fine linen, supported by 60 pillars, of which 20 were on each side, and 10 on each end. The pillars were probably of wood covered with brass. (There is strong reason for believing that the word "brass" in the Old Testament refers to copper.) They were fastened together by cords, and rested upon bases of brass, which were fastened to the ground, perhaps by spikes from the bottom. Each pillar was 7½ feet (5 cubits) high, and was covered with a silver cap. The curtain was made of linen, in sections, extending from pillar to pillar, a distance of about 8 feet, and was fastened to the pillars by hooks of silver. The entrance was on the end toward the east, 30 feet wide, and consisted of an embroidered hanging, which could be raised or lowered at pleasure. None but the priests and Levites were allowed within the court ; and the worshipers presented their offerings without at the entrance. (Review. 1. Dimensions. 2. Pillars. 3. Curtain. 4. Entrance. 5. Priests.

2. *The Altar* stood within the court, in front of the entrance, in the most prominent situation of the camp, and was the largest article of the tabernacle furniture. It was a plain structure, 7½ feet square and 4½ feet high, hollow within, and made of acacia wood, to avoid excessive weight; but covered with plates of brass, as it was exposed to the fire. Upon each corner projected a horn from the top, upon which the blood of the victim was sometimes sprinkled, and to which suppliants sometimes fled. Around the altar, midway between the top and bottom, was a "compass" (Exod. 27:5), or ledge, upon which the priest stood while sacrificing. There is mention also of "a grate" (Exod. 27:4), which was formerly supposed to have been placed inside the altar, so that the fire might be built upon it, and the ashes fall through it; but this is now by the best scholars considered to have been upright, and under the "compass," and not a grate, but a lattice-work of brass, surrounding the altar. It is believed that at each encampment the altar was filled with earth, and that upon this the fire was kindled, according to Exod. 20:24, 25. At each corner was a brass ring, and through the pair of rings on

each side a rod was passed, by which the altar was carried from place to place during the marches of Israel. The fire upon the altar was kindled miraculously (Lev. 9:24), and was never suffered to go out, but was kept alive even on the march by live coals in a vessel. Twice each day the high-priest offered the general sacrifice for the people, besides the individual offerings of worshipers. In officiating, the priest approached the altar by an ascent of earth, as steps were forbidden (Exod. 20:26), and he stood upon either the north or south side, as the ashes were thrown out on the east side. (Lev. 1:16.) The utensils of the altar were five, all of brass. 1. *Pans*, used to convey the ashes outside the camp. (Lev. 6:10, 11.) 2. *Shovels*, for taking off coals of fire to put in the censers. 3. *Basins*, for receiving and carrying the blood of offerings. 4. *Flesh-hooks*, for placing the sacrifice on the fire. 5. *Fire-pans*, for carrying the fire while on the march. (Note for Review. 1. Situation. 2. Dimensions. 3. Horns. 4. Compass. 5. Grate. 6. Earth contents. 7. Rings. 8. Fire. 9. Sacrifices. 10. Approach. 11. Utensils.)

3. *The Laver* is less minutely described than the altar. It was a large tank for holding water, an abundance of which was needed in the sacrifices, and was made out of the metallic "looking-glasses" of the women who worshiped at

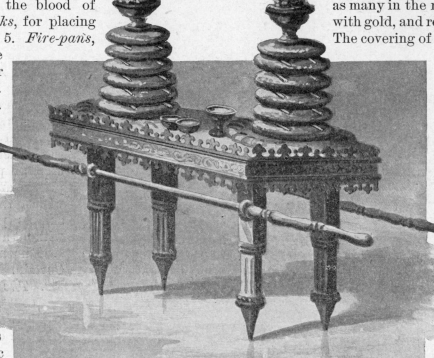

THE TABLE OF SHEW-BREAD.

the Tabernacle. (Exod. 38:8.) It stood at the door of the Tabernacle, and west of the altar. (Exod. 30:18.) With it is mentioned "its foot," which was probably a lower basin, into which the water ran from above, made to prevent the earth around from becoming saturated with water. Its size and form are not stated in the account. (Review. 1. Purpose. 2. Material. 3. Place. 4. Foot.)

4. *The Tent.* This was the Tabernacle proper, to which the court was the adjunct. It stood as the representation of God's house, wherein he dwelt in the midst of his own chosen people. It was 15 feet wide and high, and 45 feet long, divided into two rooms by a curtain, or vail. Though many details are given, yet it is not possible to give certain conclusions either concerning its plan of construction, or even its general appearance. For example: some authorities conclude that the curtained roof was flat, or even sagging downward in the middle, while others are sure that it was pointed, by means of a ridge-pole, as represented in our engraving. We consider neither as certain, but incline to the latter

opinion. The walls and rear end of the tent were made of upright boards, covered with gold, each 15 feet high, and 2 feet 3 inches wide; of which there were 20 boards on each side, and 10 in the rear, while the front was open. Upon each board were rings of gold, so arranged that, when the walls were erected, the rings were in three rows, and through them long poles were passed to hold the structure together. Each board was furnished at its lower end with two tenons, which fitted into mortises in bases of solid silver, each weighing nearly 100 pounds. These bases stood side by side, forming a firm and continuous foundation, and protecting the lower ends of the boards from decay. The roof of the tent was supported by pillars, of which there seem to have been five in the front (Exod. 36:38), and probably as many in the rear. These were covered with gold, and rested upon bases of brass. The covering of the Tabernacle consisted of four curtains, one over another. 1. A covering called the "tabernacle cloth," of linen, woven in various colors, and embroidered with figures of cherubim. 2. Over this was stretched a covering of cloth made from goat's hair, larger than the other, and therefore extending beyond it. 3. Next came a covering of "rams' skins dyed red." 4. Over all was spread a covering skin, called in the Hebrew, *tachash*, translated "badgers' skins," but supposed by many to mean *seal skin*, taken from animals found in the Red Sea, and intended to preserve the roof from the effects of the weather. The front, on the eastern end, was protected by a hanging of fine linen, embroidered in blue, purple and scarlet, and resting upon the five pillars named above. (Review. 1. Purpose. 2. Dimensions. 3. Form. 4. Walls. 5. Rings. 6. Bases. 7. Pillars. 8. Coverings. 9. Front.)

5. *The Holy Place.* This was the larger of the two rooms, and was separated from the smaller room within by the *Vail*, which was an embroidered curtain hanging upon four pillars. Its dimensions were 15 feet in width and 30 feet in length, with walls 15 feet high. There is no mention of a floor, and probably there was none. It contained three articles of furniture. On the right of a person entering, midway between the two ends of the room, stood the *Table*, made of shittim wood (acacia), covered with gold; it was 3 feet long, a foot and a half wide, 2 feet 3 inches high, and surrounded with a "crown," or ornamental band, of gold. On the corners were rings, through which rods were passed, to carry it

from place to place. On this table were kept 12 loaves of unleavened bread, which were renewed every Sabbath. On the left, opposite to the table, was the *Lampstand*, generally called the Candlestick, but incorrectly, as it contained lamps, not candles. This was a tree of gold, probably 40 inches high, having three branches on each side of the central trunk, so arranged that the seven summits, each holding a lamp, stood in a horizontal line. It is uncertain whether the lamps were kept burning at all times, or only during the night. Directly in front of the vail, at the western end of the Holy Place, stood the *Altar of Incense*. This was of acacia wood, overlaid with gold, whence it was frequently called "the golden altar." It was a foot and a half square, and three feet high. It had horns on its corners, and rings for carrying, and an opening in the top, wherein was placed daily a censer full of incense, which was lighted by live coals from the altar of burnt offering in the court. The lighting of the incense with common fire was the crime for which the two elder sons of Aaron "died before the Lord." (Lev.

THE BRAZEN ALTAR.

10:1, 2.) Into the Holy Place the priests entered daily, to trim and refill the lamps, and offer the incense. (Review. 1. Vail. 2. Dimensions. 3. Table. 4. Lampstand. 5. Altar of Incense. 6. Daily uses.)

6. *The Holy of Holies.* This was the inner room, at the western end of the building, entered only on one day in the year, the Day of Atonement, and only by the high priest. Its dimensions were those of a cube, 15 feet in breadth, length and height. It contained the most sacred *Ark of the Covenant*, which was a chest, the receptacle for the stone tables of the Law, given by the Lord to Moses. It was of shittim or acacia wood, covered without and within with gold, 3 feet 9 inches long, by 2 feet 3 inches wide and deep; furnished on the side with rings, that it might be carried. The lid was made of gold, and was called *the propitiatory*,—in our version, "mercy seat." Upon it stood golden figures of the cherubim, and between them was believed to dwell the cloud which denoted God's presence. (Review. 1. Uses. 2. Dimensions. 3. Ark.)

OUTLINE FOR TEACHING AND REVIEW

1. Draw upon the blackboard a diagram representing the ground-plan of the Court of the Tabernacle, and, within it, the Tabernacle itself. Tell the class its origin and history.

2. Locate upon the diagram each of the parts referred to, and describe them, following the outline given at the end of each paragraph.

3. Review the facts given, frequently during the lesson, and finally at the close.

THE BRAZEN ALTAR, ACCORDING TO MEYER.

THE TEMPLE IN THE TIME OF CHRIST (HEROD'S).

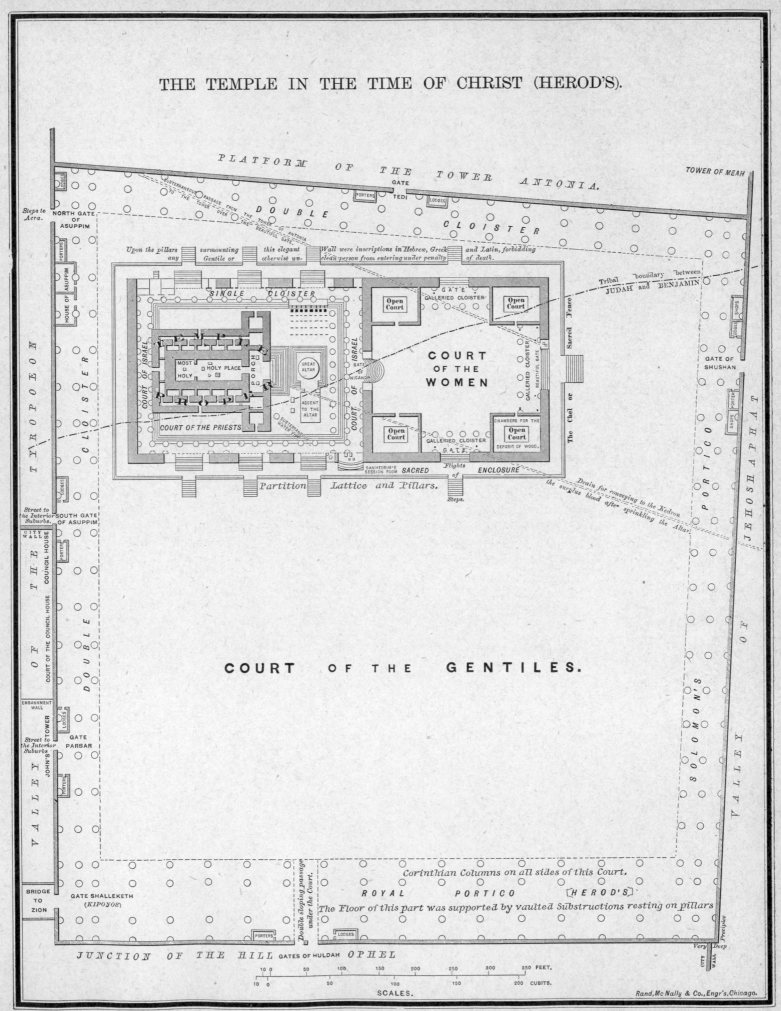

THE TEMPLE.

THE Temple was the centre of Jewish thought, not only in Palestine, but also throughout the world. Even when it lay in ruins, Daniel, in the land of captivity, opened his window toward its site when he prayed; and the front of every synagogue looked toward it. It stood on Mount Moriah, which was originally outside the wall of the city, east of Mount Zion. In order to give room for all its courts, the surface of the hill was increased by building out from its sides on successive platforms, supported by immense substructions of brick and stone, so that the entire mountain is honeycombed with artificial caves.

There were three successive Temples.

1. *Solomon's Temple* dedicated about 950 B. C. The accounts of this building are so meager, and the text is so uncertain, that it is impossible to construct its plan with any satisfaction. A conjectural ground plan is given on page 71. This temple stood until 587 B. C., when it was destroyed by Nebuchadnezzar. 2. After a period of desolation of 50 years, *Zerubbabel's Temple* was begun, 536 B. C., and finished 20 years after. Still less is known of its architecture; but it was probably on the same general plan as Solomon's, though less magnificent. It passed through many sieges, was desecrated by enemies, and reconsecrated by the Jews, but stood until 30 years before the birth of Christ. 3. *Herod's Temple* was a restoration, enlargement, and improvement upon Zerubbabel's. It was built by Herod the Great, in sections, taking down the old and building the new part by part, so that it occupied many years, and was not completed until after Herod's death, and less than ten years before its final destruction. This was the Temple standing in the time of Christ, and referred to in the allusions of

THE DOME OF THE ROCK.

the New Testament. It was destroyed by the Romans under Titus, A. D. 70, and was never rebuilt by the Jews, though its restoration was more than once attempted. Its site is now occupied by the Mohammedan "Dome of the Rock," often, but erroneously, called the Mosque of Omar.

The Temple of Herod is the one usually described in works on the subject. The authorities are: 1. The Scriptures, from which we gather references to this Temple, and analogies from the description of the Tabernacle, of which the Temple was an enlarged copy. 2. The description given by Josephus, which was written 20 years after its fall, and gives general impressions rather than accurate details. 3. The tract Middoth "measures," in the Talmud, which gives precise measurements, but not complete information. 4. The allusions in ancient Jewish literature, of more or less value and authority. 5. The results of recent explorations under the Temple area, which are very valuable. Different investigators have come to very different conclusions concerning the Temple and its courts. We present in this description those of Dr. James Strong, in McClintock & Strong's Cyclopedia, from which our diagram is taken, by permission. From the uncertainty of many dimensions, and especially the difference of opinion with regard to the length of the Jewish cubit, in which all the ancient measurements are given, most of our figures must be regarded as general estimates, rather than precise statements.

The Temple consisted of a building called "the House of God," surrounded by a number of open courts, the outer ones including the inner. On the north of it was the Tower of Antonia; east, Valley of the Kedron; south, Ophel; west, Valley of the Tyropœon; and beyond, Mount Zion.

I. **The Court of the Gentiles** was the largest, and the first entered by a visitor from without. It was so named because it was the only part of the building in which foreigners were allowed; hence not regarded as sacred by the Jews. Speaking roughly, it was an open square, of about 1,000 feet on each side; more precisely, a quadrangle, whose inside measurements were 990 feet on the north, 1,000 on the east, 910 on the south, 1,060 on the west. On two sides there was a covered corridor; Solomon's Porch on the east, Herod's Porch on the south. It was entered on the north, east and south, by a single gate in each wall : north, the Gate Tedi, a staircase leading up to the Tower Antonia, from which Paul made his speech to the Jewish mob (Acts 22); east, the Gate Shushan, directly opposite to the altar, and leading to the Valley of the Kedron; south, the Gate Huldah, a subterranean passage through the floor of the court,

fragment of this wall, with its inscription, was recently discovered in Jerusalem. Within this wall was a corridor 24 feet wide, containing an ascent of steps 8 feet high; and above them the inner wall, which was like that of a castle, very thick, from 40 to 60 feet high, and more than once used as a fortress by the Jews. Through both the outer lattice and the inner wall were nine gates, four each on the north and south; one on the east, opposite to the altar; but none on the west. Though most of the worshipers came from that side, the rear of the Temple stood toward it, and the front faced the east. The Chel, then, was a terrace of 24 feet, between two walls, an outer lattice and an inner castle. Paul was arrested under a false report of his having led Gentiles into this Sacred Enclosure. (Acts 21:28, 29.)

III. **The Court of the Women,** often called "The Treasury," occupied a square in the eastern end of the Sacred Enclosure. Passing through the thick wall, the Jewish visitor (for none other was allowed to enter) found himself in an open court, about 240 feet square,

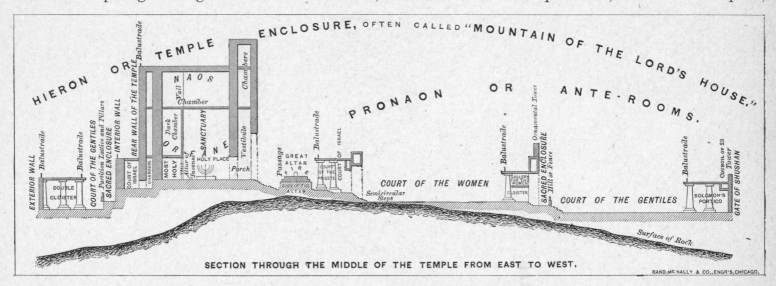

SECTION THROUGH THE MIDDLE OF THE TEMPLE FROM EAST TO WEST.

RAND, McNALLY & CO., ENGR'S, CHICAGO.

which was here much higher than the ground outside the wall; west, four gates : the southern, near the angle of the wall, the Gate Shalleketh, or Kiponos, opening to a bridge over the Tyropœon; next, Gate Parbar; then, the South Gate of Asuppim; and near the northern corner of the wall, the North Gate of Asuppim. On the floor of this court was a market for the sale of sacrificial meats, with "tables of the money changers"; twice broken up by Jesus in his ministry. (John 2:14–16; Matt. 21:12, 13.) [Notice, in this account : 1. Name. 2. Dimensions. 3. Porches. 4. Gates. 5. Market.]

II. **The Sacred Enclosure** was an elevated section in the northwestern part of the Court of the Gentiles, containing the sacred buildings. It was called by the Jews the *Chel* (pronounced *Kel*). It stood 8 feet higher than the level of the surrounding court; and its outside measurement was 630 feet on the north and south, by 300 east and west. Its outer wall was a lattice wrought in stone, called Soreg, "interwoven," 4½ feet high, containing inscriptions in many languages, warning all foreigners not to enter it, under penalty of death. A

surrounded by high walls, and 3 feet higher than the platform of the Chel. To this led four gates, or rather doors, in the middle of the wall on each side; that on the east, probably, being the Beautiful Gate (Acts 3:2), and that on the west the Gate of Nicanor, because the head of Nicanor, a Syrian enemy of the Jews, had once been hung upon it. In each corner of the court was a room, open overhead, 60 feet square. That in the southeast was used for the ceremonies of the Nazarite's vow, and was the one where Paul was seized by the Jews (Acts 21:26); in the northeast, for the preparation of wood for the altar; in the northwest, for the ceremonies of cleansing for lepers; in the southwest, for the storage of sacrificial oil. Between these rooms were galleried cloisters, of which the upper story was set apart for women, who were not allowed to penetrate further into the Temple, but from the gallery over the Gate of Nicanor could witness the sacrifices. Around the wall were fastened 13 treasure-chests, for gifts of the worshipers, from which came the name "Treasury." (Mark 12:41, 42; John 8:20.) Under the floor of this

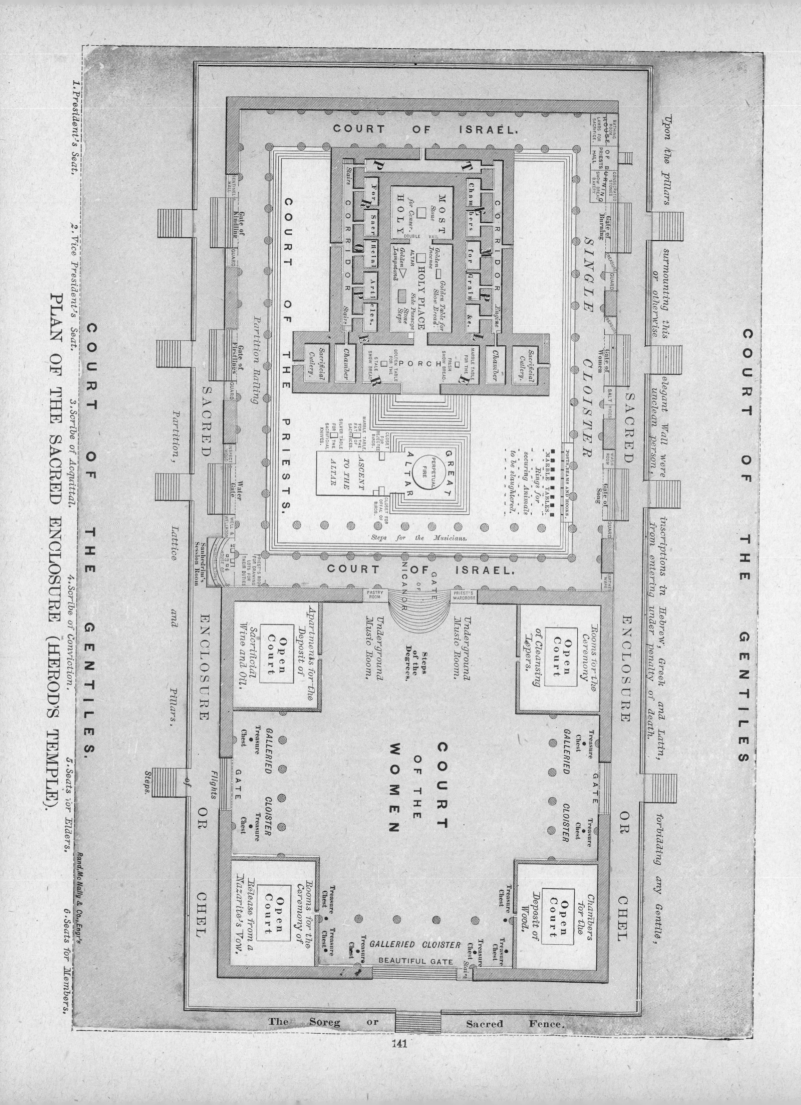

PLAN OF THE SACRED ENCLOSURE (HEROD'S TEMPLE).

1. President's Seat. 2. Vice President's Seat. 3. Scribe of Acquittal. 4. Scribe of Conviction. 5. Seats for Elders. 6. Seats for Members.

Rand, McNally & Co., Engr's

court was a subterranean passage from the Tower of Antonia, by which soldiers were sent to quell riots among the Jews, the opening being by the Gate Beautiful, over which was a guard-room. Through this passage the soldiers came who rescued Paul from the Jewish mob. (Acts 21:31, 32.) Under the steps leading up to the Gate Nicanor were two rooms in which musical instruments were stored for use at the festivals. [Review. 1. Names. 2. Dimensions. 3. Doors. 4. Rooms. 5. Galleries. 6. Treasure-chests. 7. Underground passage. 8. Music-rooms. 9. Scripture allusions.]

IV. **The Court of Israel,** or Court of the Men, occupied the western end of the Sacred Enclosure, and was a narrow corridor surrounding the Court of the Priests. It was 10 feet higher than the Court of the Women; 320 feet east and west, by 240 north and south. The width of the corridor on the north and south was 16 feet, and on the east and west 24 feet. It was the place where the men of Israel stood to view the sacrifices. On the outside of it rose the high inner wall of the Sacred Enclosure; on the inside, a low balustrade sufficed to separate it from the space set apart for the priests. Three gates led up to it on the north; as many on the south; and one, the Gate of Nicanor, on the east. In the wall on the north were chambers used severally for treasuries, guard, the storage of salt, the storage of hides and of earthenware. On the south, at its eastern corner, was the session-room of the Sanhedrim, called the Hall Gazith, and beyond it rooms in the wall for guard, storage, etc. In the Hall Gazith, the elders sat on seats of stone arranged in semicircular form. [Review. 1. Name. 2. Location. 3. Dimensions. 4. Purpose. 5. Walls. 6. Gates. 7. Rooms.]

V. **The Court of the Priests** was a raised platform within the Court of Israel, and standing 3 feet above it. It was about 275 feet long, by 200 feet wide. It was mainly occupied by the House of God, in front of which stood the great Altar of Burnt Offering, built upon the stone which now rises under the Dome of the Rock. The altar was a rude structure of rough stone, whitewashed, and 15 feet high. From its southwestern corner an underground drain passed beneath all the courts to the brook Kedron. Opposite, also, to the southwestern corner, was the Laver, supplying water for the services and washings. Around the altar were marble tables for various uses in the sacrifices, and in the pavement were rings for securing the animals to be slain. [Review. 1. Name. 2. Dimensions. 3. Altar. 4. Drain. 5. Laver. 6. Tables, rings, etc.]

VI. **The House of God,** or Temple Proper, occupied more than half the space in the Court of the Priests. Its floor was 8 feet above the level of the surrounding court; and it had four parts. 1. The Porch, or Vestibule, extended across the front: it was 120 feet high, and consisted of several stories. Its roof was steep, and covered with golden spikes to keep birds from settling upon and defiling it. It was built of marble, and richly ornamented. 2. The Chambers were on each side of the house, but separate from it, and not attached to its wall. They were three stories high, and entered from the north and south by winding stairs. Their use was to furnish homes for the priests during their two weeks of service each year. 3. The Holy Place was 30 feet wide and 60 feet long, double the dimensions of the same room in the Tabernacle. It was entered from the vestibule by double doors plated with gold; and both floor and ceiling were covered with gold. On the right side of one entering was the Table, on which 12 loaves of unleavened bread were kept standing; on the left was the Lamp-stand, generally called (but incorrectly) the Golden Candlestick, for it held seven lamps, not candles; and at its further end was the golden Altar of Incense, lighted each day by coals from the Altar of Burnt Offering. In this room Zacharias received the promise of the birth of John the Baptist. (Luke 1.) 4. The Holy of Holies was a cube, each dimension being 30 feet. It was separated from the Holy Place by a vail, said to be 8 inches thick (but probably consisting of two vails 8 inches apart), which was rent from top to bottom at the hour of the Saviour's death on the cross. (Mark 15:38.) In the first Temple this room contained the Ark of the Covenant; but in the second and third Temples the place of the lost ark was taken by a marble stone, upon which the high priest laid the censer on the Day of Atonement, the only day in the year when the Holy of Holies was entered. The Roman conqueror, Pompey, insisted upon entering it, expecting to see some object of worship, and perhaps treasure, but was surprised to find nothing within the vail. [Review. 1. Porch. 2. Chambers. 3. Holy Place and contents. 4. Holy of Holies.]

OUTLINE FOR TEACHING AND REVIEW.

I. Let the teacher relate the history of the Temple, with its three periods of building, under Solomon, Zerubbabel and Herod, and review the class on the names and events.

II. Draw the elevations of the several courts and buildings, showing how they successively rose one above another, and, as each is indicated, give its name, and its elevation above the preceding. 1. Court of Gentiles. 2. Sacred Enclosure, 8 feet elevation. 3. Court of Women, 3 feet higher. 4. Court of Israel, 10 feet. 5. Court of the Priests, 3 feet. 6. House of God, 8 feet.

III. Draw next the ground plan of the six departments as given, and describe each, following the order given in the description above. Frequently review the class upon the names, dimensions and facts.

IV. Number the Scripture references given in the description, write them on slips of paper, distribute to the class, and call for them in connection with the parts of the Temple to which they refer. At the close call upon the class to name the Scripture incidents connected with each department.

LESSONS IN THE GEOGRAPHY OF PALESTINE.

MORE than two-thirds of the events of Bible history are associated with the land of Palestine, and a knowledge of that country and its principal places is needed by every Sunday School scholar and Bible student. Any Superintendent who will take ten minutes of the Sun-

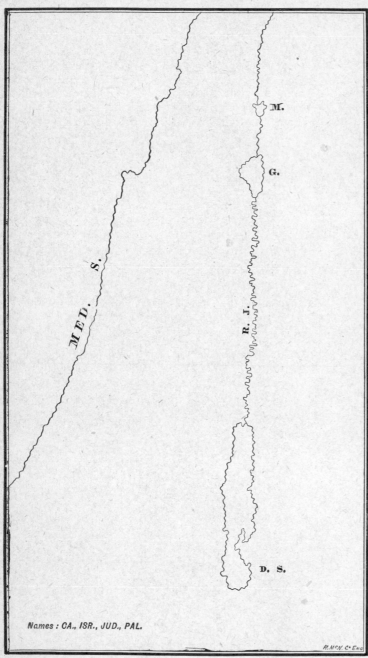

Names : CA., ISR., JUD., PAL.

LESSON I.

day School session for the purpose of teaching Bible Geography, can in less than three months give to his school a sufficient knowledge of Palestine for the general needs of Bible study. The requisites are : a blackboard; some crayons (of various colors, if possible to obtain

them); a clear idea on the part of the instructor of what he proposes to teach; precise statements of the things taught, in as few words as possible; giving nothing except the important facts which are to be remembered; and frequent reviews, from the beginning, of all the facts acquired. The lessons here given have been taught many times in Sunday Schools and children's classes at Assemblies, and are now published in the hope that they may be made generally useful.

LESSON I. LINES AND WATERS.

I. Draw in presence of the class, in white chalk, the **two lines,** one representing the Coast Line, the other, the Jordan Line. Notice that the cape on the Coast Line is one-third the distance from the top of the map; that the second of the three lakes is directly opposite to the cape; and that the distance between the second and third lakes is just six times that between the first and the second. The teacher may draw the lines in advance of the lesson, with a soapstone slate pencil, which will make a faint mark, not distinguishable at a distance, but seen by the teacher, and easily traced in presence of the class with white crayon. Let the class repeat the names of the two lines. 1. Coast Line. 2. Jordan Line.

II. Locate the different **Bodies of Water,** indicating their names by initial letters. 1. The Mediterranean Sea, on the west, called in the Bible "the Great Sea." 2. The river Jordan, flowing from north to south. 3. Lake Merom, on the north. 4. The Sea of Galilee. 5. The Dead Sea, into which the Jordan flows. Show the class that this sea lies so low, that, if a canal were cut to the Mediterranean, the ocean would run in, instead of the Dead Sea running out. Drill the class on : 1. Lines. 2. Bodies of Water.

LESSON II. NAMES AND DISTANCES.

Draw the same map as in Lesson I., but omit the lettering, and review the Lines and Waters.

I. State and drill upon the **Names** by which the land has been known in different times. 1. In the earliest ages it was called *Canaan*, because its best-known people were the Canaanites. 2. After the Israelites conquered it, it was known as the *Land of Israel*. 3. In the time of Christ it was generally called *Judæa*, because the Jews were its inhabitants. 4. Its name is now *Palestine*. [Write an initial or syllable of each name, and recall it from the class.]

II. Give the **Distances.** 1. Begin with the country best known, and state first the distance from America to Palestine, 7,800 miles. [Write on the board A. P. 7,800.]

2. The Coast Line, from a point opposite the source of the Jordan to a point opposite the lower end of the Dead Sea, 180 miles. [Write C. L. 180.] 3. The Jordan Line, from its source to the lower end of the Dead Sea, 160 miles. [J. L. 180.] 4. From the Jordan to the Mediterranean, on the north, 30 miles. [J. M. 30.] 5. From the Dead Sea, at its southern end, to the Mediterranean, 90 miles. [D. S. M. 90.] 6. The most northern

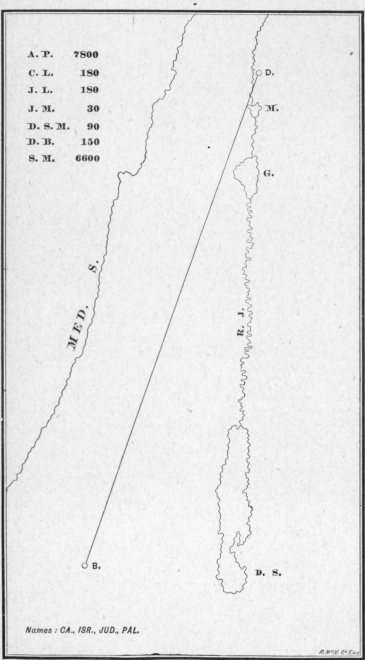

A. P.	7800
C. L.	180
J. L.	180
J. M.	30
D. S. M.	90
D. B.	150
S. M.	6600

Names: CA., ISR., JUD., PAL.

R. McN. C° Eng.

LESSON II.

town in Palestine was Dan [mark D. on the map]; the most southern was Beersheba [mark B.]. Hence, to show the extent of the land, they said "from Dan to Beersheba," which was 150 miles in a straight line. [Write D. B. 150.] 7. Palestine, between the Jordan and the sea, includes about 6,600 square miles, which is a little smaller than Massachusetts. [Write S. M. 6,600.] Review the facts already given from the beginning. 1. Lines. 2. Waters. 3. Distances.

LESSON III. NATURAL DIVISIONS.

Draw, as before, the outline of the map, and review all the facts already taught. 1. Lines. 2. Waters. 3. Names. 4. Distances. Test the memory of the class on these without giving the initials.

There are four Natural Divisions to Palestine; that is, four sections in the country, lying parallel with each other. Indicate them on the map in brown chalk, not making them very prominent.

1. We find the **Sea-Coast Plain** [S. C. P.] extending along the Coast from north to south, narrow at the north, and wider at the south.

2. Further inland, we come to the **Mountain Region** [M. R.], the backbone of the country, a section of hills and mountains, and the home of the Israelitish people.

3. Passing over the mountains, we find the **Jordan**

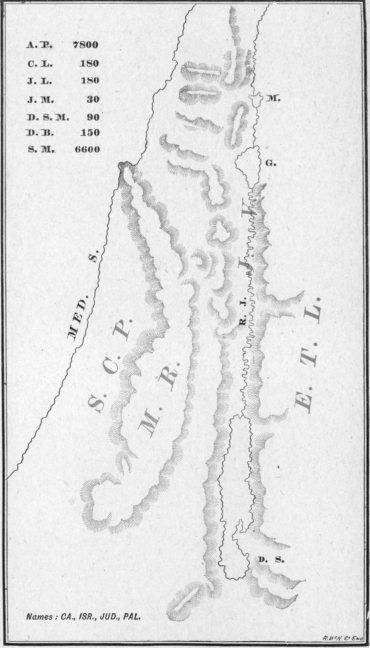

A. P.	7800
C. L.	180
J. L.	180
J. M.	30
D. S. M.	90
D. B.	150
S. M.	6600

Names: CA., ISR., JUD., PAL.

R. McN. C° Eng.

LESSON III.

Valley, a deep gorge, and deeper the further we travel southward, until, at the Dead Sea, it is more than 1,300 feet lower than the Mediterranean.

4. Still further eastward, we climb the steep mountains again, and reach the **Eastern Table-Land,** a lofty plain sloping gradually to the great desert beyond it.

Review, as before. 1. Lines. 2. Waters. 3. Names. 4. Distances. 5. Natural Divisions.

LESSON IV. MOUNTAINS.

Review, as usual, from the beginning, before commencing the advance lesson. The events of the Bible

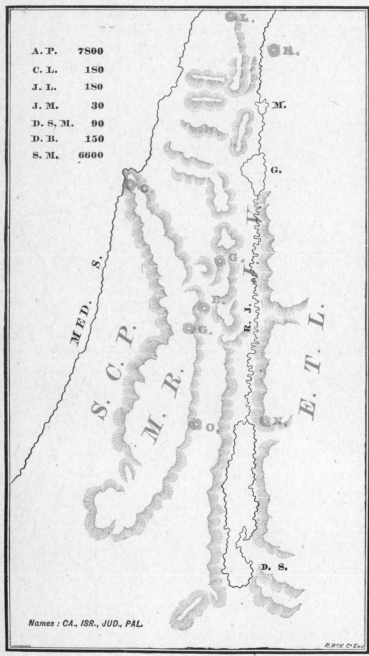

A. P.	7800
C. L.	180
J. L.	180
J. M.	30
D. S. M.	90
D. B.	150
S. M.	6600

Names : CA., ISR., JUD., PAL.

LESSON IV.

are often associated with **Mountains,** of which there are many in Palestine. We select eight of the most important, group them in pairs, and state with each the fact which gives it interest.

On the north of the country, near the source of the Jordan, we find two mountains, nearly opposite to each other. 1. *Mount Hermon,* on the east, the highest mountain in Palestine, and the place where the Saviour was transfigured. 2. *Mount Lebanon,* on the west, famous for its cedars.

Next, we find two mountains nearly in line with the Sea of Galilee, one directly west and the other southwest of it. 3. *Mount Carmel,* by the Mediterranean, where Elijah called down fire from heaven upon the altar. 4. *Mount Gilboa,* where King Saul fell in battle with the Philistines.

In the centre of the country we find two mountains, where Joshua read the law to the Israelites. 5. On the north, *Mount Ebal,* the mount of cursing. 6. On the south, *Mount Gerizim,* the mount of blessing.

In the south, directly in line with the northern end of the Dead Sea, are two mountains. 7. On the west, *Mount Olivet,* or the Mount of Olives, where Jesus ascended. 8. On the east, *Mount Nebo,* where Moses died.

With each of these mountains the event associated might be briefly related. At the close, review as before. 1. Lines. 2. Waters. 3. Names. 4. Distances. 5. Divisions. 6. Mountains. Be sure that the class can name the event with each mountain.

LESSON V. PLACES.

This lesson may well be divided into from two to four sections, according to the time which can be given to it. Draw the map, as usual, from the beginning; and, as each subject is presented upon it, review the pupils, until all their past lessons are clearly fixed in mind. 1. Lines. 2. Waters. 3. Names. 4. Distances. 5. Natural Divisions. 6. Mountains. See that with each mountain, as it is located, the event connected with it is named.

We have now to fix the most important **Places** in Palestine. We locate them by their arrangement in the Natural Divisions, and name an event for which each place is remembered.

I. **Places in the Sea-Coast Plain.** [These may constitute one lesson, if desired.] 1. *Gaza,* where Samson pulled down the idol temple upon the Philistines and himself. This lies on the Mediterranean, directly in line west of the middle point of the Dead Sea. 2. *Joppa,* the seaport of Palestine, from which the prophet Jonah started on his voyage. This lies nearly half way between Gaza and Mount Carmel. 3. *Cæsarea,* where Paul made his defense before King Agrippa, and was a prisoner for two years. This is a little more than half way between Joppa and Mount Carmel. 4. *Tyre,* the city which sent ships to all lands; a little further north of Mount Carmel than Cæsarea is south of it. As each place is named, locate it on the board, and mark it by an initial letter.

II. Another lesson may include the most important **Places in the Mountain Region.** 1. *Beersheba,* the home of Abraham; opposite the lower bay of the Dead

Sea. 2. *Hebron*, where the patriarchs were buried; opposite the middle of the Dead Sea, and in line with Gaza. 3. *Bethlehem*, where David and Jesus were born, 6 miles south of Jerusalem. 4. *Jerusalem*, the capital of Palestine, where David reigned, and where Jesus was crucified; directly in line with the northern end of the

the Sea of Galilee. 3. *Capernaum*, where Jesus lived during his ministry, and wrought many miracles; on the northwestern shore of the sea. 4. *Bethsaida*, where Jesus fed the five thousand with five loaves; on the north of the sea. 5. The last is at the source of the river Jordan, *Dan*, the most northerly town in Palestine.

IV. **Places in the Eastern Table-Land.** There are not many in this section, because few events of Bible history took place there. 1. *Machærus*, where John the Baptist was imprisoned and beheaded; opposite the northern part of the Dead Sea. 2. *Penuel*, on the brook Jab-

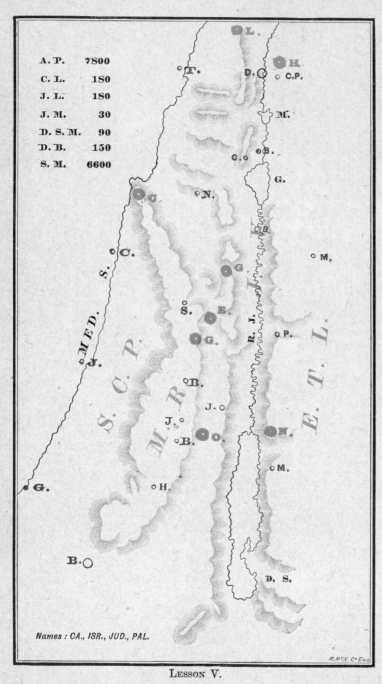

LESSON V.

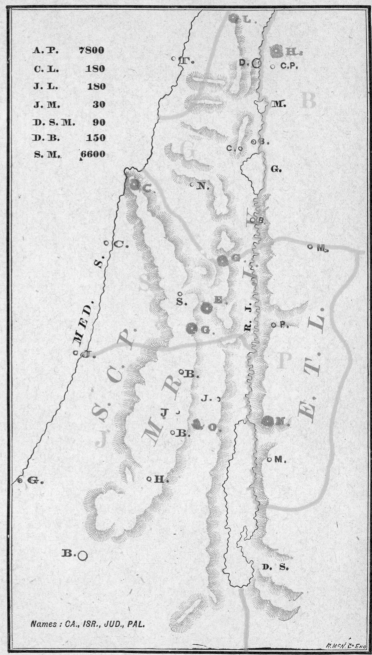

LESSON VI.

Dead Sea. 5. *Bethel*, 10 miles north of Jerusalem, where Jacob saw the vision of the heavenly ladder. 6. *Shechem*, between the twin mountains of Ebal and Gerizim, where Jesus talked with the woman of Samaria. 7. *Nazareth*, where Jesus spent his boyhood; directly in line with the southern end of the Sea of Galilee.

III. **Places in the Jordan Valley.** Two of these are near the northern end of the Dead Sea. 1. *Jericho*, west of the Jordan, where the walls fell down before the Israelites. 2. *Bethabara*, east of the Jordan, where Jesus was baptized. Two more are near the northern shore of

bok, where Jacob wrestled with the angel. This is about midway between the Dead Sea and the Sea of Galilee. 3. *Mahanaim*, where David wept over Absalom's death. This is about half way between Penuel and the Sea of Galilee. 4. *Cæsarea Philippi*, at the foot of Mount Hermon, where Jesus taught his disciples.

It may be desirable not to give these places in a single lesson, but to divide it into two, or even four sections, and give one at a session. In that case, with each lesson all the places already located should be reviewed, together with the events associated with them. If the places can be marked upon the board in bright red chalk, they will be prominent.

LESSON VI. PROVINCES.

Review from the beginning, as usual. 1. Lines. 2. Waters. 3. Names. 4. Distances. 5. Natural Divisions. 6. Mountains. 7. Places.

In this lesson we are to learn the Provinces, or parts of the country, in the time of Christ. We do not take the division by tribes; as that is more difficult to learn, and not often referred to in history. At the time when Christ was among men, Palestine was divided into five Provinces, though two of these were under one ruler.

I. Draw the boundary line of **Judæa**, and write its initial, J. This was the southern province, and the largest. [Review the names of the places contained in it.] Its people were the Jews, or men of the tribe of Judah, and its principal city was Jerusalem.

II. North of Judæa was the province known as **Samaria,** having Shechem as its principal city. Its people were the Samaritans, with whom the Jews had no dealings. In Christ's day Judæa and Samaria were under one government. It contained the twin mountains Ebal and Gerizim.

III. North of Samaria was **Galilee,** where Jesus lived during most of his life. Its people were also Jews, but were called "Galileans" by the Jews in Jerusalem; and in Christ's time it was under the rule of Herod, who slew John the Baptist. Notice the mountains and towns situated in it. Mountains: Lebanon and Gilboa; towns: Nazareth, Capernaum and Dan.

IV. On the east of the Jordan, and south of the Sea of Galilee, was the province of **Peræa,** a word which means "beyond"; so named, because it is "beyond Jordan." Here Jesus taught at one time during his ministry, and blessed the little children. The places which we have noticed in it are Machærus, Bethabara, Penuel and Mahanaim; and its mountain, Nebo. This province, in Christ's day, was also ruled by King Herod.

V. The province north of Peræa and east of the Sea of Galilee is not named in the New Testament. We will call it by its Old Testament name, **Bashan,** a word meaning "woodland." It was ruled by a brother of Herod, named Philip, whose title was "tetrarch"; hence it is sometimes called "Philip's Tetrarchy." The mountain we have noticed in it is Hermon, and the two places, Bethsaida, and Cæsarea Philippi, or "Philip's Cæsarea," to distinguish it from the other Cæsarea, by the seashore.

At the close of the lesson, review once more from the very beginning of the series; then erase the map, and, pointing to the places on an "invisible map," call for their names from the class. There can scarcely be too much reviewing of these leading facts, in order to impress them on the scholar's memory.

ARCHES IN THE TEMPLE AREA.

THE MEASURES OF THE BIBLE.

THE student of the Bible meets with some difficulty in adapting the names of weights, measures and coins, to the standards now in use, and finds that the authorities are not agreed upon the precise signification of the Bible terms used in relation to these subjects. These difficulties and discrepancies arise from three facts: 1. The Oriental mind has never been accustomed to the exactness of our systems of measurement. Among eight cubit measures found on the Egyptian monuments, no two were precisely alike. 2. The models or standards of weights and measures referred to in Hebrew history were long ago lost, and it is not easy to reproduce them. 3. The Jews adopted the measurements of peoples among whom they were dispersed, yet often retained the names of such of their own as were nearest to them in amount, so that at different periods in Bible history the standard was different. The same word may refer to different measurements at different times. We have adopted in this section the measurements of F. R. and C. R. Conder in "The Hand Book of the Bible," except where other authorities are specified.

I. **Smaller Measures of Length.** 1. The lowest dimension, as in our own table of linear measure, was the Barleycorn. 2. Two barleycorns laid endways made the Finger-breadth (Hebrew, Atzbah), two-thirds of an

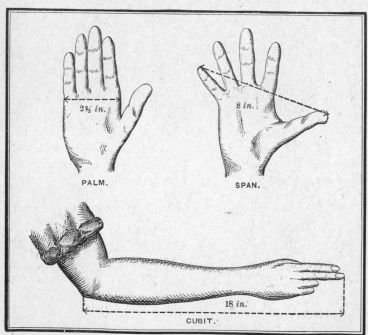

PALM.   SPAN.

CUBIT.

SMALLER MEASURES OF LENGTH.

inch. 3. Four finger-breadths made the Palm (Heb., Tupah), 2⅔ inches. 4. Sometimes the Hand-breadth and Palm are the same; elsewhere, the hand-breadth (Heb., Zereth) is double the palm, or 5⅓ inches. 5. Three palms

made the Span (Heb., Sit), 8 inches, the width of the outspread hand, from the end of the thumb to that of the little finger. 6. Four palms made the Foot (Heb., Regal), 10⅔ inches. 7. Six palms made the Cubit (Heb., Ameh), 16 inches (Conder), or the distance from the elbow to the tip of the middle finger, when held in a straight line. The cubit, however, varied (just as the pound with us varies in troy and avoirdupois weight), as indicated in the expressions "the cubit of a man" (Deut. 3:11), "a great cubit" (Ezek. 41:8), etc. In the length of the cubit, authorities vary from 15 to 21 inches. We have adopted the general opinion, and place it, conjecturally, at a foot and a half, or 18 inches.

II. **Larger Measures of Length.** The cubit (reckoned more precisely at 16 inches) is here regarded as the unit of measurement. 1. The Fathom was 6 or 6½ feet. 2. The Reed (Heb., Keneh; compare our word *cane*) was 4 cubits, according to Conder, but 6 cubits according to other authorities, thus varying between 5⅓ feet and 8 feet. 3. The Furlong (named only in the New Testament) was a Greek measurement (Stadium), of 606¾ feet, or 53¼ feet less than our furlong. 4. The Mile (Matt. 5:41) was 1,618 yards. The Hebrew mile is not referred to in the Bible, but was of two kinds, "the small mile" (Heb., Mil), being about 1,000 cubits, or about a quarter of our mile; and "the long mile," twice as far. 5. The Sabbath Day's Journey is stated by Conder at 2,000 cubits, or half an English mile; but by most other writers at seven-eighths of our mile. 6. The Day's Journey was variable, from 10 to 30 miles; generally about 20 miles. So most authorities decide, but Conder gives it at 4¾ miles.

III. **Dry Measures of Capacity.** 1. The Cab (2 Kings 6:25), 96 cubic inches, or 675 thousandths of a quart. 2. The Omer (Exod. 16:36) contained 172³⁄₁₀ cubic inches, or about 2½ quarts. 3. The Seah (in Greek, Modios) was the ordinary household measure of quantity, translated, generally, "measure" in our Bibles, but in Matt. 5:15 "bushel." It contained six times as much as the cab, or a little over a peck; according to Conder, 1.012 pecks; according to the Revised Version (Matt. 13:33, marginal note), a peck and a half. 4. The Ephah (Exod. 16:36) contained 3 seahs, or 10 omers; about three-quarters of a bushel. 5. The Cor contained 10 ephahs, or 7½ bushels. The cor is also called "the homer" (Isa. 5:10), which is to be carefully distinguished from the omer, which contained one-hundredth of its quantity. The two words are not alike in the Hebrew. It will be noticed that the omer, the ephah and the cor (or homer) formed a decimal scale of measurement.

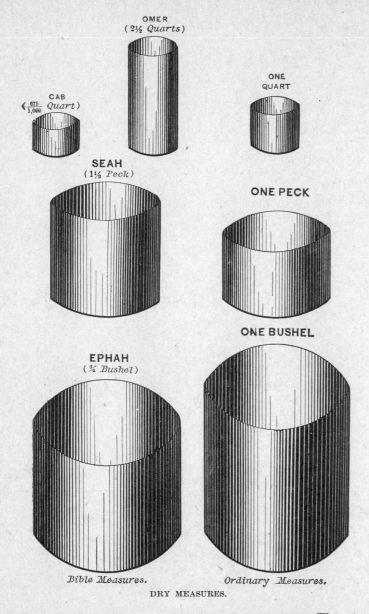

Bible Measures.   Ordinary Measures.

DRY MEASURES.

IV. Liquid Measures of Capacity.

1. The Auphauk (not named in the Bible) was the smallest, containing 6 cubic inches, or 675 thousandths of a gill. 2. The Log (Lev. 14:10), four times as large as the auphauk, was "six egg-shells full," 24 cubic inches, or a little more

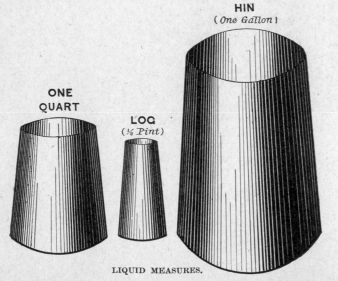

LIQUID MEASURES.

than half a pint (675 thousandths). 3. The Hin (Exod. 29:40) contained 12 logs, or a little over a gallon. 4. The Seah (see above, under Dry Measures) contained twice as much as the hin. 5. The Bath, containing 3 seahs or 6 hins, contained 1,728 cubic inches, or 6.036 gallons. Besides these, the New Testament names two Greek measures, the Metretes (John 2:6, "firkins"), equivalent to $10\frac{1}{3}$ gallons; and the Chœnix (Rev. 6:6, "measure"), about a pint and a half.

V. Measures of Weight.

(From the Oxford Teacher's Bible.) 1. The Gerah, "a bean," weighed a little less than half of a dram avoirdupois (.439 dram). 2. The Bekah, 10 gerahs, weighed about a quarter of an ounce (4.39 drams). The word means "half," i. e., of a shekel. 3. The Shekel, "weight," used as a silver coin, 2 bekahs, weighed 8.9 drams. 4. The Maneh (Greek, Mina), 60 shekels (Conder says 50 shekels, which would agree with paragraph VI., below), 2 lbs. 1 oz. 5. The Talent, "circle," meaning "an aggregate sum," 50 manehs, weighing 102 lbs. 14 ozs. The weights are of lower degree than those in common use at present, because in the early times money was weighed, and not counted, and exact weighing was necessary with gold and silver.

VI. Measures of Value.

Two systems of money are referred to in the Bible: the Hebrew, or that in use in Old Testament times and lands; and the Roman, which was used during the New Testament period. In the Hebrew system the weights referred to in paragraph V. were used in silver as measures of value. 1. The Gerah (Exod. 30:13) was the lowest, and was worth $2\frac{3}{4}$ cents. 2. The Bekah, 10 gerahs (Exod. 38:26), was worth $27\frac{37}{100}$ cents, or about 2 cents more than our quarter of a dollar. 3. The Shekel, 2 bekahs, was worth $54\frac{3}{4}$ cents, or about 5 cents more than half a dollar. 4. The Maneh, or Mina, 50 shekels (Luke 19:13, "pound"), $27.37\frac{1}{2}$. 5. The Talent of Silver, 60 manehs, $1,642.50. 6. The Talent of Gold was nearly twenty times as valuable, being estimated at $26,280. 7. So the Shekel of Gold was worth, in the same proportion of weight with the ordinary shekel of silver, $8.75. It is to be remembered that a given amount of coin in those times would purchase ten times as much as now.

This is a copper coin, a quarter-gerah, worth about half a cent; was made about the time of Alexander the Great, B. C. 325.

A silver coin, three-quarters of a shekel, called a *righia*, used especially for paying the temple tax. It was worth about 40 cents.

The Greek and Roman coins are chiefly referred to in the New Testament. The smallest was the Lepton (Mark 12:42, "mite"), worth a fifth of a cent. 2. The Quadrans (Mark 12:42, "farthing"), 2 mites, or less than half a cent. 3. The Assarion (Matt. 10:29, "farthing"), four times the quadrans, or 1⅗ cents. Notice that two coins, one worth four times as much as the other, are both translated "farthing" in our version. 4. The Denarius (Matt. 22:19, "penny"), 10 times the assarion, or 16 cents. It was the latter which in Christ's time bore the face of the Roman emperor.

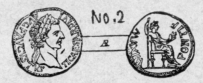

The smallest copper coin in use among the Jews, the *lepton*, called in Hebrew *chalcous*, "copper money." The widow's mite was of this coin.

The denarius, or penny, bearing the face of the emperor Tiberius.

BETHANY

INDEX TO MAP OF PALESTINE.

(SURROUNDING COUNTRY INCLUDED.)

EXPLANATION.—The letter and number following each name show its location on the map. The name will be found at or near the intersection of a vertical line drawn between the letters top and bottom and a horizontal line between the figures on either side.

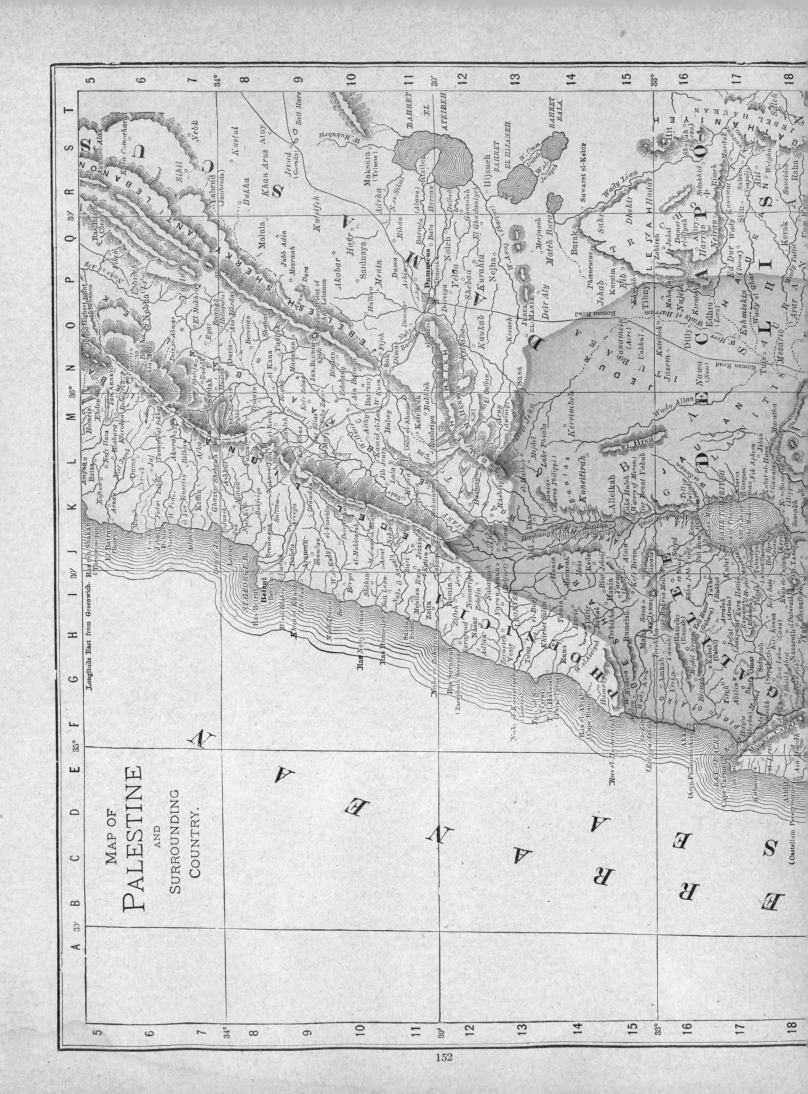

MAP OF
PALESTINE
AND
SURROUNDING
COUNTRY.

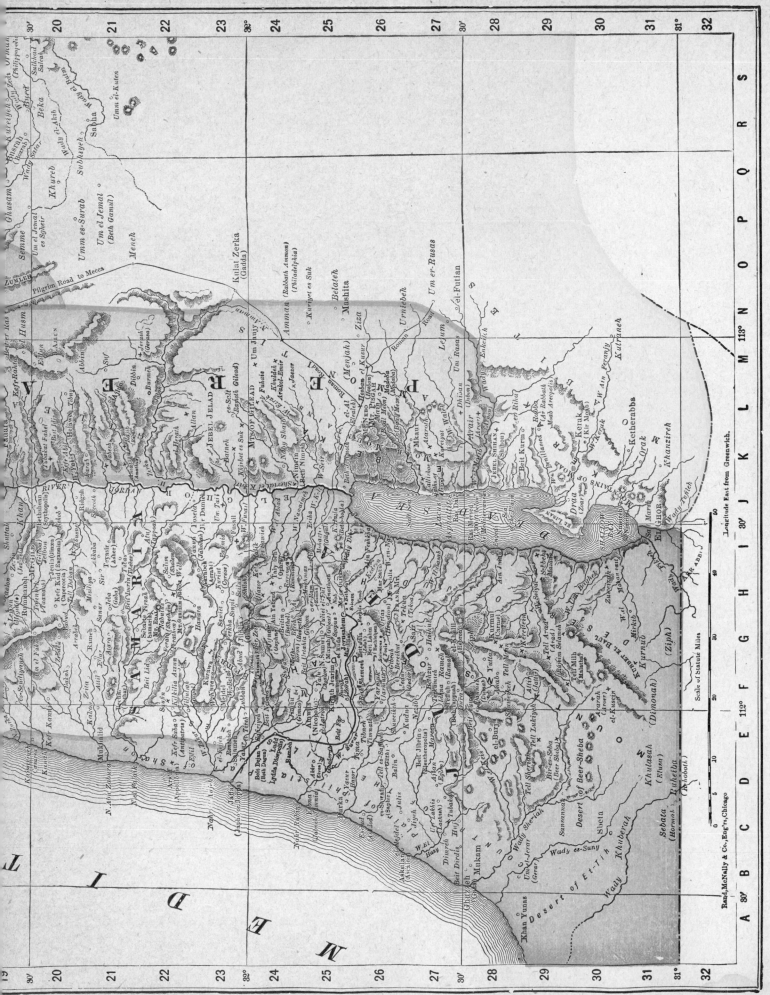

INDEX TO MAP OF OLD TESTAMENT WORLD,

GIVING ONLY BIBLE AND MODERN NAMES.

(See Map, pages 18, 19.)

EXPLANATION.—The letter and number following each name show its location on the map. The name will be found at or near the intersection of a vertical line drawn between the letters top and bottom and a horizontal line between the figures on either side. The italics designate modern names.

INDEX TO DESCRIPTIVE MATTER.